MATLAB®

Data Analysis and Visualization

MATLAB®

Data Analysis and Visualization

Antonio Siciliano
University of Bari, Italy

World Scientific

NEW JERSEY · LONDON · SINGAPORE · BEIJING · SHANGHAI · HONG KONG · TAIPEI · CHENNAI

Published by

World Scientific Publishing Co. Pte. Ltd.
5 Toh Tuck Link, Singapore 596224
USA office: 27 Warren Street, Suite 401-402, Hackensack, NJ 07601
UK office: 57 Shelton Street, Covent Garden, London WC2H 9HE

British Library Cataloguing-in-Publication Data
A catalogue record for this book is available from the British Library.

MATLAB®
Data Analysis and Visualization

ISBN-13 978-981-283-554-3
ISBN-10 981-283-554-7
ISBN-13 978-981-283-751-6 (pbk)
ISBN-10 981-283-751-5 (pbk)

Printed in Singapore.

to
Antonio
Carlo
Bianca
Beatrice

Preface

Some programming languages have been used worldwide in every branch of scientific and technical activities from the sixties of the last century. MATLAB taking the inheritance of the former Fortran, Algol, Basic, Pascal, Ada and C, is now *The Language of Technical Computing* most known and used in academia, industries and services.

MATLAB is composed by a very large set of *functions*, properties of *graphics objects* and *operators*. Their list is in MATLAB Help browser both arranged alphabetically and subdivided into *categories* and, rewritten in a more suitable form, in our Appendixes 1, 2 and 3. Quite likely the reader browsing these large appendixes could not value the depths but certainly he can comprehend the great extent of MATLAB language.

Each of two official manuals (*MATLAB Programming* and *Using MATLAB Graphics*) has about 700 pages. The Help browser, an html book that is an integrant part of MATLAB, occupies probably more space. Then a very large textbook would be necessary to cover *all* the topics and it would too require an advanced scholarship of mathematics and a high computer and programming skill: it would be improbable to find someone interested to *all* subjects and to a similar book. If this has to be useful some choices must be made.

Firstly we assume our readers are keen people with, at least, a sound education of elementary mathematics (basic algebra and trigonometry) in a secondary school. They, as it is now usual, will be skillful with a PC and Internet too. The education of a higher school would be a fine edge but it is not indispensable.

Secondly, we identify and use some *functions*, *graphics objects* and *operators* as basic and others as applications or extensions of them. For example we assume as basic a function that finds the square root of a number and as application one that determines the solutions of a complex equation. Besides we consider basic some graphics objects concerning simple 2-D plots and advanced those used, as example, for 3-D plots.

The *functions* we do not consider are however included in our long Appendix 2. We will discard, for example, functions concerning numerical calculus (vectors, matrices, systems of equations, integration, differential equations, *etc.*) or requiring specific competence (for example, object-oriented programming or handling hardware and software interfaces).

Neither will we add a chapter about Symbolic Math that, requiring an advanced mathematic expertise (for example, how to evaluate an indefinite integral), is beyond our postulated prerequisites.

Because visualization is the natural and mandatory complement of programming, even if a very complex and difficult task, we will deeply treat only some basic graphics objects (root, figure, axes, line, text and image), omitting all the others, and the large number of graphics functions necessary for programming a GUI, a Graphical User Interface.

It is an odd assumption a reader can both be interested and understand applications as how to illuminate a room, solve the heat equation, use the Fast Fourier Transform, estimate the water flow in a river, analyze a noisy signal, create a model of traffic flow, define the mortgage payments, develop a model for asset pricing or portfolio optimization, *etc.*, or how to visualize a surface with the mesh or surf functions, plot volumetric data, make a real animation application, draw plant-like objects, create lighting effects to visualize fluid flow, *etc.*

Then we will not give *applications* requiring by the reader expertise in some specialized areas but only *examples*[1] (every accurately checked) devised for a deep insight of fundamental concepts of MATLAB language so that a user will be able to write clear and clean lines of code.

When the basic *functions*, *operators* and *properties* concerning *data* and *graphics objects* and the corresponding *exercises* will be well understood the reader, owning a specific competence, can apprehend using Help browser the remaining MATLAB features if and when they could be necessary to solve its own problems.

---

[1] In the website *www.antoniosiciliano.org* are allocated all the numbered examples present in the book and the colored figures that appear black and white here.

As example, our book *Optics Problems and Solutions*, containing a hundred of MATLAB programs, makes a large use of functions concerning numerical analysis.

Our final intent is to accustom the reader to a constant use of the MATLAB Help tools that could remain his sole tutor and, if this is not adequate to fulfil its need of assistance, to make him able to find solution with a patient but alert use of the "trial and error" method: trying out to run subsequently modified versions of the same program until the requested results are obtained. The structure of our book has been defined in order to achieve this purpose. Then with our selected topics of MATLAB as its basic foundations the reader will comprehend and master the programming tools necessary for applications in every fields of scientific, engineering, industrial and services.

We first introduce the Desktop, a powerful and friendly interface between the reader and the resources of MATLAB language. The standard procedures for writing a program are the arguments of the following chapters. A distinctive feature of MATLAB is the treatment of data as arrays of every type and number: the Chapter 2 gives a summary survey about data types and M-files that are deeply treated in subsequent chapters.

Chapter 3 treats formally the two basic manners to write a program. Even if common to all programming languages known from the first era of informatics, MATLAB treats them in a new and fine way, calling the main program a script and maintaining the old name *function* for a program that is executed only if called from a main program. MATLAB defines both as M-files when they are stored in a folder of a disk. Chapters 4 and 5 give the detailed formal treatment of all types of arrays (numerical, logical, literals) and the two special ones called Structures and Cells.

The Chapter 6 concerns the essential constituents of graphics objects. The argument is very complex: in this case the adjective means both "composed of many interconnected parts" and "intricate or complicated". The treatment is quite different from that present in the other MATLAB books we hope the reader will appreciate. We consider, and explain deeply conceptually and with examples, the main graphics objects, their properties and the functions that allow us to display the objects and control their properties. Two simple and preliminary cases are considered in Chapter 7: 2-D plots and images. The final Chapter 8 treats the various types of flow control that, exploiting the speed of a computer, are another classical feature of the programming languages from the first era.

Contents

About Chapter 1

It is very difficult to define the subject which we have to begin from because MATLAB consists of many interconnected parts. Topics logically preliminary to others often assume for granted knowledge in advance of these.

This happens also in the first Chapter where MATLAB Desktop and its tools are treated: Command History, Command Window, Current Directory Browser, Editor, Figures, File Comparisons, Help Browser, Profiler, Start Button, Variable Editor (previously Array Editor), Web Browser, Workspace Browser.

Illustrating these tools inevitably one has to know, for example, what is an array, a graphics object, a script, a function or an operator, *etc.* that to be used need the acquaintance of Desktop and its tools.

Rightly the Help Browser explains itself and all other topics too.

The Desktop and its tools are formally *graphical user interfaces*: these again are arguments treated in the Chapters 6 and 7. Then we simply call them windows in the next pages.

Chapter 1

The Windows of the Desktop

1.1 Windows Properties

The MATLAB Desktop consists first of a blue bar with at the left MATLAB credits and at the right corner the usual icons of every PC, then of a *menu bar*, a *tools bar*, a blank space and the *Start* button (Fig. 1.1).

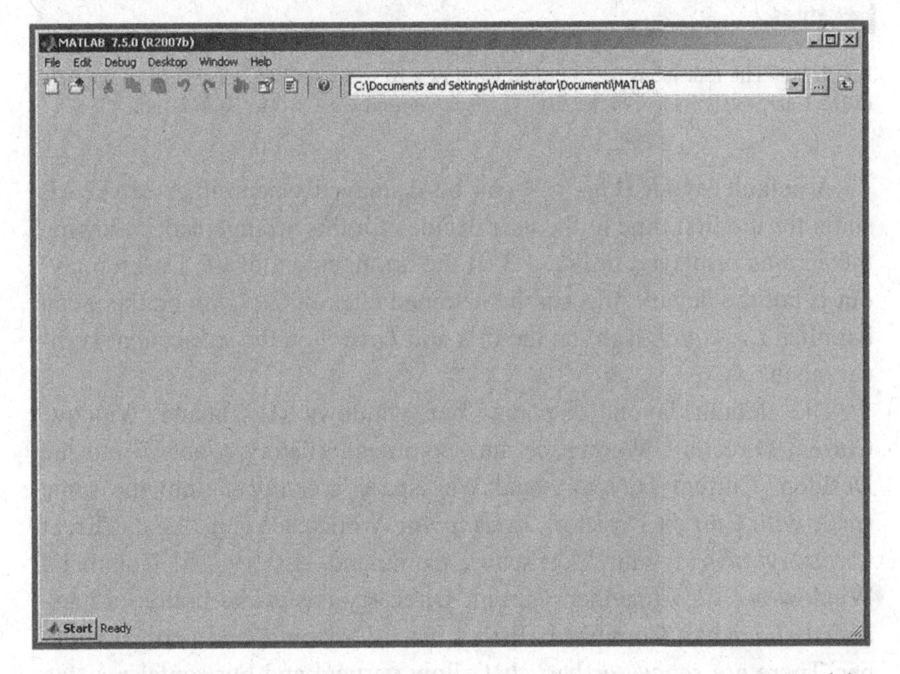

Fig. 1.1 The bare Desktop, without windows, contains three bars, an empty space and the Start button.

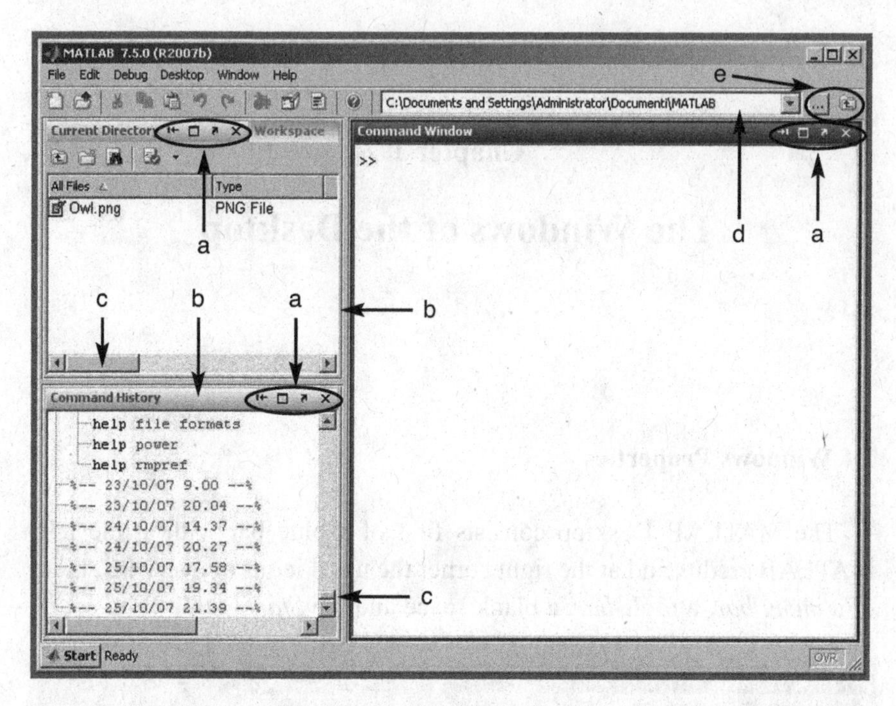

Fig. 1.2 a) The four icons belong to all windows; b) separator bars; c) sliders; d) the field of the *Current Directory*; e) the *Browse for folder* and *Go Up One Level* buttons.

A default layout (Fig. 1.2) can be displayed when either MATLAB starts for the first time or the user decides for this arrangement following the actions displayed in Fig. 1.3. If the arrangement of the Desktop layout is not the default, this can be obtained clicking *Desktop* on the menu bar, then *Desktop Layout* on the first and *Layout* on the subsequent vertical menu.

The default layout displays four windows (Command Window, Current Directory, Workspace and Command History) *docked* into the Desktop. Current Directory and Workspace are *tabbed* into the same space with Current Directory *overlapping* Workspace (Fig. 1.2); Current Directory tabbed with Workspace, Command History and Command Window are *tiled* together. Current Directory has at the bottom a horizontal *slider* bar; Command History has a horizontal and vertical slider bar. There are *separator* bars that allow vertical and horizontal *resizing* between windows: for example with the arrangement of Fig. 1.2 Com-

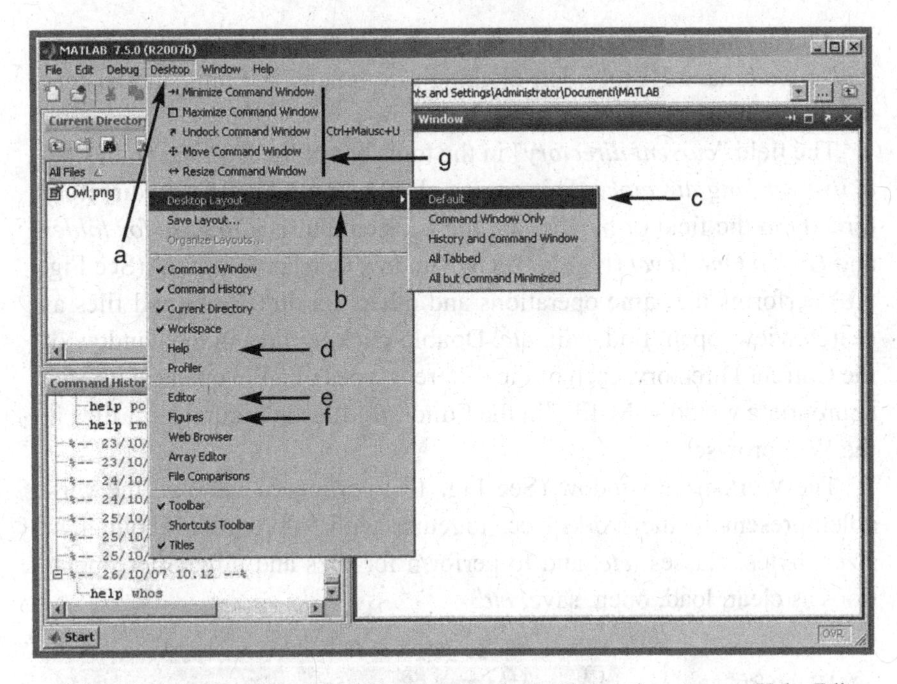

Fig. 1.3 a-b-c) How to obtain the default layout; d-e-f) other options to open Help, Editor and Figures; g) here icons refer to Command Window since this is active (its title bar is blue).

mand Window can be enlarged at the expense of the other windows on the left. So the resizing can be made too between Current Directory and Command History.

All windows have a *title bar* with four icons, at their right corners, that allow *minimize*, *maximize*, *dock/undock* and *close* a window (See their list in Fig. 1.3 for the Command Window). Each window can have one or more tools bars. When windows are docked there is *only one* menu bar whose items change accordingly to the enabled window whose title bar appears blue. One or more adjacent lists of *vertical menu* (an example is in Fig. 1.3) appear left-clicking an item of the menu bar and the item in the subsequent list.

The Command Window is a major MATLAB constituent where results are displayed, data can be entered, one or more lines of code can be typed with at once running them, typing the function *help* (See Sec. 1.2) documentation about a specific argument can be obtained.

All *commands* executed in Command Window are automatically *logged* in Command History; left-clicking a command in Command History this is again executed in Command window.

The field "*current directory*" in the tools bar of the Desktop shows the *active working directory*. This can be changed by typing a new directory directly in the field or by clicking the adjacent buttons *Browse for folder* and *Go Up One Level* (Fig. 1.2). The window Current Directory (See Fig. 1.6) performs the same operations and others on directories and files as search, view, open, find, edit, *etc*. Double-clicking files in the window of the Current Directory, each of the different types of a file opens in its own appropriate window: M-files in the Editor, fig files in Figure, html files in the Web browser.

The Workspace window (See Fig. 1.6) permits to view all the variables present in the workspace, together with information about their sizes, bytes, classes, *etc.* and to perform for files and directories operations as clear, load, open, save, *etc.*

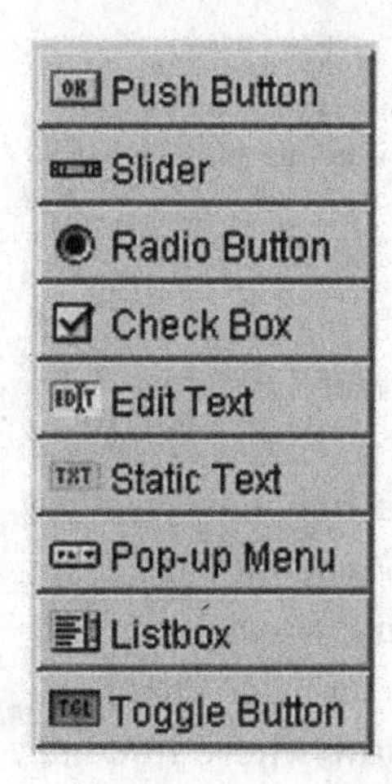

Fig. 1.4 A list of icons.

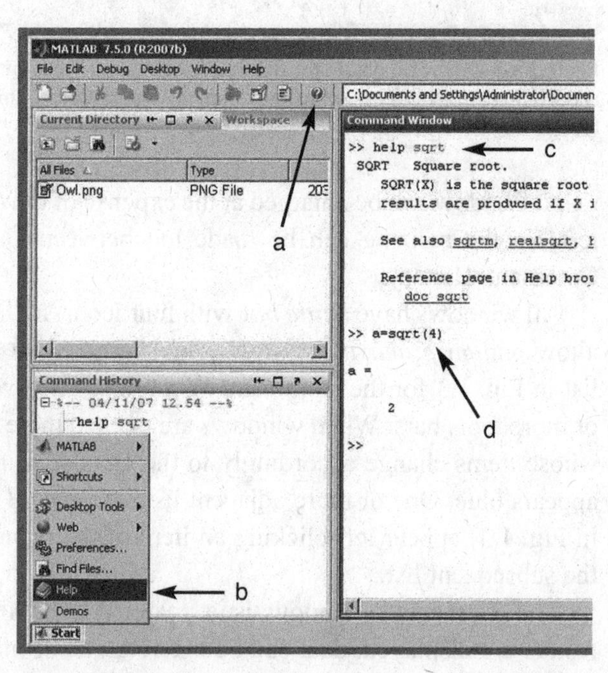

Fig. 1.5 a-b) Other two options to open Help; c) a simple help request; d) a line of code is entered and the result is displayed.

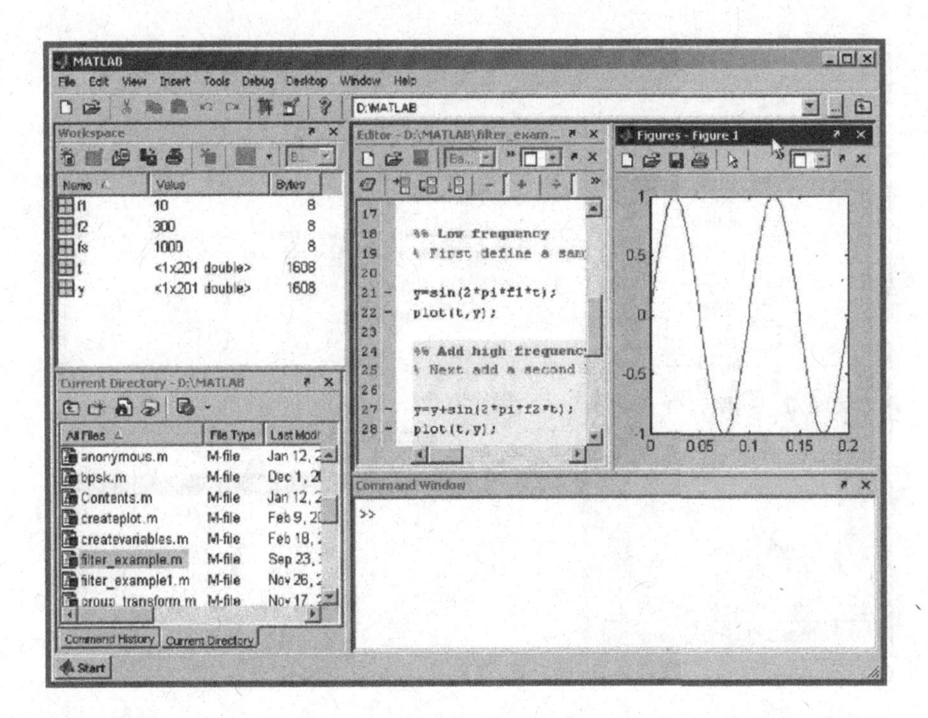

Fig. 1.6 There is only one menu bar for the six windows docked into the Desktop (The figure is part of a MATLAB Demo).

A window can have components like push buttons, radio buttons, list boxes, pop-up menu, context menu, sliders, *etc*. (Fig. 1.4). Right-clicking on the blank space of a window a *context menu* may appear where other menu items appear. Frequently the same action in every window can be performed in three different ways: *a*) clicking an item of the menu bar; *b*) using an icon of tools bars; *c*) searching the item in the associated context menu. This *triple option* must be remembered when some operations are to be operated in a window (See, for example, Sec. 1.3 where the window Editor is treated).

To move a window outside the Desktop the *undock* icon (the arrow *bent-up* on the right edge of the title bar) must be clicked and to place it again from outside into the Desktop the *dock* icon (the arrow *bent-down*) must be used.

If a window is minimized it appears as a long button on the vertical or horizontal edge of the Desktop. For example, Command Window appears

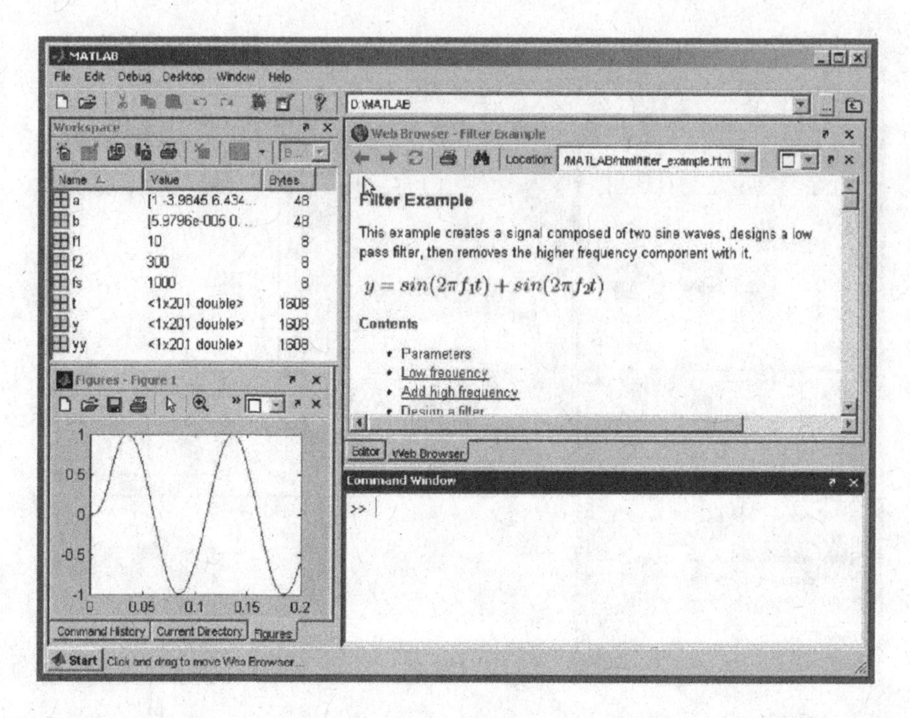

Fig. 1.7 Seven windows are docked into the Desktop (The figure is part of a MATLAB Demo).

sometimes minimized on the right side of the Desktop. Clicking this button, the window is put back into the former position.

Double-clicking on the title bar of a docked window this occupies the full space of the Desktop and with a new double-click it returns to the previous docked space.

All windows have their own *shortcuts* or mnemonics: for example, typing Ctrl+0 the Command Window is opened. Shortcuts for each window can be displayed in the corresponding context menu (Fig. 1.11 displays some *shortcuts* of the Editor window).

The *Start* button (Fig. 1.5) gives quick access to a vertical menu by which many of the MATLAB features can be obtained.

To quit MATLAB either left-click the *Close* icon on the upper right corner of the Desktop or select *Exit MATLAB* from the Desktop *File* menu or type *quit* at the Command Window *prompt* (>>).

The full list of windows contains also (See the list on the first vertical menu of the Fig. 1.3) *Array Editor*, *Editor*, *Figures*, *File Comparisons*, *Help Browser*, *Profiler* and *Web Browser*.

Arrangements of the Desktop different from the default are commonly used: two examples are given in Fig. 1.6 and in Fig. 1.7. Clearly different arrangements can be defined that could best fit the users' requirements: MATLAB demos, for example, always propose complex combinations of windows on the Desktop (Fig. 1.6 and Fig. 1.7 are two examples); we use a simple version: the Command Window docked with Help and the Editor and Figures undocked (Fig. 1.8).

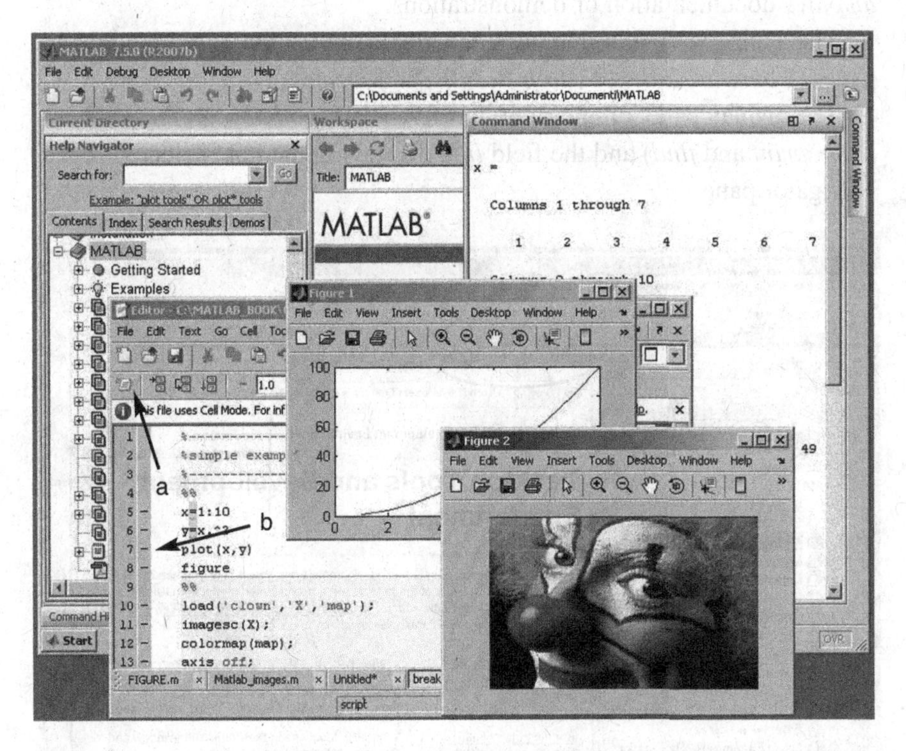

Fig. 1.8 The arrangement we use: Help and Command Window docked into the Desktop. The Editor and Figures, undocked, have their own menu bars. The M-file uses cell mode. a) The icon to publish to html; b) black dashes.

1.2 The Help Browser

The Help browser is an html window that allows the search and the view of *documentation* (Fig. 1.9) and *demonstrations* (Fig. 1.10). The Help is reached by clicking the Help button (See Fig. 1.5) on the Desktop tools bar, or by typing *helpbrowser* in Command Window, or by using the Help menu in any other undocked windows.

The Help consists of two *panes*. The first is the *Help Navigator* that provides for *searching* information or demonstration and the right pane *displays* documentation or demonstrations.

The Help Navigator includes the field *Search for* and four tabbed panes: *Contents*, *Index*, *Search Results*, and *Demos*.

The display pane, on the right, has five tools (*go back*, *go forward*, *refresh*, *print* and *find*) and the field *title* displaying the item selected in the Navigator pane.

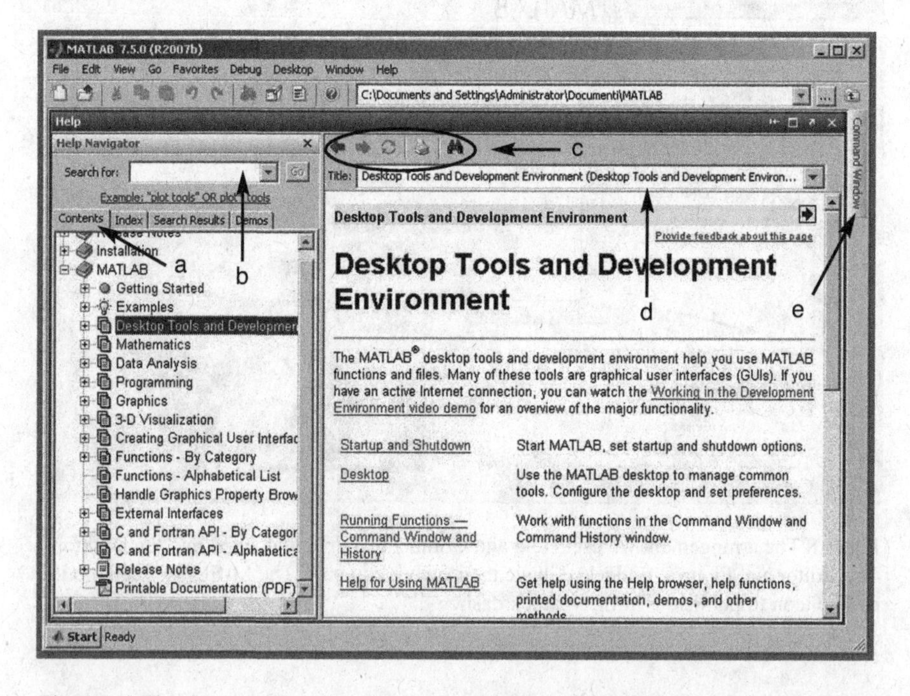

Fig. 1.9 a) The *Contents* pane is active on the left side; b) the field *Search for:* ; the right pane with the four icons (c) and the field *Title* (d). The Command Window is now minimized (e).

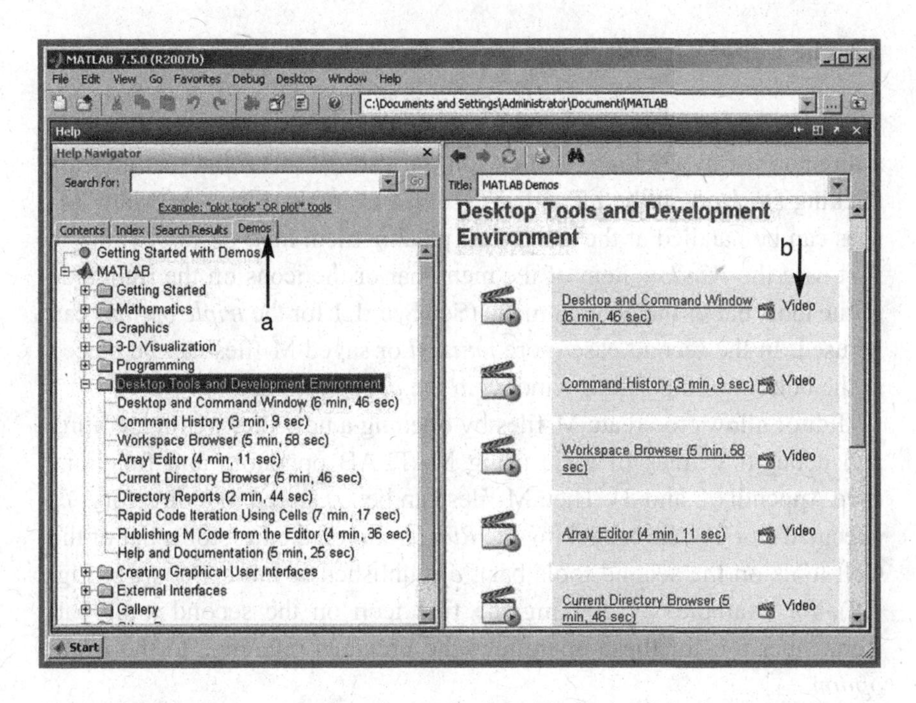

Fig. 1.10 a) The *Demos* pane is active on the left side; b) the *Video* type of the Demos appears on the right pane.

There are two relevant types of demos:

a) *M-files* give a source code with a step-by-step content including comments and output. They are published from M-file scripts to html output using the Editor.

b) *Video movies* highlight some key features of MATLAB. These movies play in PC browser, require *Flash Player* (a plug-in of the Macromedia) and sometimes also an Internet connection.

Partial and targeted aids can be obtained directly in Command Window; typing respectively *help* or *help categoryname* or *help functionname* (See Fig. 1.5) there will be displayed the list of all categories (See Appendix 1) or the list of all functions of a category or the documentation of a function.

1.3 The Editor

The Editor window is becomes active either by opening an M-file from a directory or by clicking "*Editor*" on the vertical menu list that appears clicking *Desktop* on the menu bar (See, for example, Fig. 1.3). Many M-files can be handled at the same time placing them *tiled* or *tabbed*: in the first case the *Window* item of the menu bar or the icons on the right side of the tools bar or the context menu (See Sec. 1.1 for the *triple option*) can be used. In the second case more *untitled* or saved M-files can be placed at the bottom of the Editor window in the *document bar*.

Editor allows to create M-files by opening a new file, writing, editing and debugging lines of code using MATLAB operators and functions (See Appendix 2 and 3). Then M-files can be: *a*) stored in a directory; *b*) executed (for example, clicking the *Run button* on the first tools bar or the Cell tools on the second tools bar); *c*) published to html (See a) in Fig. 1.8), for example, by clicking the first icon on the second tools bar. Remember too for these operations the previous reference to the *triple option*.

The Editor has its own *menu bar* when it is not docked. If it is docked the Editor has its own tools bars but uses the menu bar of the Desktop that serves all the docked windows.

Sometimes Editor is called *Editor/Debugger* because M-files have to be debugged too.

Usually a real M-file is large or very large: then it is a good programming rule to consider it a logical structure consisting of multiple sections. These are pressingly needed by the writers of a program and extremely useful to its readers. The MATLAB tool for this purpose is the *Cell mode*. Sections or part of these become *cells* using two percent symbols (%%) before the first row of each section (See Fig. 1.8, Fig. 1.11 and Fig. 1.12). Three icons on the second tools bar allow to *evaluate cell*, *evaluate cell and advance*, *evaluate entire file*. But also in this case remember the *triple option*.

A great help to monitor problems, bugs and potential improvements of an M-file (Fig. 1.11) is the *M-Lint automatic code analyzer*. At the top of the right edge of the Editor space reserved for writing an M-file there is a small colored *square* that becomes *red* when syntax errors are detected

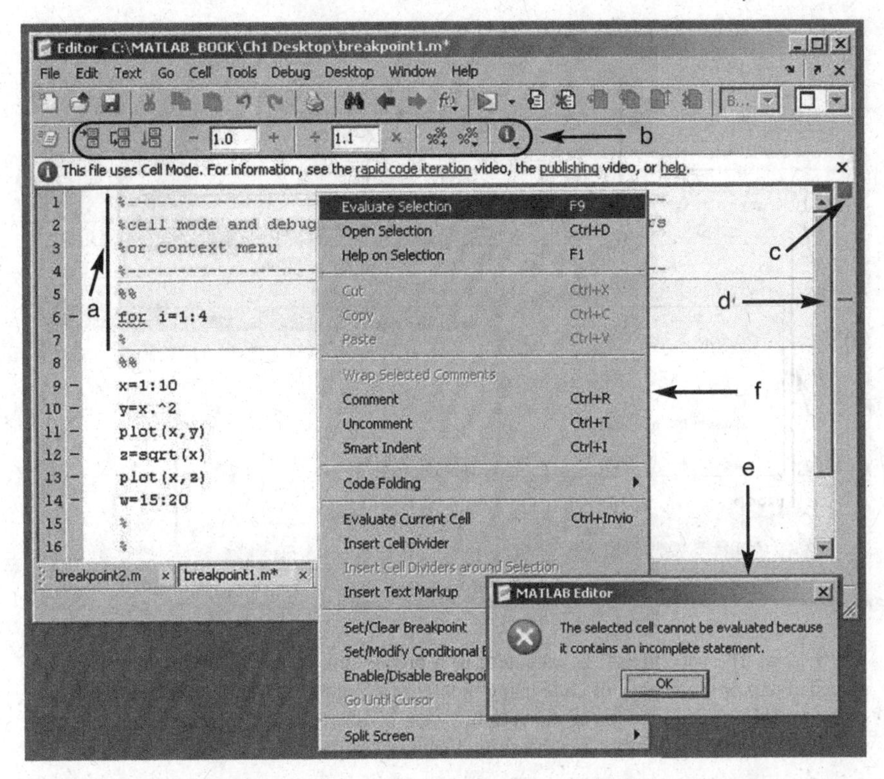

Fig. 1.11 a) The first cell is excuted; b) icons to operate with *Cell Mode*; c-d) indicators displayed by the *M-Lint analyzer*; e) additional error message; f) a *context menu* overlapping part of the Editor with on the right side some of the *shortcuts* (mnemonics) of the Editor.

(for example unmatched parentheses or, as in Fig. 1.11, an incomplete conditional function), *orange* when only warnings are found and *green* when neither errors nor warnings are present. One or more colored *dashes* appear on the bar at the right edge corresponding to the lines interested by the M-Lint analyzer. These dashes have the same color as the upper square.

When there is the need to check values of some variables of an M-file breakpoints can be set on the black dashes that identify the lines of code, passing over those beginning with a single percent (comment) or a double percent (the start of a cell mode). Breakpoints suspend temporarily the execution of a program and allow the examination of these variables: Fig. 1. 12 displays the ten values of the variable y; Fig. 1.11 shows the no

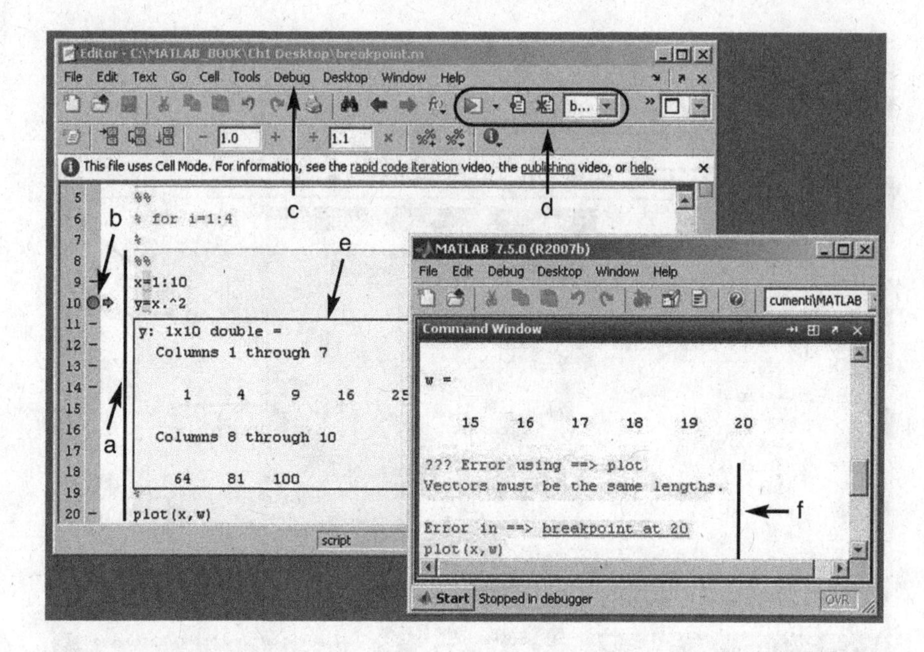

Fig. 1.12 a) The second cell is executed; b) a breakpoint at line 10; breakpoints can be placed at one or more lines of code using the item Debug of the Menu bar (c) or the icons of the tools bar (d); e) values of the variable y are displayed; f) the plot function requires variables of the same lengths for the abscissa and the ordinate.

comment rows 11-14 hidden in Fig. 1.12 by the box containing the y values. Breakpoints are handled (remember the *triple option* of Sec. 1.1) using the corresponding icons of the tools bar, *Debug* on the menu bar and the associated items in its context menu.

About Chapter 2

Now we give preliminary information about programming. Alphabetic and numerical symbols, punctuation marks, mathematical symbols, and other conventional symbols are used to name data by words, numbers and alphanumeric strings.

Data are always considered as array, an ordered set of rows, columns and pages. As examples, a single number is a one-dimensional array of size 1-by-1 and an image can be a bi- or a tri-dimensional array.

An array can contain data both of the same kind (only numerical or only literal or only logical) and of different types, like cells and structures. Graphic objects are the complementary elements of programming.

Arrays and graphics objects are identified by a list of properties: few and simple (name, size, number of bytes allocated, class, *etc*) for arrays and very long and usually more complex for graphics objects.

Some simple examples are given that emphasize properties of the arrays and graphics objects. We conclude outlining the basic components of an M-File.

Chapter 2

A Preliminary Approach to Data and M-files

2.1 Data Types

For us data are material things or products of mental activity. In computer jargon data are firstly the alphanumeric *symbols* that represent these things or products.

So data are *letters* (*a*, *b*, *c*, *etc.*), their combination as *words* and *digits* (*0*, *1*, *2*, *etc.*) with their sequence as *numbers*. A partial list of the formal signs widely recognized by languages of most Western Europe and American countries is reported in Table 2.1. An extended Table of Ascii codes is in Appendix 4 and the M-files used to obtain these tables (*ascii_codes.m* and *ext_ascii.m*) can be found in our website. These tables give the standard Ascii code (*American Standard Code for Information Interchange)* and the corresponding characters.

On the contrary universal data are *pixels*, the smallest black or colored constituents of fixed and moving images obtained from imaging equipments, *sounds* sent forth from natural and artificial sources and *pulses* or *signals* generated by technical instruments. Scientists and engineers know elementary units of sounds and pulses are harmonic waves. Then pixels, sounds and pulses lead again to digits. Data are too the logical "*yes/no*" or "*true/false*" arising as answer to an interrogative sentence and usually represented by the digits *1* and *0* that in this case lose their numerical meaning.

All data are considered by MATLAB as *array*, an ordered set of rows and/or columns. A *single data* of every type is an array of size *1-by-1*; n ordered data can be arranged horizontally (then size is *1-by-n*) or verti-

Table 2.1 MATLAB has functions for conversion between Ascii codes and characters. On every PC keyboard typing Alt+(Ascii code) the corresponding character is obtained (pad it with zeros to obtain four digits code). Remember the number of characters depends on the font used.

Ascii code	32	33	34	35	36	37	38	39	40	41	42	43
character		!	"	#	$	%	&	'	(	)	*	+
Ascii code	44	45	46	47	48	49	50	51	52	53	54	55
character	,	-	.	/	0	1	2	3	4	5	6	7
Ascii code	56	57	58	59	60	61	62	63	64	65	66	67
character	8	9	:	;	<	=	>	?	@	A	B	C
Ascii code	68	69	70	71	72	73	74	75	76	77	78	79
character	D	E	F	G	H	I	J	K	L	M	N	O
Ascii code	80	81	82	83	84	85	86	87	88	89	90	91
character	P	Q	R	S	T	U	V	W	X	Y	X	[
Ascii code	92	93	94	95	96	97	98	99	100	101	102	103
character	\	]	^	_	`	a	b	c	d	e	f	g
Ascii code	104	105	106	107	108	109	110	111	112	113	114	115
character	h	i	g	k	l	m	n	o	p	q	r	s
Ascii code	116	117	118	119	120	121	122	123	124	125	126	127
character	t	u	v	w	x	y	z	{	|	}	~	

cally (with size *n-by-1*). For a bi- or a three-dimensional array the sizes are *n-by-m* or *n-by-m-by-p* with n rows, m columns and p bi-dimensional arrays. In a similar way multidimensional arrays can be defined. An image is usually represented by a bi- or tri-dimensional array. An array can contain both data of the same kind (only numerical or only literal or only logical) and of dissimilar kinds: in this last case arrays are called *cell* (containing arrays of different types and/or sizes) and the *structure* (an array whose elements, called *fields*, are containers of any kind of data). Next Example 2.2 concerns cell and structure arrays.

2.2 Constants, Variables and Names

An array can be made of a *constant* or a set of constants if data are assumed to have a fixed value. A literal constant, always enclosed in a pair of single quote characters, can also include digits and all special characters included in Table 2.1 and in Table present in Appendix 4.

When the array can assume different values it is a *variable* and has a *name*.

A name, as we will see later, is also assigned to *functions*, *fields*, *files*, *directories and properties*.

Names of variables, functions, fields, files, directories are *case sensitive*, must begin with a letter, which may be followed by any combination of letters, digits, and underscores and have a maximum allowed length (the function NAMELENGTHMAX gives the maximum length allowed for the various identifiers). A length less than ten characters is always permitted and workable.

A *property* is an attribute of the graphics *object* that has always a *handle*, too. The handle is a number that unambiguously identifies an object. A property, as a variable, can have one or more values. For example a line represented in a plot is an object that has his handle, many properties (about 30 are counted in *Line Properties*) and one or more values for each property. The names of properties are always *quoted strings* but are *not case sensitive*.

MATLAB uses sometimes interchangeably the terms "single value" or "scalar", "one-dimensional array" or "row/column vector" and "two-dimensional array" or "matrix". As stated in the Introduction we will use always uniquely the term array.

Obviously names of the MATLAB *built-in functions* or *properties* couldn't be used, for example, to name a user-defined variable, a field, a function, a file or a directory.

2.3 Data Properties

A variable is identified by a list of properties: *name*, *size*, number of *bytes* allocated, *class* and other five fields (global, sparse, complex, nesting and persistent) that, when a variable is listed in the Command Window, appear grouped as *attributes*. So not only a graphics object has properties but also a variable has them.

Giving later (Table 2.3) an example of a list of properties we report in Table 2.2 the sequence of all classes.

Table 2.2 A list of data properties.

Class	**Definition**
double	Double precision floating point number array
single	Single precision floating point number array
logical	Logical array
char	Character array
cell	Cell array
struct	Structure array
function_handle	Function Handle
int8	8-bit signed integer array
uint8	8-bit unsigned integer array
int16	16-bit signed integer array
uint16	16-bit unsigned integer array
int32	32-bit signed integer array
uint32	32-bit unsigned integer array
int64	64-bit signed integer array
uint64	64-bit unsigned integer array
<class_name>	Custom object class
<java_class>	Java class name for java objects

A byte is a sequence of eight adjacent bits operated on as a unit by a computer. Two bytes are usually the amount of computer memory needed to store one character. The number of bytes necessary to an array depends on its type and size (See some values in Table 2.3).

2.4 Examples

All the following M-files, with a name in italic type, can be downloaded from our website; these have simple and self-explanatory lines of code and many lines of comment (text following the percent sign %). The double percent (%%) signify we are using the *Cell Mode*.

Example 2.1 (*main_data.m*)

```
a=-3
% -3 is an array of size 1x1 and class double
b=single(a)
% b is an array of size 1x1 and class single
%
% Values of a as signed integers
% of size 1x1 and class int8,int16,int32,int64
as8=int8(a); as16=int16(a); as32=int32(a); as64=int64(a)
% or as unsigned integers of size 1x1
% and class uint8,uint16,uint32,uint64
au8=uint8(a); au16=uint16(a); au32=uint32(a); au64=uint64(a)
%
% A complex number of size 1x1, class double
% and attribute complex
a_complex=3+2i
%
% array_date has size 1x6 and class uint16
% date and time have size 1x3 and class uint16
a_date=uint16(clock); date=a_date(1:3)
time=a_date(4:6)
%
% The binary 100000 corresponding to decimal 32
% becomes an array of size 1x6 and class char
a32=32; a_bin=dec2base(a32,2)
%
% A string as an array of size 1x14 and class char
a_string='red green blue'
```

```
%
% a_logical has size 1x1 and class logical
a2=2;a3=3; a_logical=a2==a3
```

Above simple data are considered and the emphasis is directed toward their sizes and classes.

The following results are displayed on the Command Window for the executable lines not terminated with a semicolon

```
a = -3
b = -3
as64 = -3
au64 = 0
a_complex = 3.0000 + 2.0000i
date = 2007     11     13
time = 18     54     55
a_bin = 100000
a_string = red green blue
a_logical = 0
```

The question "if two is equal to three", has the obvious answer "not" or "false"; so the variable a_logical assumes the logical value 0. The double equal operator (==) is used to mean "equal to".

The values of a UINT8/16/32/64 range from 0 to 255/ 65535/ 4,294,967,295/ 18,446,744,073,709,551,615. So, for example, uint8(-3) and uint8(-300) and, in our case, the variable au64 give 0 as result.

Example 2.2 (*cell_and_structure.m*)

```
%%
% A cell array of size 1x5 and class cell
a1_cell = {'Today' 'is' 'a' 'sunny' 'day'}
cellplot(a1_cell,'legend')
figure
%
% Another cell array of size 1x4 and class cell
```

```
a2_cell{1,1} = 12;a2_cell{1,2} = 'Red';...
  a2_cell{1,3} = magic(4);a2_cell{1,4}=2==3;
celldisp(a2_cell)
cellplot(a2_cell,'legend')
%
% a structure array of size 1x1 and class struct
magic_square.Name='Dürer';
magic_square.dating='21 May 1471';
magic_square.array=[16 3 2 13;5 10 11 8;...
  9 6 7 12;4 15 14 1];
magic_square.value=34;
magic_square
```

Above small examples of cell arrays and of a structure are considered.

On the Command Window two cells (a1_cell and a2_cell) and a structure (magic_square), with its four fields, are displayed

```
a1_cell = 'Today'  'is'  'a'  'sunny'  'day'

a2_cell{1} = 12
a2_cell{2} = Red
a2_cell{3} =
  16   2   3  13
   5  11  10   8
   9   7   6  12
   4  14  15   1
a2_cell{4} = 0

magic_square =
   Name: 'Dürer'
   dating: '21 May 1471'
   array: [4x4 double]
   value: 34
```

The function CELLPLOT displays with colored boxes the elements of a cell array and also puts a legend next to the plot (Fig. 2.1 and Fig.

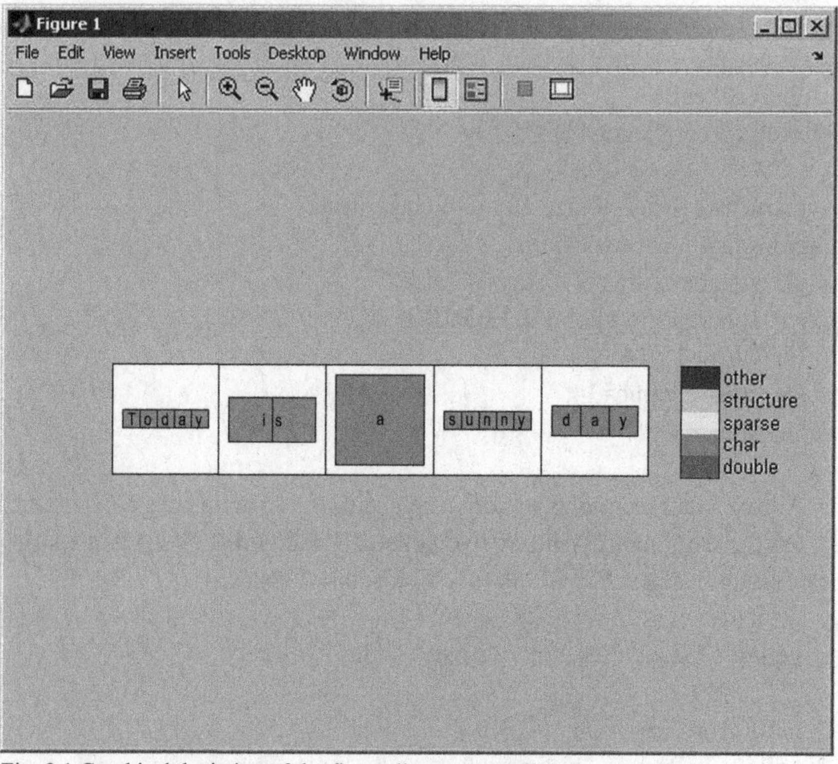

Fig. 2.1 Graphical depiction of the first cell array a1_cell.

2.2; on our website their colored versions Fig. 2.1 and Fig. 2.2 can be found).

Example 2.3 (*image.m*)

```
%%
% An image of size 960x1280x3 and class uint8
%
[x1]=imread('Owl.png');
%n1 has size 1x3 and class double
n1=size(x1)
% info1 is an array of size 1x1, class struct with 38 fields
info1=imfinfo('Owl','png')
%
```

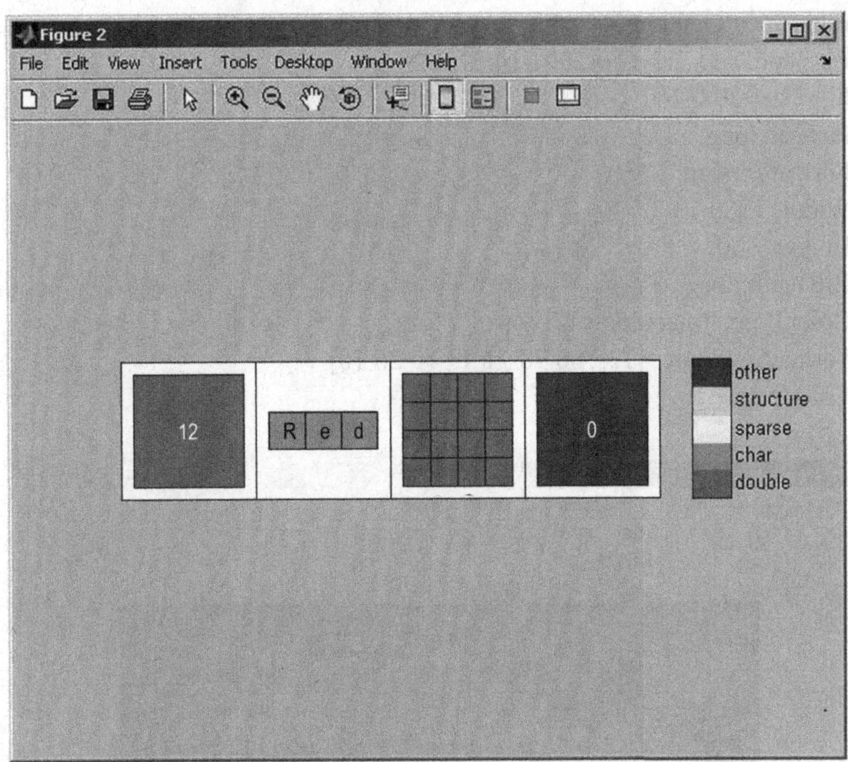

Fig. 2.2 Graphical depiction of the second cell array a2_cell.

```
% IMAGE displays array x1 as an image
image(x1)
%
%Remove axis ticks and numbers
axis off
%square pixels are requested
axis image
%
```

Now the image of an owl, available by MATLAB, is exhibited within a Figure (Fig. 2.3; its colored version is on our website). The Command Window returns structure array info1 whose 38 fields contain information about the image as a graphics file. We report only the first eleven of them:

```
Filename: 'Owl.png'
FileModDate: '13-Feb-2007 14:51:29'
FileSize: 2081760
Format: 'png'
FormatVersion: [ ]
Width: 1280
Height: 960
BitDepth: 24
ColorType: 'truecolor'
FormatSignature: [137 80 78 71 13 10 26 10]
Colormap: [ ]
```

Fig. 2.3 The Figure with the image of a owl.

Example 2.4

```
%%
%whos gives for all variables name together
%with their size, bytes, class and attributes
%IN THE WORKSPACE ARE SAVED ALL VARIABLES
%of Examples 2.1, 2.2 and 2.3
whos
%
%about_whos
%is a struct array of size 26x1 and nine fields:
%name,size,bytes,class,global,sparse,complex
%nesting and persistent. In Command Window
%the last five fields are grouped as attributes
about_whos=whos
```

Above the function WHOS allows to report about name, size, number of bytes and class of the variables used in all the previous three examples (Table 2.3). For the complex variable *a_complex* the attribute complex is added in the Class column.

After the execution of the command

```
about_whos=whos
```

the Command Window returns the following structure

```
about_whos =
26x1 struct array with fields:
name - size - bytes - class - global - sparse - complex - nesting - persistent
```

The last five fields are usually grouped within the name *attributes* in a fourth column when the results are reported in the Command Window.

Table 2.3 Data properties.

Name	Size	Bytes	Class
a	1x1	8	double
a1_cell	1x5	332	cell
a2	1x1	8	double
a1_cell	1x4	383	cell
a3	1x1	8	double
a32	1x1	8	double
a_bin	1x6	12	char
a_complex	1x1	16	double/complex
a_date	1x6	12	uint16
a_logical	1x1	1	logical
a_string	1x14	28	char
as16	1x1	2	int
as32	1x1	4	int32
as64	1x1	8	int64
as8	1x1	1	int8
au16	1x1	2	uint16
au32	1x1	4	uint32
au64	1x1	8	uint64
au8	1x1	1	uint8
b	1x1	4	single
date	1x3	6	uint16
info1	1x1	3584	struct
magic square	1x1	664	struct
n1	1x3	24	double
time	1x3	6	uint16
x1	960x1280x3	3686400	uint8

2.5 M-files

a. An executable line of an M-file is called an assignment statement when has the form
variable name = value
where meaning of the equal sign is "*assign* value *to the* variable name" and *value* can be

a1) a constant or a set of constants

a2) another variable name

a3) an expression containing variables and constants

a4) the name of a built-in or user-defined function that has, enclosed in parentheses, a list of arguments

b. The executable line can have too the short form *value* without the first member "variable name =".

In this case, for the first three previous options for *value*, MATLAB uses "*ans*" as a default variable name. For example writing as executable line only the numerical constant 4 the result is ans=4

c. If the executable line is simply the name of a function some common situations can be considered

c1) the function returns one or more data behaving as an assignment statement; for example a line with only the function

```
sqrt(4)
```

returns

```
ans=2
```

c2) the task of the function is display data (for example the function DISP returns data on Command Window without printing the array name and the function PLOT represent graphically array Y versus array X in a Figure window). In this case the executable line is usually called a command.

c3) the function name is part of functions that regulate the sequence of executable lines (as example *for*, *if*, *end*, *etc*.). Functions that control execution of a block of lines of code a specified number of times, if or while a condition is true will be treated in Chapter 8.

We have used some MATLAB functions without explaining them as being self-explanatory as, for example, DISPLAY, PLOT, WHOS, *etc.* We have assumed of immediate meaning the construction of an array, for example of five elements, with a line of the code that uses as operator a colon (:)

a=1:5

or brakets with or without the punctuation marks (,)

a = [1, 2, 3, 4, 5]

Similarly we have implicitly stated that a semicolon (;) used after an expression or a statement suppresses displaying results in Command Window and separates statements in the same line.

If a statement does not fit in one line, we use an ellipsis (three periods: . . .) to indicate the statement continues on the next line. For example,

```
s = 1 -1/2 + 1/3 -1/4 + 1/5 - 1/6 + 1/7 - 1/8 + 1/9 - 1/10;
```

can be written as

```
s = 1 -1/2 + 1/3 -1/4 ...
   + 1/5 - 1/6 + 1/7 ...
    - 1/8 + 1/9 - 1/10;
```

Blank spaces around some signs (as for example = , + , - , or punctuation marks such as the comma (,) or the period (.) *etc.*) and within parentheses, square brackets and curly braches are optional, but they improve readability.

About Chapter 3

There are two types of M-files: scripts and functions. The first autonomously executes a series of statements and it has not input/output arguments or begin/end delimiters. The second too performs statements but only if called by a script and it does not necessarily accept input arguments and/or send back results.

Variables of a function are not shared neither by the local workspaces of other functions nor by the basic Workspace of the scripts, unless they are defined *global*. Variables stored in the local workspace of a function do not remain in memory from one to the next execution of the function, unless they are defined *persistent*.

A special function of a single line, called anonymous, can be present within both a script and a function. The anonymous functions and graphics objects use a *handle*: within an anonymous function the handle operates actively to perform some actions; in the second case it defines a parental relation between two objects.

Many practicable arrangements of functions are discussed formally and by examples.

Chapter 3

Scripts and Functions as M-files

3.1 The M-file

An M-file is a sequence of MATLAB statements written using the Editor (Sec. 1.3). When it is saved a name, with the extension .m, is assigned. A stored M-file can be edited and debugged calling it into the Editor. Parts of an M-file are executable lines, lines with comments, lines defining the start of a *Cell mode* or simply blank lines (Fig. 3.1). Every line has a progressive number reported in the left column of the Editor window.

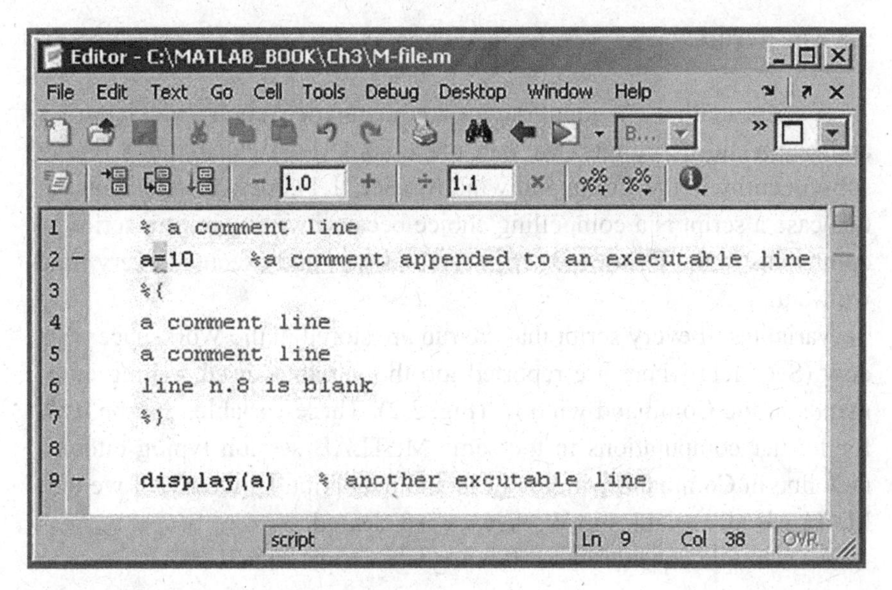

Fig. 3.1 Types of lines within an M-file.

A statement can be composed by constants, variables and functions that allow assignments, calculations, programming constructs like flow control, interactive input/output, display of data in numerical and graphical form, *etc.*

Comments are lines that begin with the percent symbol (%). Comments can appear on lines by themselves, or appended to the end of any executable line. To write comments that require more consecutive lines the block comment operators %{ and %} can be used. The %{ and %} operators must appear alone on the lines that immediately precede and follow the block of help text without including any other text on these lines.

There are two types of M-files that we can write: scripts and functions. A script simply autonomously executes a series of statements; a function too performs statements but only if called by a script accepting input arguments and sending back some results. The *function definition line* (Sec. 3.3) is a feature that applies to the functions only. The *cell mode* (Sec. 1.3) however is a characteristic that is useful only within a script. Scripts and functions have different workspace where to store their variables.

3.2 The Script

A script neither has input/output arguments nor requires declarations and begin/end delimiters. We can make some long calculations typing subsequenthy in the Command window (Sec. 1.1) lines of statements: in this case a script is a compelling choice because writing once a series of commands in the Editor the script can be saved and executed every time we want.

Variables of every script that we run are stored in the Workspace window (Sec. 1.1) where are reported too the variables used writing commands in the Command window (Fig. 3.2). These variables can be used for further computations in the same MATLAB session typing either a new line in Command window or in another script. Obviously if we quit MATLAB all variables in Workspace are cleared.

As example consider the following two scripts *sa* and *sb*.

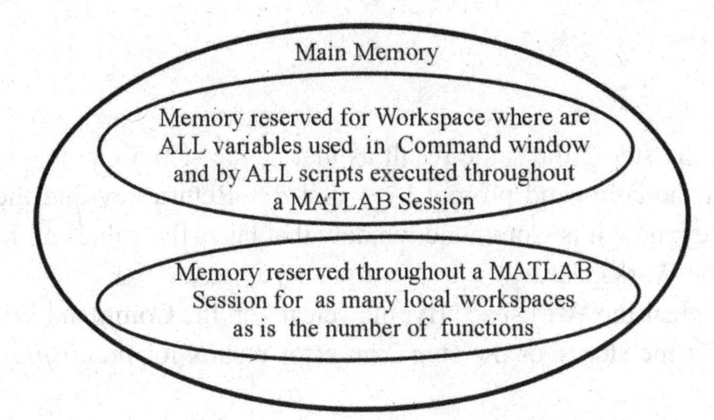

Fig. 3.2 The Workspace and local workspace.

Step 1. Executing the script *sa* composed of two lines

```
a=10
display(b)
```

we have on Command Window

```
a = 10
??? Undefined function or variable 'b'.
```

Step 2. Executing immediately afterward the script *sb*, composed by two lines too

```
b=100
display(a)
```

we have on Command Window

```
b = 100
a = 10
```

Step 3. Executing again the script *sa* Command Window returns the values of the two variables even if *a* is not defined into the script *sb*. This takes the value of *a* from the Workspace.

```
a = 10
b =  100
```

After the step 2 the same result as that of the step 3 can be obtained typing at the command prompt (>>) first *a* + Return key and then *b* + Return key: now it is Command window that takes the values of *a* and of *b* from the Workspace.

If we clear the Workspace (typing "clear" on the Command Window) and repeat the step 1 or the step 2 an error results for the *display* command.

3.3 The Anonymous Function

An anonymous function is made of a single line and can be used both by a script and by a function (Sec. 3.4). Its general form is

```
fh=@(arg1, arg2, . . .) expr
```

where
- arg1, arg2,... is a list of input arguments
- expr is an expression
- @ is the MATLAB operator that constructs a function handle
- fh is the function handle.

The general form to call an anonymous function in a script or in a function is

```
var = fh(arg1,arg2, ...)
```

where var is the name of the variable that receives the calculated value of the expression.

As a simple example, we define an anonymous function with only one input argument x:

```
fh=@(x) x*x
```

We can call this with the assignment statement

```
square=fh(2)
```

that returns

```
square=4
```

Here the function handle fh "*handles*" (as a virtual human hand) the value *2*, put it into the expression *x*x*, calculate the result *4* and transfers back it to the variable *square*.

The following example has two input arguments

```
sin_cos=@(x,y) sin(x)+cos(y)
alfa1=3.1416/2
alfa2=3.1416*2
result=sin_cos(alfa1,alfa2)
```

When the script is executed, it returns

```
result=2.0000
```

In the two preceding examples the variables *square* and *result* are numerical values of class *double*, whereas the variables *fh* and *sin_cos* are values of class *function_handle*.

If the anonymous function doesn't have input argument empty parentheses must be used for the list of arguments and for the calling function; here is an example (*date* is a MATLAB function that returns the actual day, See Sec. 5.3)

```
t=@ ( ) date
t ( )
```

When executed it returns

```
ans = 05-Dec-2007
```

Here the MATLAB variable *ans* has class *char* and *t* has class *function_handle*.

We can pass a function to another function using function handles as in the following example

```
f=@(x) x^2
g=@(x)2*x
h=@(x)g(f(x))
a=h(2)
```

Running the script the return is

```
a=8
```

where *f*, g and *h* have class *function handle* and *a* has class *double.*

We can use function handles in structures and cell arrays but not in the standard arrays. For example

```
S.a = @sin;  S.b = @cos;  S.c = @tan
C = {@sin, @cos, @tan}
```

are respectively supported structure and cell arrays whereas the following standard array it isn't

```
A = [@sin, @cos, @tan]
```

3.4 Examples of Anonymous Function

The following two M-files have simple and self-explanatory lines of code and many lines of comment. The double percent (%%) signify we are using the *Cell Mode.*

Example 3.1 (*AnonymF1.m*)

```
%anonymous function
%that converts degrees into radians
conv=@(deg)(pi/180)*(deg);
%the array deg 1x4 is defined
deg=0:30:90;
%the function_handle conv is used for conversion
radian=conv(deg);
%properties of conv and radian are ascertained
%through the final command WHOS
% ------------------------------------------------------------
%%
%the anonymous function is defined
h=@(x)sin(x);
%input argument x is defined into the function_handle h
y1=h(-2*pi:0.1:2*pi);
plot(-2*pi:0.1:2*pi,y1),title('sin')
figure
% ------------------------------------------------------------
%%
%EZPLOT can have a function_handle as argument
%whereas PLOT must have as arguments arrays of class double
%conversion to double from function_handle is not possible
ezplot(@cos)
%plot(@cos) would return an error
% ------------------------------------------------------------
%%
%the anonymous function uses cell array
%to calculate a polynomial of degree two
%each element of the cell is an anonymous function
A={@(a,x)a*x^2,@(b,x)b*x,@(c)c};
%when the function is called, the values of  corresponding
%input arguments are defined for each element of the cell
y2=A{1}(-2,10)+A{2}(3.5,10)+A{3}(2.75);
whos
```

The following results are displayed in the Command Window for the executable lines not terminated with a semicolon

Name	Size	Bytes	Class
A	1x3	228	cell
conv	1x1	16	function_handle
deg	1x4	32	double
h	1x1	16	function_handle
radian	1x4	32	double
y1	1x126	1008	double
y2	1x1	8	double

Example 3.2 (*AnonymF2.m*)

```
%%
%polynomial of degree two is defined in the range (-40,40)
x=-40:0.5:40;
%coefficients of polynomial a, b, c
%are the arguments of the anonymous function
pol_degree2=@(a,b,c)(a*x.^2+b*x+c);
%a, b, c are input argoments of the function
%polinomial is calculated
y=pol_degree2(-2,3.5,2.75);
%y being a variable of class double can be used
%with PLOT function
plot(x,y),title('polinomial of degree two')
%___________________________________________________
%%
%anonymous function uses a cell array
%for calculation of a polynomial of degree two
A={@(a1,x1)a1*x1.^2,@(b1,x1)b1*x1,@(c1)c1};
%values of a1, b1, c1 and x1
%are the input arguments
y1=A{1}(-2,[-5:1:5])+A{2}(3.5,[-5:1:5])+A{3}(2.75);
%but the PLOT function cannot be used
%since the x1 array is implicitly defined
```

```
% ______________________________________________
%%
B={@(a2,x2)a2*x2.^2,@(b2,x2)b2*x2,@(c2)c2};
%now the PLOT function can be used
%the x2 array is explicitly defined
x2=-10:1:10;
%the returning argument y2 is calculated
y2=B{1}(-2,x2)+B{2}(3.5,x2)+B{3}(2.75);
%since arrays x2 and y2 are explicitly defined
%the PLOT function can be used
figure
plot(x2,y2),title('polinomial of degree two using cell')
whos
```

The following results are displayed in the Command Window for the executable lines not terminated with a semicolon

Name	Size	Bytes	Class
A	1x3	228	cell
B	1x3	228	cell
pol_degree2	1x1	16	function_handle
x	1x161	1288	double
x2	1x21	168	double
y	1x161	1288	double
y1	1x11	88	double
y2	1x21	168	double

3.5 The Function: Basic Syntax

The function is an M-file that has the following *declaration* as first *line*

```
function [arg1_out, arg2_out, ...] = d_name(arg1_in, arg2_in, ...)
```

A function can accept input arguments and return output arguments. These input/output arguments are optional. If output arguments, arg1_out, arg2_out, ...,, are present some values must be assigned in the body of the function to them.

A function is executed when it is called by an M-file (a script or another function) with the following *call statement*

```
[var1_out var2_out ...] = f_name(var1_in, var2_in, ...)
```

The calling name *f_name* is the name of the M-file saved to permanent storage on disk: the name *d_name* of the definition line can be equal to f_name. But the d_name can be a dummy name too. When MATLAB does not recognize the function name d_name, it searches for a file with name f_name on the disk.

Variables enclosed in square brackets that are returned by the called function may be absent; so may be too for the variables enclosed in parentheses to the right of the name of the M-file f_name.

Remember that the *last updated* version of the file f_name *must always be saved before it is called* and the "Current Directory" (see the arrow d in Fig. 1.2 of Sec. 1.1) on the Tool bar of the Command Window *must display the directory* where this file is saved. Many errors using functions occur if this rule is disregarded.

The following two examples have deceitfully simple but self-explanatory lines of code. The double percent (%%) signify we are using the *Cell Mode* for the scripts.

Example 3.3 (*script: s1.m - function:f1.m*)

Script s1

```
x=-2:2; %the array x is defined
y=f1(x); %the array y is defined calling function f1
```

Function f1

%VERSION 1:the function name f1 appears on the right

```
function z=f1(x1)
xq1=x1.^2
z=18-xq1/8 %z must be on the left part of the assignment
```

```
%-----------------------------------------------------------------------
%VERSION 2: f1 is on the left and becomes output argument
% function f1=a(x2)
% xq2=x2.^2
% f1=18-xq2/8 %f1 must be on the left part of the line
%-----------------------------------------------------------------------
%VERSION 3: the function name f1 is completely absent
% function c=b(x3)
% xq3=x3.^2
% c=18-xq3/8 %a must be on the left part of the line
%-----------------------------------------------------------------------
```

Whichever version of the function f1 is made "Uncomment" on the Editor, the Command Window displays the values of y returned by the function

```
y = 7.5000   17.8750   18.0000   17.8750   17.5000
```

The version 1 of the function displays too

```
xq1 = 4    1    0    1    4
z = 7.5000   17.8750   18.0000   17.8750   17.5000
```

the version 2 gives (f1 replaces z)

```
xq2 = 4    1    0    1    4
f1 = 17.5000   17.8750   18.0000   17.8750   17.5000
```

and for version 3 we have (c replaces the previous values)

```
xq3 = 4    1    0    1    4
c = 17.5000   17.8750   18.0000   17.8750   17.5000
```

Example 3.4 (*script: s2.m - function: f2.m*)

Script s2

```
%%
%VERSION 1 of s2
f2 %the correct call for a function without arguments
%―――――――――――――――――――――――――――――――――――――――――――――――――――――
%%
%VERSION 2 of s2
% y=f2 %incorrect call: there is nothing to assign to y
```

Function f2

```
%UNCOMMENT ONLY ONE OF THE TWO VERSIONS
%―――――――――――――――――――――――――――――――――――――――――――――――――――――
%VERSION 1 of f2
function y1=F10
x=-12:12;xq=x.^2;y=18-xq/8;
plot(x,y)
%VERSION 2 of f2
% function F20
% x=-12:12;xq=x.^2;y=18-xq/8;
% plot(x,y)
```

This example shows the two versions of the script with only one line of code containing the call to the function f2 that has two options too. The four results that may occur are shown in Table 3.1.

Table 3.1 Results using different options of the script and function.

Script s2	Function f2	Plot execution	Error
Version 1	Version 1	yes	not
Version 1	Version 2	yes	not
Version 2	Version 1	yes	Error in = = > f2 at 7
Version 2	Version 2	not	Error using = = > f2

3.6 The Local Workspace of a Function

Variables of each function are called *local* because they operate within their own workspace, called too *function workspace*, that is separate from the Workspace we access at the MATLAB command prompt or used by the scripts. Consider the following example with the following script *s3*

```
c=10
y1=f3a(20);
y2=f3b(30);
```

that calls functions *f3a*

```
function f3a
function a1= f3a(x1)
a1=x1*x1
```

and function *f3b*

```
function a2=f3b(x2)
a2=x2*x2
display(a1)
```

These M-files have been stored on the same directory of a disk and this directory have been selected in the field of the *Current Directory* (see the arrow d in Fig. 1.2 of Sec. 1.1) of the Command window.

Running the script s3, the functions are called and the following results are obtained in the Command window:

```
c = 10
a1 = 400
a2 = 900
??? Undefined function or variable 'a1'.
Error in ==> f3b at 3 display(a1)
```

The function *f3b* does not recognize the variable *a1* of the function *f3a*. The situation is depicted in Fig. 3.3.

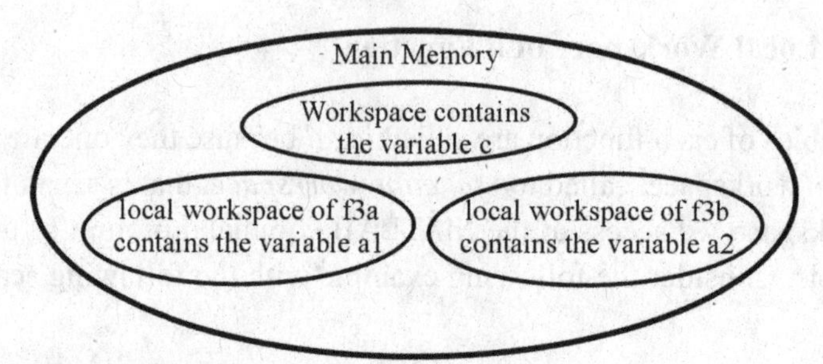

Fig. 3.3 Functions have their own workspaces.

Variables defined in the workspace of a function are not shared neither with the local workspaces of other functions nor with the basic Workspace of the scripts, unless they are defined *global*. Variables defined in the same workspace of a function do not remain in memory from one function call to the next, unless they are defined as *persistent*. These declarations of a variable as GLOBAL or as PERSISTENT are clarified with the following examples.

We define the script s4

```
c=10
y1=f4a_G1(20);
y2=f4b_G1(30);
```

the function f4a_G1

```
global c
c_f4a=c
a1=x1*x1;
```

and the function f4b_G1

```
global c
c_f4b=c
a2=x2*x2
```

Running the script s4 (remember the advice of the Sec. 3.5), the functions are called and executed with the following results (Fig. 3.4a)

```
c = 10
c_f4a = [ ]
c_f4b =  [ ]
a2 =  900
```

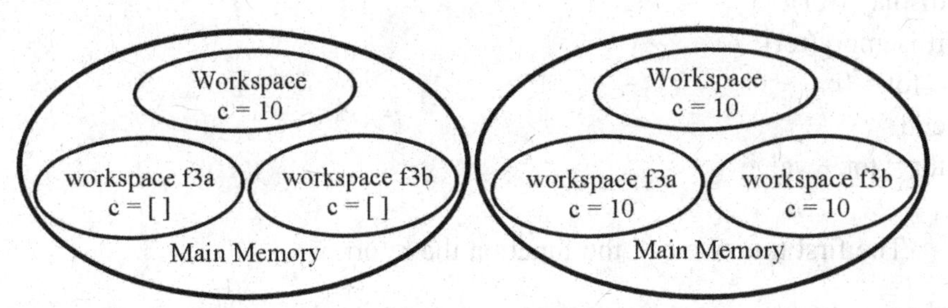

Fig. 3.4a The variable c isn't declared global in the script.

Fig. 3.4b The variable c is declared global in the script too.

The *value* of the variable c, defined in the script where c is not declared GLOBAL, is not transferred to the two functions. However, since c is declared GLOBAL in both functions, it becomes here an empty array and so assigned to the variables c_f4a and c_f4b. If c is declared GLOBAL also in the script the Command window returns (Fig. 3.4b)

```
c = 10
c_f4a = 10
c_f4b = 10
a2 = 900
```

The declaration PERSISTENT is not permitted for a variable of a script: it is allowed only in a function. Persistent variables are known only to the function in which they are declared. This prevents persistent variables from being changed by other functions or from a command line in Command window. Persistent variables are cleared when the function is deleted or we quit MATLAB. The global and persistent variables are similar as they create permanent storage for both. An example of use of persistent variables follows. The script is composed by the single line

```
f5_P(5)
```

calling the function f5_P

```
function f5_P(value)
persistent tot
display (tot)
if isempty(tot)
  tot = 0;
end
tot = tot + value
```

The first time we call the function the return is

```
tot =  [ ]
tot = 5
```

Calling f5_P again, we have

```
tot = 5
tot = 10
```

and so on.

3.7 The Types of Functions: Primary, Subfunction and Nested

In the previous Sections 3.5 and 3.6 we have defined function an M-file executed when is called by a script or invoked by a command line in Command Window. This is a *primary*, or outer or external, function. Besides can be defined an *internal* function too. This is a function that is executed only if it is invoked by a primary function or by another internal function. There are many practicable arrangements of functions internal to other functions that one can devise in accordance with the requirements of its own programming task. Two basic types of internal functions are *subfunctions* and *nested* functions.

A subfunction must begin with its own *function definition line* as it is required for the primary function. The subfunctions must immediately follow each other in any order, as long as the primary function appears first. Here is an example.

Example 3.5 (*script: s_primF.m - function: f_primF.m*)

Script s_primF

```
% ____________________________________________________________
%the array t;
t=[66 69 65 66 68 61 62 64 62 63];
%mean and plot of t
mean=f_primF(t);
% ____________________________________________________________
```

Function f_primF

```
% ____________________________________________________________
%Two subfunctions (f_subF1 and f_subF2) are defined
%within a function (SubF)
% ____________________________________________________________
function value = f_primF(u) % Primary function
n = length(u);
testP=10;
value = f_subF1(u,n);
f_subF2(u,n);
% ____________________________________________________________
function a = f_subF1(v,m)  % Subfunction
testS1=20;
% Calculate average.
a=sum(v)/m;
% ____________________________________________________________
function f_subF2(w,p)       % Subfunction
testS2=30;
z=1:p;
plot(z,w);
% ____________________________________________________________
```

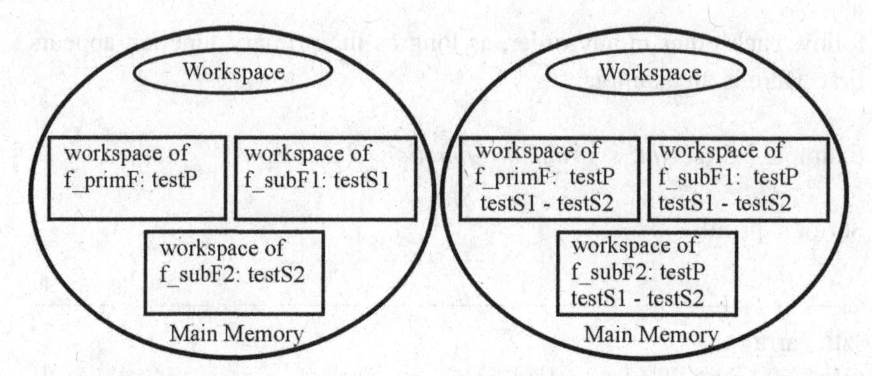

Fig. 3.5a Subfunctions have their own workspaces.

Fig. 3.5b Situation whem global command is used in the three functions.

In Command window doesn't appear any result. Only the Figure window displays the plot requested. Using a display command in the primary and in each of the two subfunctions, the variables testP, testS1 and testS2 could be used to check if the primary function can share a variable with each of the two subfunctions or if a subfunction can share a variable with the other subfunction. The answer would be in any case a message of error. In fact the primary function and the two subfunctions have their own workspace (Fig. 3.5a). Declaring GLOBAL all the three variables in the primary function and in each subfunction, these are present in each of the three workspaces (Fig. 3.5b).

A function defined within another function and with its own *function definition line*, as it is required for the primary function and for a subfunction, becomes nested when this and its primary function are terminated with the END statement. It is possible that nested functions can be nested within other nested functions and can call subfunctions defined within them. The following two examples elucidate the basic features.

We have the script *s_nest1*

```
%%
value=1000; perc=0.15;
y=f_nest1(value,perc)
```

that calls the function *f_nest1* and its nested function *perc*

```
function y1 =f_nest1(x1,x2)
y1=perc

   function y2=perc
      y3=x2*x1
      y2=y3
   end
test1=y3
end
```

After execution Command window returns y = 150 (1000x0.15). The same value is assigned to the variable test1 external to the nested function.

Even if the calculation is very simple the example clarifies the structure of a nested function. We observe that the variable test1, external to the nested function, can assume a value defined within the nested function.

Here is the last example that uses a function handle.

The script s_nest2

```
%%
b=10;
expo=3;
value = f_nest2;
result=value(b,expo)
```

calls the function f_nest2

```
function h = f_nest2
h = @power

   function y = power(b,expo)
   y = b^expo
   end

%test2=y
end
```

Now Command window returns the function handle and the result

```
h = @f_nest2/power
y = 1000 (10^3)
```

To understand the action of the function handle in this example remember what has been said in Sec. 3.3 about the task the function handle can accomplish.

Now the variable test2 defined within the outer function cannot share the value of the variable y defined within the nested function. If we made uncomment the line

```
test2=y
```

an error message returns in Command window.

About Chapter 4

Treating numerical arrays MATLAB reserves a great space (about 20% of all the functions present in the Appendix 2) to their applications in mathematics grouped in the following subjects: *Linear algebra, Polynomials, Interpolation and Computational Geometry, Cartesian Coordinate System Conversion, Nonlinear Numerical Methods, Specialized Math, Sparse Matrices*.

We concern instead the formal characteristics of the arrays and the simple operations we can perform on them using numbers.

We will give general rules to create an array, specify a part of it, expand or diminish its size, change its shape, shift or sort its elements, and define its measure.

Then we will consider how numbers are displayed and stored in memory and elementary functions which provide some basic constants, operators and operations.

Chapter 4

Numerical Arrays

4.1 Creating an Array

Treating images (Sec. 7.2) we will use three-dimensional numerical arrays having p rectangular pages of m rows and n columns. Quite often we will consider two-dimensional arrays with sizes 1-by-1 (a single value), 1-by-n and m-by-1 (a row- and column-wise array) and n-by-m. An array can be also empty with dimensions equal to zero (0-by-0).

As stated in our Introduction we do not consider some special numerical arrays, with their related MATLAB built-in functions, that have specific meaning in advanced mathematics (linear algebra): scalars of size 1-by-1, vectors of sizes 1-by-m or n-by-1, and matrices with m-by-n elements.

Some general rules are valid to build an array:

- The elements of a row can be separated with blanks or commas
- If there are more rows, a semicolon (;) has to be used at the end of each row
- Clearly all rows must have the same number of elements
- The list of elements becomes an array if it is placed within square brackets, [ ]. These are used not only as a constructor operator to create an array but also as a concatenation operator to make greater an array by combining together more arrays and to delete rows or columns from an array (Sec. 4.4)
- The square brackets operator constructs only two-dimensional arrays.

Each of the following two lines can define an array 2-by-2:

```
a = [1 2; 3 4]
```

or

```
a = [1, 2; 3, 4]
```

Writing b = [ ], we define *b* as an empty array of size 0-by-0.

Subscripts are used to determine an element of an array. The element in row i and column j of an array is denoted by a (i, j). For example, looking for the element (3) in the second row and first column of the previous example we write a (2,1).

We have used implicitly the colon operator just from the Chapter 2 to create simple arrays. The colon operator (:) is used to *create arrays* of numerical elements with regularly spaced increments between them. We assume i, j and k are defined variables containing *real* numbers, as 1, -1, 0.1, -0.1, *etc*. The rule to create an array is

```
i : j : k
```

where i is the first term, j the increment and k the last term.

The keyword END can be used to designate the last element k in a row or column of an existent array. This keyword can be useful in instances where we don't know the value of k.

This keyword is also used (Sec. 3.7) to terminate a nested function or a conditional block of code such as *if* and *for* blocks (Ch. 8).

The increment term j cannot be equal to zero and can be omitted if equal to one. If j > 0, k must be greater than i; but if j < 0, k must be smaller than i. Some examples are reported in Table 4.1

Table 4.1 Some uses of colon operator to create arrays.

Command	Condition	Result
1: 5 or 1 : 1 : 5	j > 0 and k>i	1 2 3 4 5
1 : 2 : 6	j > 0 and k>i	1 3 5
1 : 0.3 : 2	j > 0 and k>i	1.0 1.3 1.6 1.9
1:-3:-6	j<0 and i > k	1 -2 -5
10:-2:4	j<0 and i > k	10 8 6 4
(0 : pi/3 : 2*pi)*180/pi	j > 0 and k>i	60 120 180 240 300 360
1:0:5 or 1:0:-5	j = 0	Empty array: 1-by-0
10:2:4	j > 0 and i > k	Empty array: 1-by-0
4:-2:10	j<0 and i < k	Empty array: 1-by-0

Strictly speaking the colon operator creates arrays of size 1-by-m: it is with the aid of the semicolon and of the square brackets that it allows to create two- or three-dimensional arrays.

Special arrays of size 1-by-m can be created using the function LINSPACE

```
y = linspace(i, k, m)
```

where i and k are the first and the last elements of the array and m is the number of elements including i and k. If m is omitted it is assumed equal to 100.

The m elements are *linearly* spaced, that is, if y is plotted versus m a line is displayed.

In this interval LINSPACE calculates, linearly spaced and including i and k, m elements. The colon operator (:) doesn't determine the number m for the size of the array whereas LINSPACE gives direct control over it.

The difference between the colon operator and the linspace function is clearly highlighted in the following simple script

```
y1=linspace(1,30,10)
x=1:10
plot(x,y1)
figure
y2=1 : 2.2 : 30
m=length(y2)
plot(1:m,y2)
```

Both *y1* and *y2* define arrays with elements *linearly* (as we can verify by the plots) spaced between 1 and 30; but the length (10) of y1 is fixed within the function whereas that (14) of y2 depends from the value (2.2) assigned to the increment.

An array can be built starting from the elements of the diagonal using the function DIAG. The syntax is

```
a = diag(x, dim)
```

where *x* is an array of size 1-by-n. If $d = 0$, *x* defines the main diagonal, if it is positive/negative element of *x* are placed above/below the main diagonal.

Here are some examples.

We define *x*

```
x=[1 2 3]'
```

as

```
x =
    1
    2
    3
```

An array of size 3-by-3 with *x* as main diagonal:

```
b=diag(x,0)
```

is

```
b =
    1   0   0
    0   2   0
    0   0   3
```

An array of size 4-by-4 with *x* above the main diagonal:

```
c=diag(x,1)
```

is

```
c =
     0     1     0     0
     0     0     2     0
     0     0     0     3
     0     0     0     0
```

An array of size 4-by-4 with *x* below the main diagonal:

```
d=diag(x,-1)
```

is

```
d =
     0     0     0     0
     1     0     0     0
     0     2     0     0
     0     0     3     0
```

4.2 Specifying a Part of an Array

The colon operator (:) is used to pick out a portion of an array as a selected row or column and a portion of a selected row or column of an array.

If *a* is a one-dimensional array

```
a(j:k)
```

selects a portion of the array: a(j), a(j+1),...,a(k); its length is k – j + 1.

For a two-dimensional we can chose among the following options (Fig. 4.1):

```
a(i,:)
```

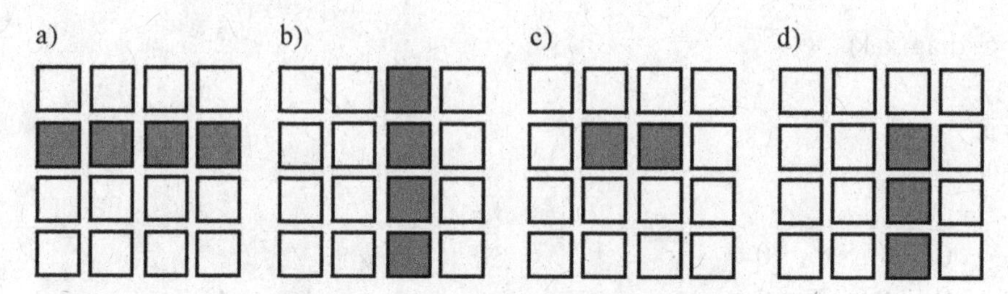

Fig. 4.1 We can extract all or some elements of a row or a column.

selects the full ith row of the array.

```
a(:,j)
```

selects the full jth column of the array.

```
a(i,j:k)
```

selects a portion of the ith row of the array: a(i:,j), a(i,j+1),...,a(i:,k). And

```
a(i:k,:j)
```

selects a portion of the jth column of the array: a(i,j), a(i+1,j),...,a(k,j).

These options can be extended to a three-dimensional array.

The diagonal elements of an array can be extracted from an array using the function DIAG.

If we have the array

```
a =
    1  2  3
    4  5  6
    7  8  9
```

the following command

```
diag(a,0)
```

pull out the main diagonal

```
ans =
   1
   5
   9
```

Omitting the parameter 0:

```
diag(a)
```

The same result is obtained

```
ans =
   1
   5
   9
```

Using the parameter 1

```
diag(a,1)
```

we draw out the diagonal immediately above the main one

```
ans =
   2
   6
```

and with the parameter -1

```
diag(a,-1)
```

that immediately below

```
ans =
   4
   8
```

A two-dimensional array can be used to create a three-dimensional one with p pages writing a (:, :, p). If we have the array a = [1, 2; 3, 4], to add a third page to it we write

```
a(:,:,3)=[5 6;7 8]
```

with result

```
a(:,:,1) =
    1   2
    3   4
a(:,:,2) =
    0   0
    0   0
a(:,:,3) =
    5   6
    7   8
```

Assigning values to the third page, Command window puts zeros into all elements of the second page.

The element in row i, column j and page k of the array is denoted by a (i, j, k). For example, looking for the element (7) in the second row, first column of the third page we write a (2,1,3).

Writing a (:), a previous defined two- or three-dimensional array becomes a one-dimensional array *regarded as a single column*. Really, arrays are not stored as we write them or they appear on Command Window, but as a single column composed of all the columns subsequently appended. Usually we refer to an element of an array, for example of size n-by-m, assigning values to the two subscripts i and j. If we consider this array as a single column, as is stored in memory only one *linear index* is necessary to pick out an element: there are two functions (SUB2IND and IND2SUB) that allow conversion between the subscripts and the linear index.

4.3 Built-in Arrays

MATLAB supplies some basic arrays. To create an array of zero with size n-by-m we write

```
a = zeros(n,m)
```

If n = m or if m is omitted the size is n-by-n. As example

```
a = zeros (2, 2)
```

gives

```
a =
   0  0
   0  0
```

An array with all elements equal to one is given by

```
a=ones(n,m)
```

If n = m or if m is omitted the size is n-by-n. This array allows to define arrays with all elements equal to any number x; for example, writing

```
a=(ones(2,3)*2.5
```

we have

```
a =
  2.5  2.5  2.5
  2.5  2.5  2.5
```

The functions RAND and RANDN gives arrays with uniformly and normally distributed random elements on the unit interval. These probably will not sound as simple as the previous ones even if the syntax is the same. For example

```
a = rand(3)
```

gives

```
a =
   0.8147   0.9134   0.2785
   0.9058   0.6324   0.5469
   0.1270   0.0975   0.9575
```

If we want elements on different interval (1, n) we have to multiply the array by n. For example, writing

```
a=fix(100*rand(3))
```

the result is a range of integer random numbers in the interval (1, 100)

```
a =
   81   91   27
   90   63   54
   12    9   95
```

For a didactic use there is also the magic array that we used in Chapter 2. Its syntax is

```
a=magic(n)
```

where n must be greater than 2. The result is a square array n-by-n that has the same value if we sum all elements of each row or of each column and of the main diagonal.

4.4 Expanding or Diminishing Size of an Array

To join small matrices to make a bigger one we use the pair of square brackets, [ ] as a concatenation operator. As example, from the 2-by-2 array a =

  1 1
  1 1

An array 4-by-4 is obtained writing

```
a=[a a+2;a+3 a+4]
```

The result is

```
a =
  1  1  3  3
  1  1  3  3
  4  4  5  5
  4  4  5  5
```

Clearly we can enlarge arrays using concatenation as long as the resulting array maintains a rectangular shape. So adding an array to another one horizontally, each must have the same number of rows and adding them vertically each will have the same number of columns.

Also the functions CAT, HORZCAT, VERTCAT can enlarge an array using concatenation.

Another function allows to make larger an array replicating and grouping tile-wise a minor one. The syntax is

```
b = repmat(a,m,n)
```

where a is the array to replicate as if it was a single element in m rows and n column. For example applying to the array

a =

  1 2
  3 4

the command

```
b=repmat(a,2,2)
```

we obtain

```
b =
    1   2   1   2
    3   4   3   4
    1   2   1   2
    3   4   3   4
```

A pair of empty square brackets can be used to delete rows and columns from an array. Starting with the following 3-by-3 array

```
a =
    1   2   3
    4   5   6
    7   8   9
```

we can delete the second row with the command

```
a(2, :)=[ ]
```

Now the array becomes

```
a =
    1   2   3
    7   8   9
```

From the new array 2-by-3 we can obtain a 2-by-2 array cutting, for example, the third column writing

```
a(;, 3) = [ ]
```

The result is

```
a=
    1   2
    7   8
```

Finally with

```
a(1:2)=[ ]
```

the result is the last column considered as a row

```
a =
   2   8
```

As another example, the array of size 4-by-3

```
a =
   1    2    3
   4    5    6
   7    8    9
  10   11   12
```

can be resized to 2-by-3 by cutting the second and the third row if we write

```
a(2: 3, :)=[ ]
```

Now the result is

```
a =
   1    2    3
  10   11   12
```

4.5 Changing the Shape of an Array

There are some functions that can change the form of an array (Table 4.2)

Table 4.2 Options to modify an array.

Function	Description
RESHAPE	Modify the shape
ROT90	Rotate the array by 90 degrees
FLIPLR	Flip the array about a vertical axis
FLIPUD	Flip the array about a horizontal axis
FLIPDIM	Flip the array along the specified direction
TRANSPOSE	Flip an array about its main diagonal, turning rows into columns and vice versa
CTRANSPOSE	Transpose an array and replace each element with its complex conjugate

An array can be modified in its form changing the number of rows from n to n1 and of columns from m to m1 on condition to keep up equal their products: n*m = n1*m1. To change the array

```
a =
    1   2   3
    4   5   6
```

of size 2-by-3 into the array *b* of size 3-by2 we use the function RESHAPE in its simplest form

```
b = reshape (a,3,2)
```

to obtain as result

```
b =
    1   5
    4   3
    2   6
```

The elements of the array *b* are taken column-wise from *a*.

For the transpose operation (See Table 4.6 in the Sec. 4.9) we can use either the TRANSPOSE function or the dot-apostrophe operator (.'); for the operation of complex conjugate transpose the equivalent operator of CTRANPOSE is simply the sign ('). The apostrophe operator (e.g., a') performs a complex conjugate transposition. It flips an array about its main diagonal and also changes the sign of the imaginary component of any complex elements of the array. The dot-apostrophe operator (e.g., a.'), transposes without affecting the sign of complex elements. For arrays containing all real elements, the two operators return the same result. Here are some examples:

From

```
a =
    1   2
    3   4
```

its transpose *b* is given writing

```
b=a'
```

and the result is

```
b =
   1   3
   2   4
```

If *a* has complex elements

```
a =
   1.0000 + 1.0000i      2.0000
   3.0000                4.0000 - 1.0000i
```

we have the transpose simply writing

```
b = a.'
```

The result is

```
b =
   1.0000 + 1.0000i    3.0000
   2.0000              4.0000 - 1.0000i
```

For the complex conjugate transpose we write

```
c = a'
```

Now the result is

```
c =
   1.0000 - 1.0000i    3.0000
   2.0000              4.0000 + 1.0000i
```

We see what happens using the ROT90, FLIPLR, FLIPUD and FLIPDIM functions using the array

```
a =
    1    2
    3    4
```

Writing

```
b=rot90(a)
```

we have

```
b =
    2    4
    1    3
```

And from

```
c=fliplr(a)
```

we obtain

```
c =
    2    1
    4    3
```

Then from

```
d=flipud(a)
```

we have

```
d =
    3    4
    1    2
```

If we use

```
flipdim(a,dim)
```

it returns *a* with dimension *dim* flipped. For dim = 1, the array is flipped row-wise down and for dim = 2, the array is flipped column-wise left to right. Hence flipdim(a,1) is the same as flipud(a), and flipdim(a, 2) is the same as fliplr(a).

4.6 Shifting and Sorting an Array

To shift circularly an array *a* into an array *b* we write

```
b = circshift(a,shiftsize)
```

where shiftsize = [r c] with r and c integer numbers; we consider the simplest cases: [r 0] and [0 c]. Under the first assumption we have (See next example)

– a number r of circular shift of the rows up if r is positive and down if r is negative without any shifting of the columns because the second element within the square brackets is 0.

Under the second assumption we have (See next example)

– a number c of circular shift of the columns from right to left if c is positive and from left to right if c is negative without any shifting of the rows because the second element within the square brackets is 0.

Here are the examples assuming as starting point the array

```
a =
   1   2   3
   4   5   6
   7   8   9
```

One circular shift up of the rows for the array a is given by the command

```
b=circshift(a,[1 0])
```

with result

```
b =
   7   8   9
   1   2   3
   4   5   6
```

One circular shift down of the rows for the array *a* is given by the command

```
c=circshift(a,[-1 0])
```

with result

```
c =
   4   5   6
   7   8   9
   1   2   3
```

One circular shift right of the columns for the array *a* is given by the command

```
d=circshift(a,[0 1])
```

that returns

```
d =
   3   1   2
   6   4   5
   9   7   8
```

One circular shift left of the columns for the array *a* is given by the command

```
e=circshift(a,[0 -1])
```

with result

```
e =
   2   3   1
   5   6   4
   8   9   7
```

If we need to put into ascending or descending order the rows or the columns of an array a we use the SORT function

```
b = sort (a, dim, string)
```

where *dim* = 1 if the function must act on the columns and *dim* = 2 if the function must act on the rows; *string* is 'ascend' (default) or 'descend'. If *dim* and *string* are omitted the function acts in ascending order on the columns. Here are some simple examples assuming as starting point the array

```
a =
   56   18   70
   25   44   13
   85   27   64
```

The function acts in ascending order on the columns with command

```
b=sort(a)
```

with the result

```
b =
   25   18   13
   56   27   64
   85   44   70
```

Adding the parameter dim = 1 the result doesn't change.

```
c=sort(a, 1)
```

The result is again

```
c =
   25   18   13
   56   27   64
   85   44   70
```

The function acts in ascending order on the rows specifying dim = 2

```
d=sort(a, 2)
```

The result is

```
d =
  18   56   70
  13   25   44
  27   64   85
```

The function acts in descending order on the rows specifying dim = 2 and string = 'descend'

```
e=sort(a,2,'descend')
```

with result

```
e =
  70   56   18
  44   25   13
  85   64   27
```

4.7 Measuring an Array

The functions that return general information about an array are LENGTH, SIZE, NDIMS and NUMEL.

The first function returns the value of the longest dimension. It returns 0 if the array is empty.

As examples, for the arrays a = ones (1, 10), b = ones (2, 5) and c = ones (8, 3, 2), the corresponding lengths are 10, 5, 8

The main syntactic patterns of the function SIZE are

```
d = size(a)
v = size(a,dim)
```

where d is an array 1-by-m containing the sizes of each dimension of array a and v is the size of the dimension specified with *dim*.

For the previous three arrays typing

```
sa = size ( a )
sb = size ( b )
sc = size ( c, 2 )
```

the results are respectively

```
1   10
2   5
3
```

The function NDIMS returns the number of dimensions. The main syntactic pattern is

```
n = ndims (a)
```

For the previous three arrays typing sa = ndims (a), sb = ndims (b), sc = ndims (c) the results are respectively 2, 2, 3.

The function NUMEL gives the number of elements in array. The main syntactic pattern is

```
n = numel (a)
```

For the previous three arrays the results are respectively 10, 10 and 48.

We can observe that the same result is obtained writing either ndims (a) or length (size (a)) and that length (a) is equivalent to the maximum value obtained with size (a).

From the beginning we have given to a value of every type (numerical, *etc.*) a name and considered this formally as an array. Every array, being graphically a square or rectangular form, needs always two dimensions. Then the least possible degree for an array is n-by-m, with n and m positive integer numbers equal to or greater than one (when n or/and m are equal to zero the array is defined empty). Therefore the term "one-dimensional" isn't formally correct even if sometimes it is used for array of sizes 1-by-m or n-by-1 (a row- or column-wise arrays). The simplest cases, we know, are summarized in Table 4.3 where is included the singleton qualifier of a dimension. A singleton dimension is any dimension dim of an array a for which size (a, dim) = 1. For example, for the following array 4-by-1

```
a =
   1
   2
   3
   4
```

we can make the sum of the elements along the first (*dim* = 4) non-singleton dimension with the result 10; but it has not a meaning "make a sum" about the second (*dim* = 1) singleton dimension.

Table 4.3 Cases of singleton arrays.

First dimension	Second dimension	Number of values represented	Qualifier of the first dimension	Qualifier of the second dimension
1	1	one	singleton	singleton
1	m	m in a single row	singleton	non-singleton
n	1	n in a single column	non-singleton	singleton
n	m	In n rows with m columns	non-singleton	non-singleton

Consider now the following three-dimensional array

```
a=repmat(1,[1,1,3])
```

that has as a result a single value on each of its three pages

```
a(:,:,1) = 1
a(:,:,2) = 1
a(:,:,3) = 1
```

Here the size of the array *a* is 1-by-1-by-3, and each page has size 1-

by-1. We have now two singleton dimensions into each page. The previous array *a*, of size 1-by-1-by3 can be squeezed to an array *b* of size 3-by-1 using the functions SHIFTDIM or SQEEZE.

By the first function:

```
[b,nshifts] = shiftdim(a)
```

we obtain

```
b =
    1
    1
    1
nshifts =
    2
```

where nshifts is the number of dimensions removed.

Or by the second function:

```
b=squeeze(a)
```

the result is

```
b =
    1
    1
    1
```

The second formal pattern of the function SHIFTDIM is

```
b = shiftdim(a,n)
```

Using this function with the initial array *a* of size 2-by-3

```
a =
    1   2   3
    4   5   6
```

when n = 1, 2, 3 the corresponding sizes of *b* become first 3-by-2, then 2-by-3, and again 3-by-2. If n = -1 and the initial array is always *a*, the corresponding size becomes 1-by-2-by-3 (each of the three pages having two elements). Writing

```
b=shiftdim(a,-1)
```

we obtain

```
b(:,:,1) =
   1    4
b(:,:,2) =
   2    5
b(:,:,3) =
   3    6
```

If n = -2 and the initial array is always *a*, the corresponding sizes of the array *b* become 1-by-1-by-2-by-3. Writing

```
b=shiftdim(a,-2)
```

the result is

```
b(:,:,1,1) =
   1
b(:,:,2,1) =
   4
b(:,:,1,2) =
   2
b(:,:,2,2) =
   5
b(:,:,1,3) =
   3
b(:,:,2,3) =
   6
```

We have now three three-dimensional arrays with each having only two pages and each page padded with singletons. In fact each page has only one element. This last array *b* can return the initial array *a* typing

```
a=shiftdim(b,2)
```

4.8 The Numbers as Elements of an Array

Firstly we have to distinguish between how a number is displayed setting a format for it and how it is stored in memory and used in computations.

Secondly, no matter how it is displayed, a number can be stored and used in computations in appropriate precision either as a floating-point

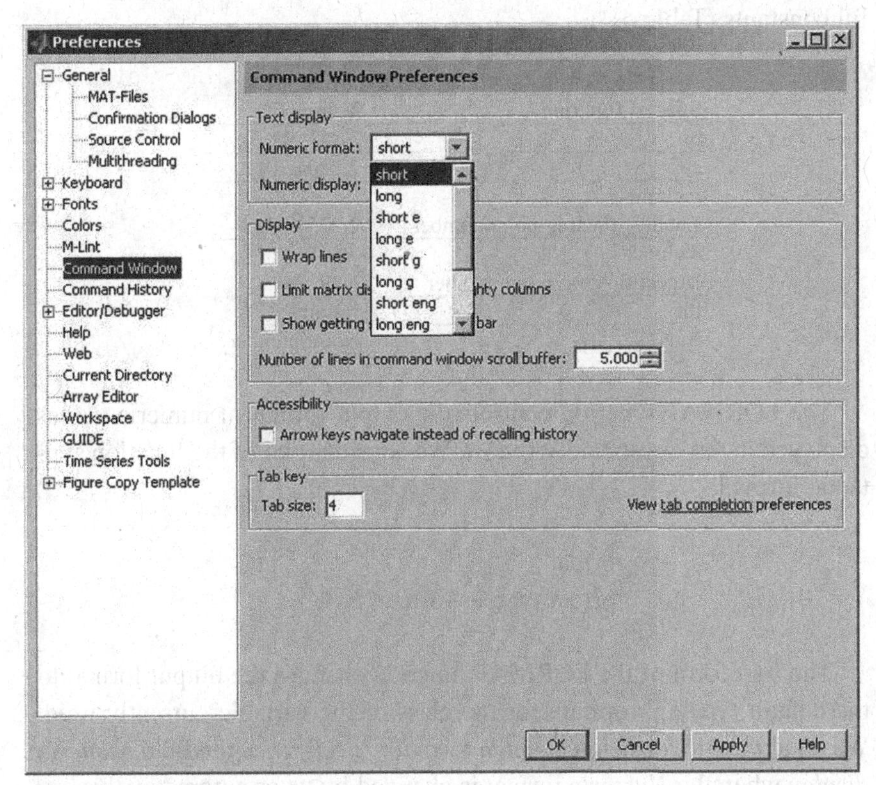

Fig. 4.2 The Preferences dialog box.

variable, namely single or double, or as an integer variable (See Sec. 2.3).

In this last case computations are done natively in integer mode and setting format, for example to short or long, does not affect the display of an integer variable.

The display for a number can be set either in the *Preferences* dialog box, accessible from the File menu in the MATLAB desktop (Fig. 4.2) or using the FORMAT function. In the first case the defined format is maintained from one session to the next while in the second case it is applied only to the current session.

Floating numbers uses conventional decimal notation, with an optional decimal point and leading plus or minus sign, for numbers. Scientific notation uses the letter *e* to specify a power-of-ten scale factor (for example 3e5 means 300000). Imaginary numbers use either i or j as a suffix (as examples: -3.14159j, 3e5i). Special functions provide values of some useful constants (Table 4.4).

Table 4.4 Constants defined by MATLAB.

Special function	**Value**
pi	3.14159265...
eps	2.2204e-016
realmin smallest floating-point number	2.2251e-308
realmax largest floating-point number	1.7977e+308
Inf	Infinity
NaN	Not-a-number

The FORMAT function controls the output format of numeric values displayed in the Command Window. We consider two of the function syntactic forms

```
format
format type or format('type')
```

The first form of the FORMAT function changes the output format to the default type appropriate for the class of the variable currently used. We set always to *loose* in *Command window Preference* the field *Numeric display* when the *Numeric format* is changed by us or automatically.

For floating-point variables, for example, the default is short format. In fact if we first set in *Command window Preference* the field *Numeric format* to *long* and then we execute the following two lines

```
format
pi
```

in Command window returns

```
ans =
   3.1416
```

and in *Command window Preference* the field *Numeric format* is by MATLAB set to *short.*

If with the field *Numeric format* set to *short* in *Command window Preference* we execute the following two lines

```
format long
pi
```

in Command window returns

```
ans =
   3.141592653589793
```

and in *Command window Preference* the field *Numeric format* returns to long.

The two options of the second form change the format to the specified type (Table 4.5). Typing the variable eps (Table 4.4) in Command window and then clicking the Return key its value is displayed

```
ans =
   2.220446049250313e-016
```

Before and after the execution of the command in *Command window Preference* the field *Numeric format* was and remains set to *long*. Then after the execution of the commands

```
format short e
pi
```

the returning value in Command window is

```
ans =
  3.1416e+000
```

and in *Command window Preference* the field *Numeric format* is set to *short e.*

Starting with the field *Numeric format* set to *short* and writing and executing again *pi* in Command window we have

```
ans =
   3.1416
```

and the field *Numeric format* remains set to *short.*

Then writing pi_double=double(pi) or pi_single=single(pi), the result is always 3.1416; whereas typing

```
format long
pi1_double=double(pi)
```

the result is

```
pi1_double =
  3.141592653589793
```

And with

```
pi1_single=single(pi)
```

we have as result

```
pi1_single =
   3.1415927
```

Hence the number of decimal digits for a double and single precision variable is respectively 15 and 7 (See Sec. 2.3 too).

Table 4.5 Format types for floating-point variables.

Type	**Result using pi**
short	3.1416
long	3.14159265358979
short e	3.1416e+000
long e	3.141592653589793e+000
short g	3.1416
long g	3.14159265358979
short eng	3.1416e+000
long eng	3.14159265358979e+000
bank	3.14
hex	400921fb54442d18
rat	355/113

The following are other useful functions: DOUBLE (Convert to double precision), SINGLE (Convert to single precision), DEC2BASE (Convert decimal to base N number in string) and BASE2DEC (Convert base N number string to decimal number) where the usual value for N are 2, 8 and 16 respectively for binary, octal and hexadecimal system of numeration.

4.9 The Simplest Arithmetic Operators and Operations

MATLAB has two different types of arithmetic operations. Matrix arithmetic operations are defined by the rules of linear algebra. When they are taken away from the world of linear algebra, matrices become two-dimensional numeric arrays where arithmetic operations are carried out element by element that can be used by multidimensional arrays too. The period character (.) distinguishes the array operations from the matrix operations (The full list of operators is in Appendix 3).

Expressions use the familiar arithmetic operators and precedence rules provided by the Table 4.6.

Table 4.6 Simplest arithmetic operators.

Symbol	Element-by-element operation
+	addition
-	subtraction
.*	multiplication
./	division
.^	power
.'	unconjugated transpose
'	conjugated transpose
.	decimal point
=	assignment

Some simple and usual mathematical operation can be performed using the functions of the Table 4.7.

Table 4.7 Simplest mathematical functions.

Function name	Operation carried out
ACOS	Inverse cosine; result in radians
ASIN	Inverse sine; result in radians
ATAN	Inverse tangent; result in radians
CEIL	Round toward infinity
COS	Cosine of argument in radians
FIX	Round toward zero
FLOOR	Round toward minus infinity
IMAG	Imaginary part of complex number
MAX	Largest elements in array
MEDIAN	Median value of array
MIN	Smallest elements in array
MOD	Modulus after division
REAL	Real part of complex number
REM	Remainder after division
ROUND	Round to nearest integer
SIN	Sine of argument in radians
TAN	Tangent of argument in radians

About Chapter 5

Also logical and literal data are considered by MATLAB arrays. The numerical, logical and literal data are used to build arrays of type Dates/Times, Structures and Cells. Logical data, representing a true or false state, are obtained using a long list of functions and operators supplied by MATLAB (See in Appendix 2 the 43 items whose first two letters are "is").

The relational operators perform element-by-element comparisons between two arrays returning a logical array of the same size.

A literal data, or string, is an array composed by a sequence of characters.

Information about date and time are represented by a string array, or a numerical array composed by many or a single numerical value.

The basic element of a structure and a cell and the functions allowing operating with both are clarified formally and with examples.

Advantages and disadvantages between structures and cells and their correlations are also discussed.

Chapter 5

Other Types of Arrays

As numerical so logical, characters and strings values are inherently array oriented. These data form arrays of class logical, char, struct and cell (See Table 2.2 in Sec. 2.3).

5.1 Logical Types

A logical data represents a true or false state using, as symbols, the numbers 1 and 0 respectively. These values are obtained using some functions and operators.

5.1.1 *Basic logical functions*

The following examples clarify the meaning of the functions TRUE, FALSE, LOGICAL.

```
a=-5;
true(a)
ans =
   [ ]

 a=1;
true(a)
ans =
   1

a=2;
```

```
true(a)
ans =
    1   1
    1   1
```

The functions TRUE, FALSE always give rise to an array. Now an example of the function LOGICAL that allows conversion of numeric values to logical ones. The commands and the corresponding results are

```
a=[1 -2 eps; 0.5 4 0]
a =
   1.0000  -2.0000   0.0000
   0.5000   4.0000        0
b=logical(a)
b =
    1   1   1
    1   1   0
```

We observe that the result is false for a(2,3) and true for the other elements including a(1,3) = eps displayed as 0.0000.

5.1.2 *Logical operators*

Table 5.1 gives implicitly definition of the operators and their precedence in the evaluations (first the NOT function, then AND and so on). Also logical expression are evaluated from left to right; if we want a different order of execution parentheses must be used to specify the intended precedence.

Table 5.1 Operators and functions used for logical expressions.

Logical A	**Logical B**	**Operator ~A Function not(A)**	**Operator A&B Function and(A,B)**	**Operator A | B Function or(A,B)**	**Function xor(A,B)**
0	0	1	0	0	0
0	1	1	0	1	1
1	0	0	0	1	1
1	1	0	1	1	0

These operators are called element-wise because they operate on corresponding elements of a logical array. There are too bit-wise logical operators that operate on corresponding bits of one or more bytes representing data of any type. The AND and OR operators can be too called short-circuit and represented by different symbols (&& and ||, respectively). For A && B if A equals zero, then the entire expression is evaluated to logical 0 (false), regardless of (i.e. short-circuiting) the value of B. Similarly for A || B, if the first term is true the expression will be assumed as true regardless of the value of B. These short-circuit operators are useful when A and B are themselves logical expressions containing, for example, relational operators.

5.1.3 *Relational operators*

Table 5.2 Relational operators.

Operator	Function	description
= =	eq	equal to
~=	ne	not equal to
<	lt	less than
>	gt	greater than
<=	le	less than or equal to
>=	ge	greater than or equal to

The relational operators (Table 5.2) perform element-by-element comparisons between two arrays returning a logical array of the same size, with elements set to logical 1 (true) where the relation is true, and elements set to logical 0 (false) where it is not. If elements are complex, the operators <, >, <=, and >= use only the real part of their operands for the comparison. The operators = = and ~= test real and imaginary part of complex elements. The following example use the array

```
a =
    8   1   6
    3   5   7
    4   9   2
```

The command and the corresponding results are

```
a(a >6) = 10
```

```
a =
  10   1   6
   3   5  10
   4  10   2
```

5.1.4 *Other logical functions*

The long list of the functions of type is* (See Appendix 2) that return logical values will be examined when the corresponding topic is treated. Part of these, regarding arguments of this Chapter, is reported in Table 5.3. The functions ANY and ALL return logical values, too. The first return a true value if any element of the array is a nonzero number or is a logical 1;

Table 5.3 Some (28) functions returning logical values.

Function	State detected
isa	Determine whether input is object of given class
iscell	Determine whether input is cell array
iscellstr	Determine whether input is cell array of strings
ischar	Determine whether item is character array
isdir	Determine whether input is a directory
isempty	Determine whether array is empty
isequal	Test arrays for equality
isequalwithequalnans	Test arrays for equality, treating NaNs as equal
isfield	Determine whether input is structure array field
isfinite	Array elements that are finite
isfloat	Determine whether input is floating-point array
isglobal	Determine whether input is global variable
ishandle	Is object handle valid
isinf	Array elements that are infinite
isinteger	Determine whether input is integer array
isletter	Array elements that are alphabetic letters
islogical	Determine whether input is logical array
isnan	Array elements that are NaN
isnumeric	Determine whether input is numeric array
isprime	Array elements that are prime numbers
isreal	Determine whether input is real array
isscalar	Determine whether input is scalar
issorted	Determine whether elements are in sorted order
isspace	Array elements that are space characters
isstr	Determine whether input is character array
isstrprop	Determine whether string is of specified category
isstruct	Determine whether input is structure array
isvarname	Determine whether input is valid variable name

the second gives true if all elements are nonzero. The following Table 5.4 shows the results of four applications of the function ANY on the array

```
a =
   1   0   2
   3  -2   4
```

Table 5.4 Some applications of any function.

Command	Result
a1 = any(a= =4)	a1 = 0 0 1
a2 = any(a(:)= =4)	a2 = 1
a3 = any(a(2,:)<0)	a3 =1
a4 = any(any(a)= =4)	a4 = 0

We observe in Table 5.4 that a1 is an array 1-by-3, whereas a2, a3 and a4 are single values. If the result must be a single logical value the linear indexing (See Sec. 4.2) is used for a2. A single value a3 is too obtained if we restrict the check to a single row (or column). The same value a4 would be obtained if we had written a4 = (any(a1)= =4).

5.1.5 *Logical values in array indexing*

The main use of the logical values and expressions is in conditional and loop control of a block of lines of code in a M-file (See Ch.8). They are useful too in array indexing, as appear from the following examples.

We want to put in the array *a* the elements of third column equal to zero

```
a =
  1  2  3
  4  5  6
```

The commands and subsequent result are

```
a=[1 2 3;4 5 6];
a(a= =3|a= =6)=0
a =
  1  2  0
  4  5  0
```

Then we consider the following lines of code and their corresponding results

```
a = [1 0 0;0 1 0;0 0 1]
a =
    1   0   0
    0   1   0
    0   0   1
b = magic(3)
b =
    8   1   6
    3   5   7
    4   9   2
b(~a) = 0
b =
    8   0   0
    0   5   0
    0   0   2
```

Above the expression ~a refers to the zero elements of the array *a* and put to zero the corresponding elements of the array *b*.

5.2 Characters and Strings

The term string refers to an array composed of any characters of the Table 2.1 and of the extended Table (Appendix 4), where are shown too the corresponding numeric values stored internally (for example, the lowercase letter *a* has the code 97). As we have seen (Table 2.3 of Sec. 2. 4) each character uses 2 bytes of internal memory. Besides when a character is converted to a numeric value using an UINT* function (See Table 2.2 of Sec. 2.3) the number of bytes changes as we can see from the following example were all functions give the same result (97) but use a different number of bytes to store it; the CHAR function returns the literal value *a* that uses the standard number (2) of bytes. After the code the results follow.

```
a8=uint8('a')
a16=uint16('a');
a32=uint32('a');
a64=uint64('a');
char_a=char(97)
whos
```

```
a8 =
  97
char_a =
a
Name      Size      Bytes   Class
a16       1x1       2       uint16
a32       1x1       4       uint32
a64       1x1       8       uint64
a8        1x1       1       uint8
char_a    1x1       2       char
```

5.2.1 ***Creating string arrays***

An m-by-n array of strings, as any other type of arrays, must have for each row the same length. Arrays of strings of unequal length are allowed only in a cell array (Sec. 5.5). We can join two or more string arrays together to create a new array, using concatenation either with function STRCAT or the operator [ ]. In the next example we have the initial arrays s1, s2 and s3 that we concatenate horizontally in *sch* using the function STRCAT (s1,s2 and s3 are not separated by blanks) and in *sph* using the operator [ ] (we add two blanks to separate s1,s2 and s3). The functions STRVCAT and CHAR form an array with s1, s2 and s3 as rows. Using DEBLANK we remove trailing blanks padded by the functions STRV-CAT and CHAR.

Example 5.1 (*string1.m*)

```
s1 = 'Every step brought him';
s2 = 'nearer to London';
s3 = 'farther from his own life';
```

```
sch=strcat(s1,s2,s3)
sph=[s1,' ',s2,' ',s3]
scv=strvcat(s1,s2,s3)
spv=char(s1,s2,s3)
s2_new=deblank(spv(2,:))
whos
```

The displayed results are

```
sch =
Every step brought himnearer to Londonfarther from his own life
sph =
Every step brought him nearer to London farther from his own life
scv =
Every step brought him
nearer to London
farther from his own life
spv =
Every step brought him
nearer to London
farther from his own life
s2_new =
nearer to London
Name     Size    Bytes   Class
s1       1x22    44      char
s2       1x16    32      char
s2_new   1x16    32      char
s3       1x25    50      char
sch      1x63    126     char
scv      3x25    150     char
sph      1x65    130     char
spv      3x25    150     char
```

It follows the syntax of the function CHAR

```
s = char(x)
s = char(c)
s = char(s1,s2,s3,..)
```

In the first case the array x, containing nonnegative integers representing character codes, is converted into a character array (char (97) = a). The second case refers to cell arrays and will be treated later (Sec. 5.5). In the third case the function forms the character array s containing strings s1,s2,s3,... as rows, padding automatically each string with blanks in order to form a valid array (See Example 5.1).

It follows the syntax of the other functions

```
s = strcat(s1, s2, s3,...)
```

returns a 1-by-m array *s* concatenating horizontally s1, s2, s3, ...

```
s = strvcat(s1,s2, s3,..)
```

returns a n-by-m array *s* containing s1, s2, s3,... as rows, automatically padded with blanks if they doesn't have the same length.

```
s_new = deblank(s)
```

the function removes trailing blanks from the array *s*.

5.2.2 *Strings comparisons*

There are functions that allow to examine single characters or strings for equality and to determine whether an element of a string is a character or white space. These functions work for cell arrays of strings, too (Sec. 5.5). The syntax for the function that determines if two strings s1 and s2 are identical is

```
tf = strcmp(s1,s2)
```

where *tf* is the logical 1 (true) if the strings are identical and logical 0 (false) otherwise.

The syntax of the function that determines if the first n characters of two strings are identical is

```
tf = strncmp(s1,s2,n)
```

where *tf* is the logical 1 (true) if the first n characters of the strings are identical and logical 0 (false) otherwise.

The function STRCMPI and STRNCMPI are the same as the previous two functions, except that they ignore case.

Relational operators (>, > =, <, < =, = =, ~ =) compare too strings arrays using the numerical value corresponding to each character (Table 2.2). We write some simple clarifying lines of code and their corresponding results

```
sa = 'a';
sb ='b';
sa = = 97
ans =
   1
sb < 97
ans =
   0
s=[sa sb]
s =
ab
cod_ab=[97 98]
cod_ab =
   97   98
s = = cod_ab
ans =
   1   1
s ~ = cod_ab
ans =
   0   0
```

The following example is a modified version of a previous one

(Example 5.1). It clarifies the difference between the use of a function and the equal (= =) operator in the comparison operation. After the lines of code, the results follow.

Example 5.2 (*string2.m*)

```
s1 = 'Every step brought him';
s2 = 'nearer to London';
spv=char(s1,s2)
row1=spv(1,:);
row2=spv(2,:)
a1=strcmp(row1,row2)
s_logical=row1= =row2
ind=find(s_logical)
```

```
spv =
    Every step brought him
    nearer to London
a1 =
    0
s_logical =
    0  0  0  1  0  0  0  1  0  0  0  0  0  0  0  0  0  0  1  0  0  0
ind =

    4   8   19
```

The array *ind* gives indices of nonzero elements corresponding to identical characters in row1 and row2 (r, t and blank in corresponding positions 4, 8 and 19). We observe the function returns a single logical value whereas the operator displays an array of the same size as that of row1 and row2.

5.2.3 *Other functions relating string arrays*

There are functions operating on the strings arrays as, for example, for categorizing characters inside a string, for searching and replacing characters in a string, to parse a sentence into words, to convert strings arrays to numeric data and conversely, *etc*. (Table 5.5).

Table 5.5 Functions for working with character arrays.

Function	Description
base2dec	Convert a positive integer to a character type of any base from 2 through 36
bin2dec	Convert a positive integer to a character type of binary base
blanks	Create a string of blanks
cellstr	Convert a character array to a cell array of strings
char	Convert to a character or string
deblank	Remove trailing blanks
double	Convert a string to numeric codes
find	Find indices of nonzero elements
findstr	Find one string within another
hex2dec	Convert a character type of hexadecimal base to a positive integer
hex2num	Convert a numeric type to a character type of specified precision
int2str	Convert an integer to a string.
iscellstr	Return true for a cell array of strings
ischar	Return true for a character array
isletter	Return true for letters of the alphabet
isspace	Return true for white-space characters
isstrprop	Determine if a string is of the specified category
lower	Make all letters lowercase
num2str	Convert a number to a string
sort	Sort elements in ascending or descending order.
sprintf	Write formatted data to a string
'str'	Create the string specified between quotes
str2double	Convert a string to a double-precision value.
str2num	Convert a character type to a numeric type
strcat	Concatenate strings
strcmp	Compare strings
strcmpi	Compare strings, ignoring case.
strjust	Justify a string.
strmatch	Find matches for a string
strncmp	Compare the first N characters of strings
strncmpi	Compare the first N characters, ignoring case
strrep	Replace one string with another.
strtok	Find a token in a string
strtrim	Remove leading and trailing white space
strvcat	Concatenate strings vertically
uint8/16/32/64	Convert a character to an integer code using 1/2/4/8 bytes
upper	Make all letters uppercase

5.3 Dates and Times

Information about date and time are given in three formats:

a. a *string array* of class char (by MATLAB called *date string*), using the function DATE

```
a_date=date
a_date =
06-Jan-2008
```

b. a *numerical array* of class double (by MATLAB called *date vector*), using the function CLOCK

```
c_clock=fix(clock)
c_clock =
2008    1    6    10    47    23
```

The function CLOCK returns a six element numeric array containing the current date (year month day) and time (hour minute seconds). The FIX function rounds numbers to an integer display format.

c. a *single numerical value* of class double (by MATLAB called *serial date number*), using the function NOW

```
b_now=now
b_now =
7.3341e+005
```

MATLAB works internally with *single numerical value*. Handling large numbers of dates or doing extensive calculations with dates, this last format allows a better performance. This represents the number of days that has passed assuming for the January 1, 0000 a date number equal to 1. This format allows to represent fractions of days beginning at midnight; for example, 6 p.m. equals 0.75 serial day and for the string array '31-Oct-2003, 6:00 pm' the corresponding *serial date number* is 731885.75.

5.3.1 *Format conversions*

The main functions handling conversion of date and time format are DATENUM, DATESTR and DATEVEC.

The simplest syntax form for DATENUM is

```
nv = datenum(a)
```

This converts m *numerical arrays* or m *string arrays* into *single numerical values nv*. The variable *a* can be m-by-6 or m-by-3 array containing m full or partial date arrays respectively. The function returns a column-wise array of m *single numerical values*.

The simplest syntax form for DATESTR is

```
sa = datestr(a)
```

This converts m *numerical arrays* or m *single numerical values* to m *strings array sa*. If the variable *a* is of the first type, it must be an m-by-6 array containing m six-elements rows. If the variable *a* is of the second type each element of *a* must be a positive double-precision number. The function returns a column-wise array of m *string arrays*.

The simplest syntax form for DATEVEC is

```
na = datevec(nv)
```

This converts m *single numerical values* to m *numerical arrays na*. The function returns an m-by-6 array containing m numerical arrays.

The following example explains the mean of these format conversion functions.

Example 5.3 (*date1.m*)

```
%we start from a string format
sa='01-Jan-2008 00:00:01'
%its corresponding
%single value format
nv=datenum(sa)
%numeric array format
na=fix(datevec(nv))
%
%the same day of the next year
%
% with a single value format
nv1=addtodate(nv,1,'year')
%with a string array format
sa1=datestr(nv1)
%with a numeric array format
na1=datevec(sa1)
%
%we form an array with two rows
%of the two previous numeric arrays
two_na=[na;na1]
%and of the two previous string arrays
two_sa=[sa;sa1]
%
%the corresponding single value format
%
%using numeric arrays
two_nv_n=datenum(two_na)
%using string arrays
two_nv_s=datenum(two_sa)
%
%their expected differences
%2008 is a leap year
diff_n=two_nv_n(2)-two_nv_n(1)
diff_s=two_nv_s(2)-two_nv_s(1)
```

The corresponding results displayed on Command window are:

```
sa =
01-Jan-2008 00:00:01
nv =
  7.3341e+005
na =
       2008        1        1        0        0        1
nv1 =
  7.3377e+005
sa1 =
01-Jan-2009 00:00:01
na1 =
       2009        1        1        0        0        1
two_na =
       2008        1        1        0        0        1
       2009        1        1        0        0        1
two_sa =
01-Jan-2008 00:00:01
01-Jan-2009 00:00:01
two_nv_n =
   7.3341e+005
   7.3377e+005
two_nv_s =
   7.3341e+005
   7.3377e+005
diff_n =
  366
diff_s =
  366
```

Example 5.4 (*date2.m*)

```
%2008 starts
sa='01-Jan-2008 00:00:01'
%its corresponding
%single value format
```

```
nv=datenum(sa)
%numeric array format
na=datevec(nv)
sav=datestr(nv)
saa=datestr(na)
%
%2009 starts
sa1='01-Jan-2009 00:00:01'
%its corresponding
%single value format
nv1=datenum(sa1)
%numeric array format
na1=datevec(nv1)
saa1=datestr(nv1)
saa2=datestr(na1)
%
%conversion to string arrays
bna=[na;na1]
bsv=[nv;nv1]
csa1=datestr(bna)
csa2=datestr(bsv)
%
%conversion to numeric array
cnv=[nv;nv1]
cna=datevec(cnv)
```

The corresponding results displayed in Command window are:

```
sa =
01-Jan-2008 00:00:01
nv =
  7.3341e+005
na =
  1.0e+003 *
    2.0080    0.0010    0.0010         0         0    0.0010
sav =
```

```
01-Jan-2008 00:00:01
saa =
01-Jan-2008 00:00:01
sa1 =
01-Jan-2009 00:00:01
nv1 =
  7.3377e+005
na1 =
  1.0e+003 *
    2.0090    0.0010    0.0010         0         0    0.0010
saa1 =
01-Jan-2009 00:00:01
saa2 =
01-Jan-2009 00:00:01
bna =
  1.0e+003 *
    2.0080    0.0010    0.0010         0         0    0.0010
    2.0090    0.0010    0.0010         0         0    0.0010
bsv =
  1.0e+005 *
    7.3341
    7.3377
csa1 =
01-Jan-2008 00:00:01
01-Jan-2009 00:00:01
csa2 =
01-Jan-2008 00:00:01
01-Jan-2009 00:00:01
cnv =
  1.0e+005 *
    7.3341
    7.3377
cna =
  1.0e+003 *
    2.0080    0.0010    0.0010         0         0    0.0010
    2.0090    0.0010    0.0010         0         0    0.0010
```

5.3.2 Other date and time functions

Additional functions handling date and time operations are listed in the Table 5.6.

Table 5.6 Other functions handling date and time.

Function	Description
addtodate	Modify a date number by field
calendar	Return an array representing a calendar
clock	Return the current date and time as a date array
cputime	Return the total CPU time usedby MATLAB since it was started
date	Return the current date as date string
datenum	Convert to a serial date number
datestr	Convert to a string representation of the dat
datetick	Label axis tick lines with dates
datevec	Convert to a date array
eomday	Return the last day of a year and month
etime	Return the time elapsed between two date arrays
now	Return the current date and time as serial date numbe
tic, toc	Measure the time elapsed between invoking tic and toc
weekday	Return the current day of the week

5.4 Structures

Like numerical, logical and string arrays, structures are another type of array. First of all we see an example:

Example 5.5 (*structl_1x1.m*)

```
image.size = [960 1280 3];
image.Filename= 'Owl.png';
image.FileModDate= '13-feb-2007 14:51:30';
image.FileSize= 2081760;
image.BitDepth= 24;
image.ColorType= 'truecolor';
image.Colormap= [ ];
image
whos
```

When it is executed, the Command window returns

```
image =
size: [960 1280 3]
Filename: 'Owl.png'
FileModDate: '13-feb-2007 14:51:30'
FileSize: 2081760
BitDepth: 24
ColorType: 'truecolor'
Colormap: [ ]
Name      Size      Bytes    Class
image     1x1       980      struct
```

We observe that
- the name, image in the previous example, of the structure array follows the rules defined in Sec. 2.2 and must be separated with the punctuation symbol comma by the next name, called field;
- the name of a field must too follow rules of Sec. 2.2;
- a structure can have many fields. These are called data containers since they can contain any data types: numerical, logical, literal, date and time either as single values or as arrays of any dimension. An empty array is also permitted.

The size of the structure does not depend on the number of the fields: the structure of the previous example is an array of size 1-by-1 (as that of a single numerical value, 3.14 for example) although the number of the fields is seven.

To increment the size of the structure, indices within parentheses must be placed after the name of the structure and before the period as in the following example (this define some properties of the images of Fig. 5.1)

Example 5.6 (*struct2_1x2.m*)

```
image(1).size = [960 1280 3];
image(1).Filename= 'Owl.png';
image(1).FileModDate= '13-feb-2007 14:51:30';
image(1).FileSize= 2081760;
image(1).BitDepth= 24;
image(1).ColorType= 'truecolor';
```

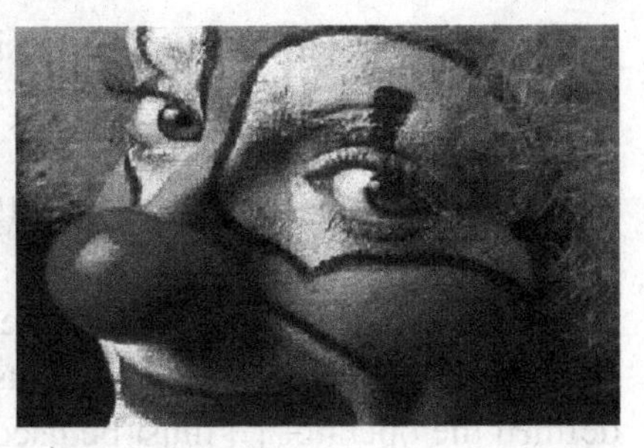

Fig. 5.1 A structure array is used to define properties of an image.

```
image(1,1).Colormap= [ ];
%
image(2).size = [200 20];
image(2).Filename =  'clown.bmp';
image(2).FileModDate  = '10-feb-2007 18:02:38';
image(2).FileSize  = 65078;
image(2).BitDepth  = 8;
image(2).ColorType =  'indexed';
image(2).Colormap =  ['256x3 double'];
image
```

Now the Command window returns a more compact result than in the previous example

```
image =
1x2 struct array with fields:
    size
    Filename
    FileModDate
    FileSize
    BitDepth
    ColorType
    Colormap
```

We can build a structure too using the function STRUCT. Its basic form is

```
a_struct = struct('field1', val1, 'field2', val2, ...)
```

where the arguments are fields names and their corresponding values. All fields must be entered as arguments. If any corresponding value is not defined the operator [ ] must be used to declare it empty.

We can preallocate a third row for the structure array of the previous example as follows

Example 5.7 (*struct3_1x3.m*)

```
image(3)=struct('size',[ ] ,'Filename','another',...
  'FileModDate',[ ],'FileSize',[ ],'BitDepth',[ ],...
  'ColorType', [ ],'Colormap',[ ]);
image(3)
```

with the following results displayed in Command window

```
ans =
        size: [ ]
        Filename: 'another'
        FileModDate: [ ]
        FileSize: [ ]
        BitDepth: [ ]
        ColorType: [ ]
        Colormap: [ ]
Name     Size     Bytes     Class
ans      1x1      882       struct
image    1x3      1962      struct
```

We can preallocate a structure array of size 2-by-2 (or n-by-m-by-p) for the structure of previous example as follows

Example 5.8 (*struct4_2x2.m*)

```
image(1,1)=struct('size',[ ] ,'Filename','another1',...
   'FileModDate',[ ],'FileSize',[ ],'BitDepth',[ ],...
   'ColorType', [ ],'Colormap',[ ]);
image(1,2)=struct('size',[ ] ,'Filename','another2',...
   'FileModDate',[ ],'FileSize',[ ],'BitDepth',[ ],...
   'ColorType', [ ],'Colormap',[ ]);
image(2,1)=struct('size',[ ] ,'Filename','another3',...
   'FileModDate',[ ],'FileSize',[ ],'BitDepth',[ ],...
   'ColorType', [ ],'Colormap',[ ]);
image(2,2)=struct('size',[ ] ,'Filename','another4',...
   'FileModDate',[ ],'FileSize',[ ],'BitDepth',[ ],...
   'ColorType', [ ],'Colormap',[ ]);
image(2,2)
whos
```

The Command window returns the element (2,2) of the second row and second column and the properties of the full array image of size 2-by-2:

```
ans =
        size: [ ]
        Filename: 'another4'
        FileModDate: [ ]
        FileSize: [ ]
        BitDepth: [ ]
        ColorType: [ ]
        Colormap: [ ]
Name     Size     Bytes    Class
ans      1x1      884      struct
image    2x2      2192     struct
```

We can extract a structure of minor size from one of greater size. With reference to the Example 5.8 defining a structure of size 1-by-2 we can remove the second row making this a stand alone structure of size 1-by-1 with the simple lines of code

```
clown_struct=image(2)
whos
```

giving rise in Command window as result to the structure *clown_struct*

```
clown_struct =
size: [200 20]
Filename: 'clown.bmp'
FileModDate: '10-feb-2007 18:02:38'
FileSize: 65078
BitDepth: 8
ColorType: 'indexed'
Colormap: '256x3 double'
Name            Size      Bytes    Class
clown_struct    1x1        996     struct
image           1x2       1528     struct
```

We can access to a value of a field or modify its value using the function struct or in simpler mode with an assignment; the next example refer to the Example 5.6 where it extract the value and the size of the field FileModDate of the first row and modifies the field FileSize from 65078 to 100000 and the field Filename from clown.bmp to mandrill

Example 5.9 (*struct5.m*)
This example refers to the structure array of the Example 5.6.

```
image1_date=image(1).FileModDate
str_date=size(image(2).FileModDate)
%
image(2)=struct('size',[200 20] ,'Filename','clown.bmp',...
 'FileModDate',['10-feb-2007 18:02:38'],'FileSize',[100000],'BitDepth',[8],...
 'ColorType', 'indexed','Colormap',['256x3 double']);
image(2)
%
image(2).Filename =  'mandrill';
image(2)
```

The results are

```
image1_date =
13-feb-2007 14:51:30
str_date =
1   20

ans =
        size: [200 20]
        Filename: 'clown.bmp'
        FileModDate: '10-feb-2007 18:02:38'
        FileSize: 100000
        BitDepth: 8
        ColorType: 'indexed'
        Colormap: '256x3 double'

ans =
        size: [200 20]
        Filename: 'mandrill'
        FileModDate: '10-feb-2007 18:02:38'
        FileSize: 100000
        BitDepth: 8
        ColorType: 'indexed'
        Colormap: '256x3 double'
```

The next Table 5.7 contains a list of functions concerning the structure arrays.

Table 5.7 Other functions used for structures.

Function	Definition
setfield	Set structure field contents
getfield	Get structure field contents
isfield	True if field is in structure array
fieldnames	Get structure field names
orderfields	Order fields of a structure array
rmfield	Remove fields from a structure array
struct	Create or convert to structure array
isstruct	True for structures
struct2cell	Convert a structure array into a cell array

5.5 Cell Arrays

A cell array provides the data storage of dissimilar kinds (single values or arrays of different types and sizes) within a cell array that uses curly braces, { } (instead of square brackets or parentheses) around the elements, now called cells. The curly braces are cell array constructors; the square brackets are used for all types of array. A cell array, as other types of arrays, uses commas or spaces to separate elements and semicolons to terminate rows. To access data in a cell array, the same type of indexing is used as with other arrays (Table 5.8). The notation { } denotes the empty cell array, just as [ ] denotes the empty numeric array.

The advantage over structures is that cell arrays are referenced by indices, allowing you to loop through a cell array and access each argument passed in or out of the function. The disadvantage is that you do not have field names to describe each variable.

However structure and cell are correlated by functions that allow conversion between them. The next example, that illustrates the arrangement of a cell array and its correlation with the structure array, has as a starting point a reduced form of a previous one with a shorter name for the structure. We have directly made the structure array s1 and the cell array c2, as a row-wise array, with an assignment whereas s2 and c1 are constructed by the functions CELL2STRUCT and STRUCT2CELL (Fig. 5.2). The array c1 is made column-wise by the second function.

Example 5.10 (*cell_struct.m*)

```
s1.Filename= 'Owl.png';
s1.FileDate= '13-feb-2007';
s1.FileSize= 2081760;
s1
c1=struct2cell(s1)
c2={'Owl.png','13-feb-2007',2081760};
c2
F={'Filename','FileDate','FileSize'};
s2=cell2struct(c2,F,2)
whos
```

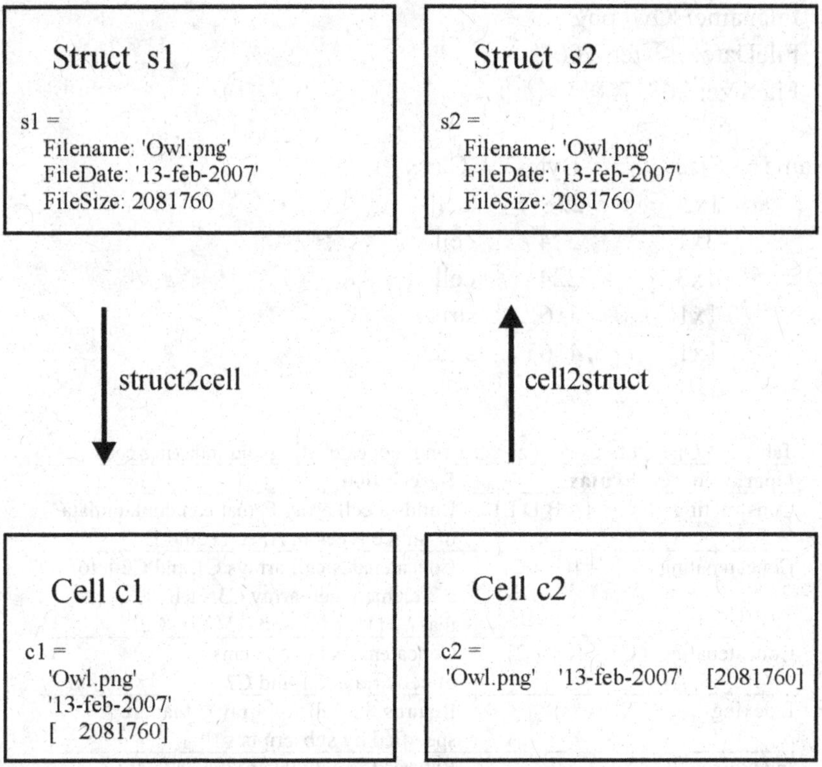

Struct s1

s1 =
Filename: 'Owl.png'
FileDate: '13-feb-2007'
FileSize: 2081760

Struct s2

s2 =
Filename: 'Owl.png'
FileDate: '13-feb-2007'
FileSize: 2081760

struct2cell

cell2struct

Cell c1

c1 =
'Owl.png'
'13-feb-2007'
[2081760]

Cell c2

c2 =
'Owl.png' '13-feb-2007' [2081760]

Fig. 5.2 Functions used for conversion between cell and structure arrays.

The results displayed in Command window are

```
s1 =
  Filename: 'Owl.png'
  FileDate: '13-feb-2007'
  FileSize: 2081760
c1 =
  'Owl.png'
  '13-feb-2007'
  [2081760]
c2 =
  'Owl.png'   '13-feb-2007'   [2081760]
s2 =
```

```
Filename: 'Owl.png'
FileDate: '13-feb-2007'
FileSize: 2081760
```

```
Name   Size   Bytes   Class
F      1x3    228     cell
c1     3x1    224     cell
c2     1x3    224     cell
s1     1x1    416     struct
s2     1x1    416     struct
```

Table 5.8 Operators used in constructing, concatenating and indexing cells.

Operation	**Syntax**	**Description**
Constructing	C = {A B D E}	Builds a cell array C that can contain data of unlike types in A, B, D, and E
Concatenating	C3 = {C1 C2}	Concatenates cell arrays C1 and C2 into a 2-element cell array C3 such that C3{1} = C1 and C3{2} = C2
Concatenating	C3 = [C1 C2]	Concatenates the contents of cell arrays C1 and C2
Indexing	X = C(s)	Returns the cells of array C that are specified by subscripts s
Indexing	X = C{s}	Returns the contents of the cells of C that are specified by subscripts s
Indexing	X = C{s}(t)	References one or more elements of an array that resides within a cell. Subscript *s* selects the cell, and subscript *t* selects the array element(s)

We can create an empty cell of any dimensions with the CELL function whose syntax is

```
c = cell(m,n,p)
```

that preallocates memory for a cell array *c* of size m-by-n-by-p. For example if p is greater than 1 the cell is three-dimensional; the least case is m = n = p =1 as for a single value of every type of array.

We can create cell arrays, as with other type of arrays, with a assignment statement using now as a concatenating operator not only the square brackets but also curly braces. Next example clarifies how cell arrays can be created.

Example 5.11 (*cell_3D.m*)

```
%we define six cell arrays
%four are of size 1x1 and two 1x2
c111={'James'};
c121={'Joyce'};
c112={'Ulysses'};
c122={'Finnegans Wake'};
c21={1882 1941};
c22={1922 1939};
%cells are concatenated
%using curly braces
%into cells of sizes 2x2
cp1={c111 c121;c21(1),c21(2)}
cp2={c112 c122;c22(1),c22(2)}
%we see their contents
%it they are concatenated
%if we use square brackets
c_p1=[c111 c121;c21]
c_p2=[c112 c122;c22]
%cells are concatenated
%using curly braces
%into a cell of size 1x2
c_row_curly={c_p1 c_p2}
%into a cell of size 2x1
c_col_curly={c_p1;c_p2}
%we see their contents
%it they are concatenated
%if we use square brackets
c_row_brackets=[c_p1 c_p2]
c_col_brackets=[c_p1;c_p2]
%cells are concatenated
%using square brackets
```

```
%into a cell of size 2x2x2
c_3D(:,:,1)=c_p1;
c_3D(:,:,2)=c_p2;
c_3D
whos
```

The results are

```
cp1 =
    {1x1 cell}    {1x1 cell}
    {1x1 cell}    {1x1 cell}
cp2 =
    {1x1 cell}    {1x1 cell}
    {1x1 cell}    {1x1 cell}
c_p1 =
    'James'    'Joyce'
    [ 1882]    [ 1941]
c_p2 =
    'Ulysses'    'Finnegans Wake'
    [   1922]    [          1939]
c_row_curly =
    {2x2 cell}    {2x2 cell}
c_col_curly =
    {2x2 cell}
    {2x2 cell}
c_row_brackets =
    'James'    'Joyce'    'Ulysses'    'Finnegans Wake'
    [ 1882]    [ 1941]    [   1922]    [          1939]
c_col_brackets =
    'James'      'Joyce'
    [   1882]    [          1941]
    'Ulysses'    'Finnegans Wake'
    [   1922]    [          1939]
c_3D(:,:,1) =
    'James'    'Joyce'
    [ 1882]    [ 1941]
```

```
c_3D(:,:,2) =
   'Ulysses'    'Finnegans Wake'
   [   1922]    [          1939]
```

Name	Size (*Bytes and Class, always cell, are omitted*)
c111	1x1
c112	1x1
c121	1x1
c122	1x1
c21	1x2
c22	1x2
c_3D	2x2x2
c_col_brackets	4x2
c_col_curly	2x1
c_p1	2x2
c_p2	2x2
c_row_brackets	2x4
c_row_curly	1x2
cp1	2x2
cp2	2x2

We have stated a cell array can contain arrays of any other type. These can be also a structure array or another cell array. Cell array indexing has two subscript components: the indices within curly braces { } specify which cell to get the contents of. The indices within parentheses ( ) specify a particular element of that cell.

The syntax for indexing to the content X of field F of a structure array that resides in a cell of array C is

```
X = C{CellArrayIndex}(StructArrayIndex).F(FieldArrayIndex)
```

The syntax for indexing to the content X of a cell of a cell array that resides in a cell of array C is

```
X = C{OuterCellArrayIndex}{InnerCellArrayIndex}
```

The next example creates a structure and an inner cell into an outer cell and uses the content indexing of the structure and of the inner cell.

Example 5.12 (*struct_cell_cell.m*)

```
%A Structure and a Cell within a Cell
%We define numerical, string,
%cell and logical arrays
a_num=[19 9 4; 17 3 5];
a_char=['January ';'February'];
a_cell={1 4;8 2;9 2};
a_logical=a_num<10;
%then a struct arrays
a_struct(1).month=a_char(1,:);
a_struct(2).month=a_char(2,:);
a_struct(1).log=a_logical(1,:);
a_struct(2).log=a_logical(2,:);
a_struct
% and at end we assemble all arrays
%in a new cell array
A_cell={a_num, a_cell, a_struct}
%INDEXING
%using indexing with parentheses
%we find only the type of an element
%using curly braces we obtain its content
%in a simple way for the first two elements
%and in a less simple mode for the third
%element that is a structure
a_par1=A_cell(1)
a_cur1=A_cell{1}
a_par2=A_cell(2)
a_cur2=A_cell{2}
a_cur31=A_cell{2}{3,1}
a_cur32=A_cell{2}{3,2}
a_par3=A_cell(3)
a_cur3_month=A_cell{3}(1).month(1,:)
```

```
a_cur3_log=A_cell{3}(1).log(1,:)
```

The results are:

```
a_struct =
1x2 struct array with fields:
   month
   log
A_cell =
   [2x3 double]    {3x2 cell}    [1x2 struct]
a_par1 =
   [2x3 double]
a_cur1 =
   19    9    4
   17    3    5
a_par2 =
   {3x2 cell}
a_cur2 =
   [1]    [4]
   [8]    [2]
   [9]    [2]
a_cur31 =
   9
a_cur32 =
   2
a_par3 =
   [1x2 struct]
a_cur3_month =
January
a_cur3_log =
   0    1    1
```

Clearly the simplest way to create a cell array of strings is by using the curly braces. However we can create a cell array of strings c from a string array s with the function CELLSTR

```
c = cellstr(s)
```

that places each row of the string array s into separate cells of c. We can use the function CHAR to convert back a cell array c into a string array s.

```
s = char(c)
```

The following example uses the previous two functions.

Example 5.13 (*string_cell.m*)

```
%We define three strings
s1 = 'Every step brought him';
s2 = 'nearer to London';
s3 = 'farther from his own life';
%
sch=strcat(s1,s2,s3)
sph=[s1,' ',s2,' ',s3]
scv=strvcat(s1,s2,s3)
spv=char(s1,s2,s3)
%
ch1=cellstr(sch)
ch2=cellstr(sph)
cv1=cellstr(scv)
cv2=cellstr(spv)
%
cs1=char(ch1)
cs1=char(ch2)
cs1=char(cv1)
cs1=char(cv2)
```

We do not give the obvious and same results that return both the string and the cell arrays: in fact the formal symbols defining a string (the pair of quotes, ' ') and a cell (the pair of curly braches, { }) do not appear in results displayed in Command window but only in the M-file typed in the Editor window.

About Chapter 6

The Figure is the window where *graphics objects* are displayed. As matter of fact the same Figure is a graphics object too. The screen of our PC, called Root is also a graphics object and the grandparent of all other graphics objects. Each of these has a *handle* and acts for other objects as a parent or a child.

Figure by means of Axes and GUIs (Graphical User Interfaces) is the container of all other graphics objects.

Of the long list of objects Axes or GUIs can contain we will treat the "core objects" *line* and *text* (necessary to build 2-D plots, and many other graphs) in this Chapter and the *image* in the next.

We will discuss some fundamental functions, both formally and by examples that allow knowing or modifying the properties of all graphics objects: *set, get, gcf* and *gca*.

Each graphics object has a number (usually greater than 30) of properties; each of these is represented by one or more values (usually numerical or literal). Their abridged lists are reported in the final pages of this Chapter.

Chapter 6

The Figure Window for Graphics Objects

6.1 Figure, Root and Their Properties

In its bare, not usual, form the Figure window appear as in Fig. 6.1 centered at the top of the PC screen. We have seen in the previous chapters that operations on data return results in the Command window. Writing special lines of code we can obtain also *graphics objects* that are directed to the Figure, a window separate from the Command window. However the Figure window can be docked in the Desktop, if we want it (See, for example, Fig. 1.6 and Fig. 1.7). The '*DockControls*' property (Table 6.3) determines whether you can dock the Figure or not. By default, the dock/undock arrows are '*visible*' in Figure.

The characteristics of Figure are controlled by PC windowing system and by MATLAB Figure properties. The appearance of Figure as in Fig. 6.1 will be useful in cases when we are displaying images (See for example Fig. 7.17). In its usual aspect Figure, as all other MATLAB windows, has a menu bar and tools bars. In Fig. 6.2 the Figure appears first with the menu bar only and then a tools bar is added. To display these three Figure windows we write:

```
figure ('Name', 'A BARE FIGURE WINDOW',...
        'NumberTitle', 'off ', 'Color', 'blue', 'Menubar', 'none')
figure ('Color', 'green', 'Toolbar', 'none')
figure ('Color', 'red')
```

The command is the function FIGURE. The resulting Figure, dis-

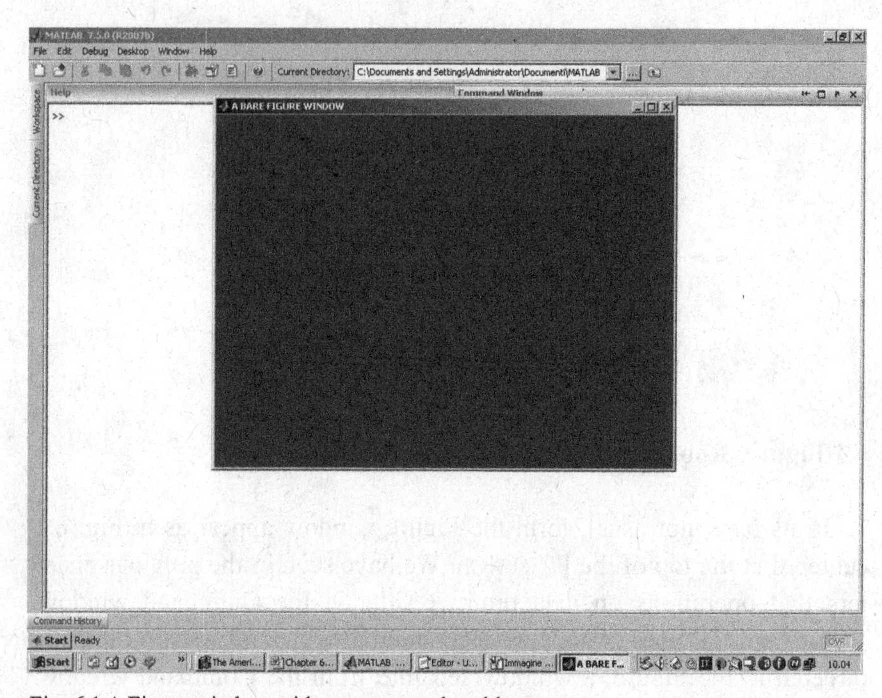

Fig. 6.1 A Figure window without menu and tool bars.

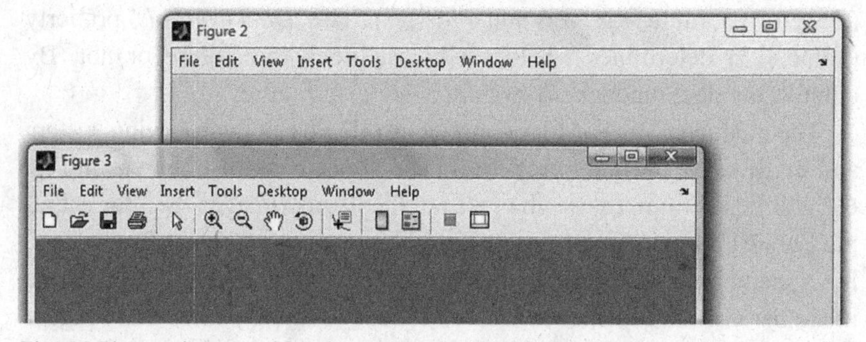

Fig. 6.2 Figure windows with only menu and with added tool bars.

played on the screen, is itself considered a graphics object. The screen of our PC is regarded as a graphics object too and is called *Root*. Screen, Figure and all other graphics objects we are considering now and in the next chapter, have a large number of *properties* and each of these has one or more *values* (Sec. 6.6).

In the first line of the previous example we change the default name

(Figure) in the title bar with a different one using the property '*Name*' and the literal value '*A BARE FIGURE WINDOW*'. The other properties used '*NumberTitle*', '*Color*', '*Menubar*' and '*Toolbar*' contain literal values. In the first line assigning to the property '*Menubar*' the value '*none*' we hide the Toolbar too.

Blue, green and red colors are assigned to the background of Figure that, by default, is dark gray corresponding to the RGB triplet [0.8 0.8 0.8] as can be verified with the following simple lines of code

```
h=figure
h =
   3
get (h, 'color')
ans =
   0.8000    0.8000    0.8000
```

Here *h* is called the *handle* of Figure. Every graphics object has a handle and acts for another object as a parent or a child. Figures are children of the Root but they are parent of the Axes (Fig. 6.3). The handle of the Root has value 0. The handle of a Figure is the same as the number that appears in title bar after the title 'Figure'. There is only one Root object and this has no parent. The Root object exists when we start MATLAB and we cannot create or destroy it. The Root maintains information on the state of MATLAB and of our PC system through its properties (See Table 6.2 in Sec. 6.6). All graphics objects, Root's descendants, are interdependent, so a graphics object typically is related to other objects that, grouped, produce a meaningful graph (we will consider, for example in the next chapter, 2-D plots).

The functions SET and GET allow us to access to the properties of the Root, Figure and all other graphics objects (Sec. 6.2). The first allows to obtain for a given object, identified by the handle, its value or values. The second allows to assign a value or values to a given object, identified by its handle.

We have introduced, as self-explanatory, the functions FIGURE and

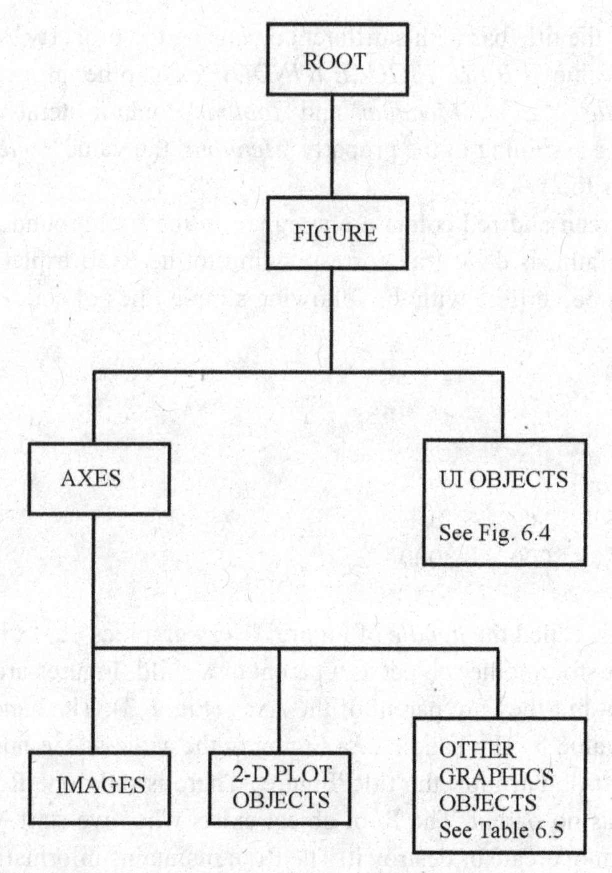

Fig. 6.3 The hierarchy between parent and child objects.

GET in the previous example. We give now the main syntactic forms of the FIGURE function:

```
figure
figure ( 'PropertyName', propertyvalue,...)
h = figure (...)
```

where the first form creates a new Figure using for properties default values (Table 6.3 in Sec. 6.6); the second form creates a new Figure using the values of the properties specified. All other properties not explicitly defined will assume their default values. The third form returns the handle of the Figure; if parentheses are omitted a Figure is simply created; if parentheses are included some properties of an object can be explicitly defined within them.

6.2 The Functions SET, GET and GCF

These functions are the basic tools to modify (SET) or to obtain (GET) the value or values of specified properties of an object. The syntax of the main forms of the first function is

```
set ( h, 'PropertyName', PropertyValue )
```

that sets the value of the specified property for the graphics object with handle h. This can be an array of handles, in which case SET sets the properties' values for all the objects.

```
set ( h, s )
```

where *s* is a structure whose field names are object property names; the function sets the properties named in each field name with the values contained in the structure.

```
set (h, pn, pv )
```

sets the named properties specified in the cell array of strings *pn* to the corresponding values in the cell array *pv* for all objects specified in h. The cell array pn must be 1-by-n, but the cell array *pv* can be m-by-n where m is equal to length(h) so that each object will be updated with a different set of values from the list of property names contained in *pn* (See an application in Example 6.4).

The syntax of the main forms of the function GET is:

```
v = get ( h, 'PropertyName' )
```

that returns the value of the specified property for the graphics object with handle h. If h is an array of handles, then GET returns an m-by-1 cell array of values where m is equal to length (h). If 'PropertyName' is replaced by a 1-by-n or n-by-1 cell array of strings containing property names, then GET will return an m-by-n cell array of values.

```
get ( h )
```

displays all property names and their current values for the graphics object with handle h. Whereas

```
s = get ( h )
```

where h is a single value, returns a structure *s* where each field name is the name of a property of h and each field contains the value of that property.

There is another very useful function, GCF, that returns the handle of the *current* Figure

```
h = gcf
```

The current Figure is the window in which a graphics command such as IMAGE or PLOT draws their results. If no Figure exists, the function creates one and returns its handle. The function GCF is usually an argument of the SET and GET commands when these are involved with the Figure proprieties.

These functions concern *all* graphics objects, as we will see in the following pages and in the next chapter. We give now some simple applications on the graphics objects we have considered: Root and Figure.

a. Writing

```
get ( 0, 'CurrentFigure')
```

we obtain the handle of the current Figure, if any is active; otherwise the

Command window returns the empty array [ ].

b. Entering the command

```
get ( gcf )
```

the Figure window is displayed and in Command window returns the full list of its properties and default values

c. The following statement displays a Figure with a pink colored background

```
set ( gcf, 'Color', [1, 0.4, 0.6])
```

d. Writing

```
set (0, 'Units', 'pixel' )
get (0, 'ScreenSize' )
```

the Command window returns the size in pixels of our PC screen (Root has the handle 0)

```
ans =
        1     1     1024     768
```

6.3 Axes and UI Objects

The graphics commands allow to create graphics objects: for example, if x and y are two arrays of numerical data (both of size 1-by-m) we can plot x versus y or if the array I (of size n-by-m or n-by-m-by-3) contains the data of an image this can be displayed. These are two examples of final graphics objects we are concerned with.

In all cases the frame of reference that defines where to place the final graphical picture is the coordinate system, defined by the Axes, that shifts, orients and scales graphs to produce the view we want to see on screen.

Axes are always contained within a Figure and themselves contain all other graphics objects that make up a final graphics object (Fig. 6.3). As for all graphics objects also Axes have a long list of properties that control aspects of how they are displayed (See Table 6.5 in Sec. 6.6).

Figure is the container of two basic graphics objects: Axes and UI Object (or GUI Graphical User Interface) are the containers of all other graphics objects (Fig. 6.3). As explained in the Introduction we do not treat the features of the GUI (Fig. 6.4) and the long list of related objects and corresponding properties. However a list of the main graphics objects that can be contained in the Axes (and in a GUI) is given in Table 6.6. Of these graphics objects we will directly treat in the next chapter few "core objects": the *line* and *text* (Sec. 6.5), necessary to build 2-D plots (and many other graphs), and the *image* (Sec. 7.2).

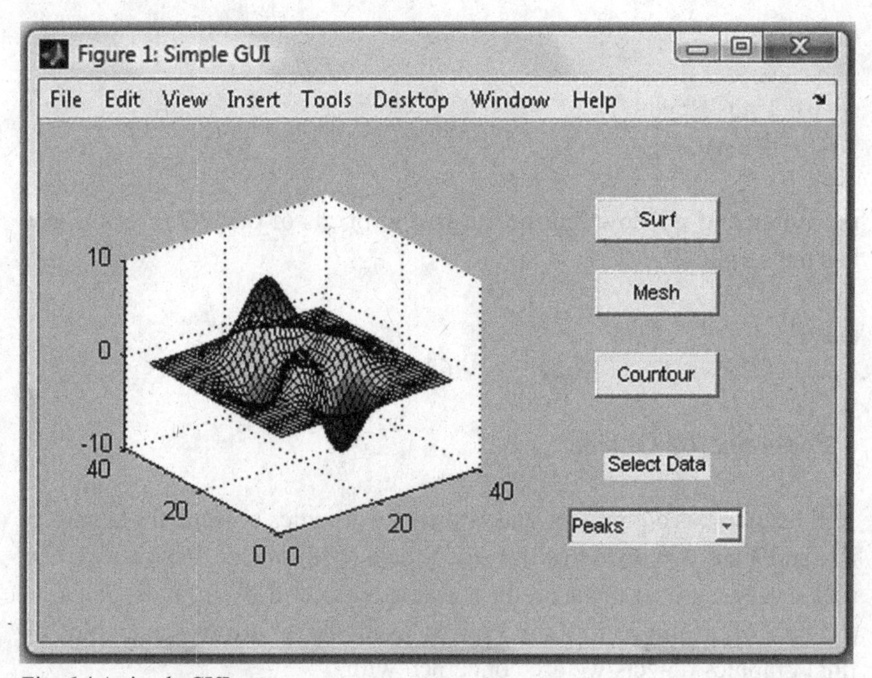

Fig. 6.4 A simple GUI.

6.4 Axes Related Functions

The function AXES that allows to create Axes has the following main syntactic forms.

```
axes ( 'position', rect )
```

this form of the function opens up the Axes at the specified location defined in *rect* and returns a handle to it. Here rect = [left, bottom, width, height] specifies the size of the Axes box and its location relative to the lower-left corner of the Figure. If normalized units (Table 6.5c) are used, (0,0) is the lower-left corner and (1,1) the upper-right corner of Figure.

The following simple form of the function

```
axes
```

creates the default Axes within a Figure and returns a handle to it.

Then the form of function

```
axes ( h )
```

makes *current* the Axes with handle h. *Current* are the Axes created by commands like AXES or AXIS (and others, like PLOT for example). The AXIS function that controls scaling and appearance of the current plot if typed alone

```
axis
```

creates too an Axes object within a Figure. In addition the scaling values (minimum and maximum of the x and y coordinates) are returned in Command window.

If h is the handle of a current Axes and we execute

```
get ( h )
```

a list of Axes object properties and their *current* values is displayed in

Command window (for example: Box = off).
If we execute

```
set ( h )
```

a list of Axes object properties and legal (i.e possible) property values is displayed (for example: Box: [on | { off }]).

The function GCA has for the Axes the same role that GCF has for the Figure. Its syntax is

```
h = gca
```

Its execution returns the handle of the current Axes in the current Figure. The function GCA is usually an argument of the SET and GET commands when these are involved with the Axes properties (Table 6.5).

We now consider some examples.

Example 6.1 (*Fig&Ax.m*)

Figures and corresponding Axes are placed in different positions and both have different dimensions.

```
% Part a
h1=figure ('color', [.5 .5 .5])
h2=axes ('color', [1 1 1])
%%
%part b
pos1=get (gcf, 'position')
unit1=get (gcf, 'units')
pos2=get (gca, 'position')
unit2=get (gca, 'units')
set (gcf, 'position', [100  200  400  400])
set (gcf, 'color', [.5 .5 .5])
set (gca, 'position', [0.2  0.2  0.6  0.7])
set (gca, 'color' ,[1 1 1])
```

Running only the first two lines of code (Part a) a Figure with Axes is

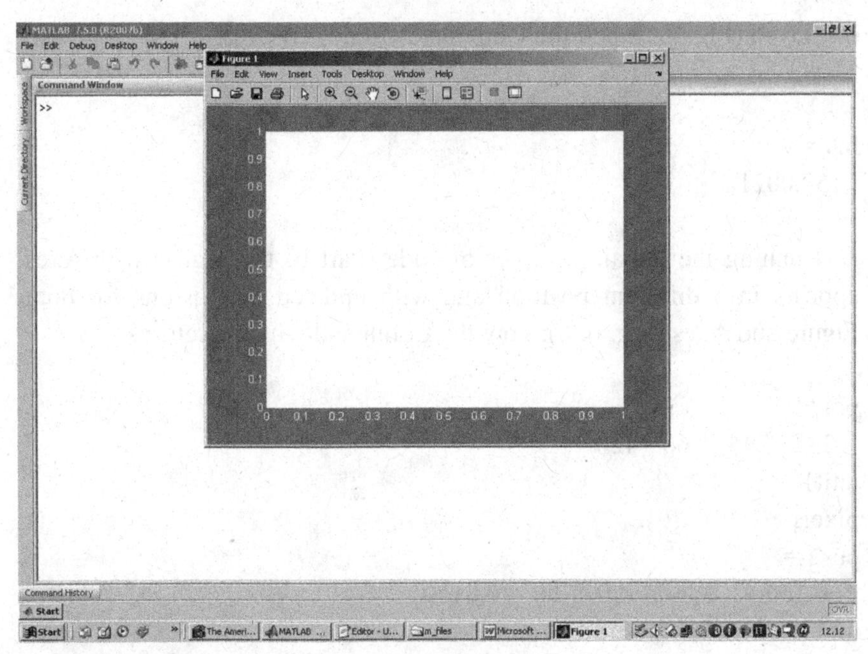

Fig. 6.5 Standard positions of a Figure on the Desktop.

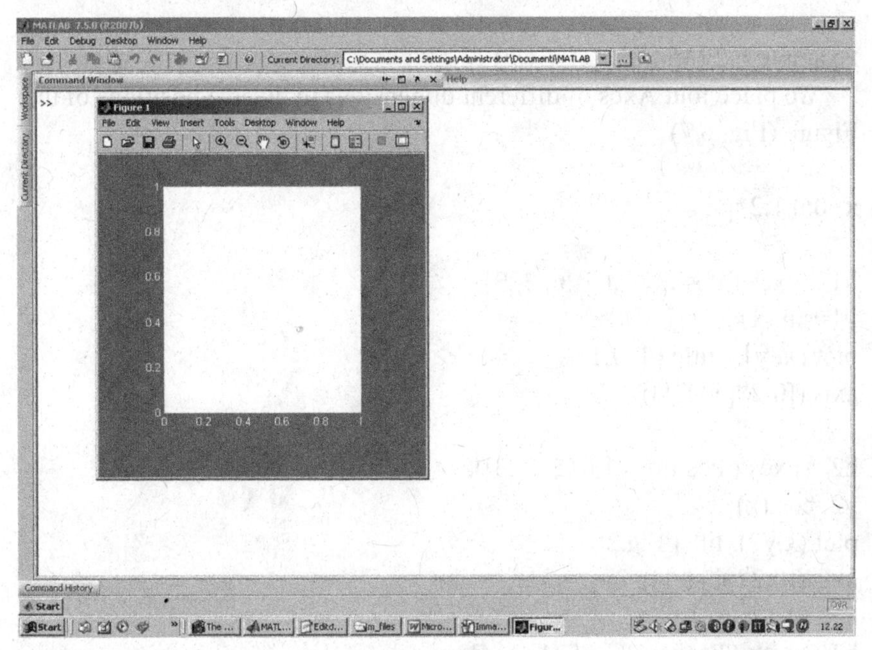

Fig. 6.6 Figure has a new position and dimensions.

displayed (Fig. 6. 5) and the Command window returns

```
h1 =
    1
h2 =
  158.0021
```

Running the remaining lines of code (Part b) the Figure with Axes appears in a different position and with updated dimensions for both Figure and Axes (Fig. 6. 6); now the Command window returns

```
pos1 =
  232  246  560  420
unit1 =
pixels
pos2 =
   0.1300   0.1100   0.7750   0.8150
unit2 =
normalized
```

Example 6.2 (*Multiple_Axes.m*)

We place four Axes of different dimensions in diverse positions of the Figure (Fig. 6.7)

```
x=0:0.1:2*pi;

h1 = axes ('Position' ,[.1 .6 .3 .3])
y1=sin (x);
plot (x, y1), title ('Fig.1')
axis ([0 2*pi -1 1])

h2 = axes ('Position', [.6 .5 .3 .3])
y2=cos (x);
plot (x,y2), title('Fig.2')
axis ([0 2*pi -1 1])

h3 = axes ('Position', [.15 .1 .2 .4])
```

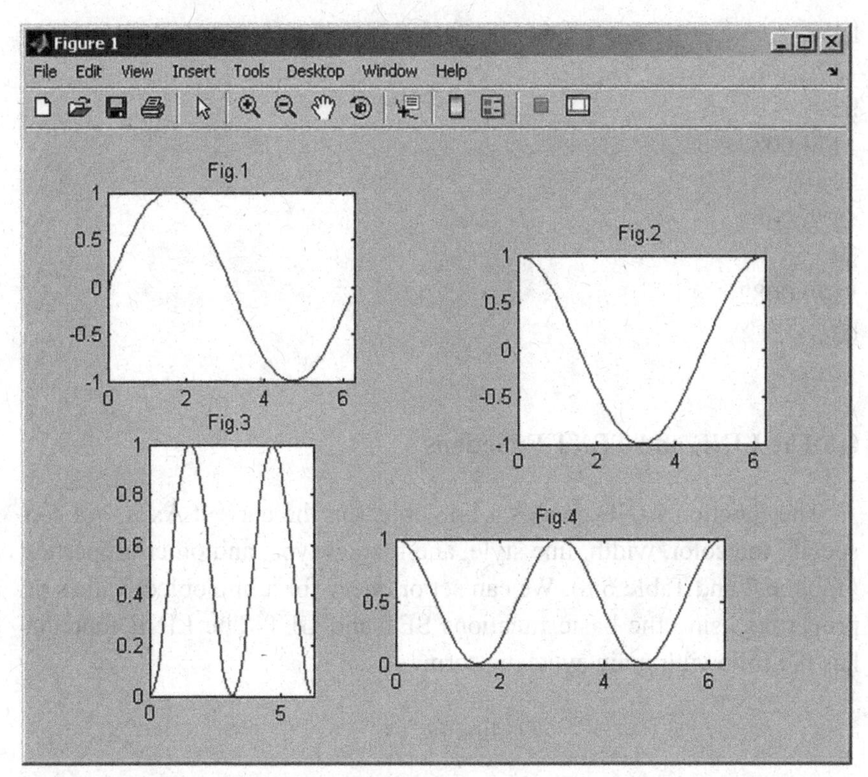

Fig. 6.7 Four plots are positioned in a Figure.

```
y3=sin(x).^2;
plot(x,y3), title('Fig.3')
axis ([0 2*pi 0 1])

h4 = axes ('Position', [.45 .15 .4 .2])
y4=cos (x).^2;
plot (x,y4), title ('Fig.4')
axis([0 2*pi 0 1])

h=gcf
```

The Command window returns the handles of the four Axes and of the Figure

```
h1 =
  170.0082
h2 =
  173.0082
h3 =
  176.0082
h4 =
  179.0082
h =
  1
```

6.5 The LINE and TEXT Functions

The function LINE creates a line object in the current Axes. We can specify the color, width, line style, and marker type, and other properties (Table 6.7 and Table 6.8). We can set or query for a line object values of properties using the basic functions SET and GET. The LINE function has the following main syntactic form

```
line (x, y)
```

that adds the line in arrays x and y to the current Axes. Whereas

```
line
```

returns a column array of handles of the line objects, one handle per line. The line objects are children of Axes objects.

Executing get (h) or set (h) , where h is a line handle, we have the list of line object properties and their current or admissible values (as we have seen for these function when h is the handle of the Axes, Sec. 6.4).

The function TEXT creates, in current Axes, text graphics objects placing a characters string at a specified position in the Axes. We can also specify properties relating to the font (Name, Weight, *etc.*), the alignment, size, color and other properties (some of these are listed in Table 6.9) using the usual basic functions SET and GET. The main syntactic form is

```
text (x, y, 'string')
```

that adds the text in the quotes to location (x, y) on the current Axes, where (x, y) is in units defined for the current plot. If x and y are contained in an array *a* of size n-by-2, TEXT writes the text at all the n locations specified. If 'string' is too an array having the number of rows equal to n, TEXT marks each of the n points with the corresponding row of the 'string' array. The simple command

```
text
```

returns a column vector of handles of Text objects, one handle per text object. Text objects are clearly children of Axes objects.

Executing get(h) or set(h) , where h is a text handle, we have the list of text object properties and their current or legal values (as we have seen for these function when h is the handle of the Axes, Sec. 6.4).

We now consider the following two examples that use the properties of LINE and TEXT functions.

Example 6.3 (*two_axes.m*)

We place an Axes into another ones in the same Figure (Fig. 6.8).

```
h1=figure ('color', 'w')
h2=axes ('Position', [0.06 0.06 0.90 0.90],...
   'color', [0.8 0.8 0.8], 'box','on')

h3=axes ('Position', [.38 .15 .5 .75])

x=-pi:0.1:pi;y = sin (x);
plot(x,y), grid on

str(1) = {'Plot of the sine'};
str(2) = {'function'};
str(3) = {'from'};
str(4) = {'-3.14'};
str(5) = {'to'};
```

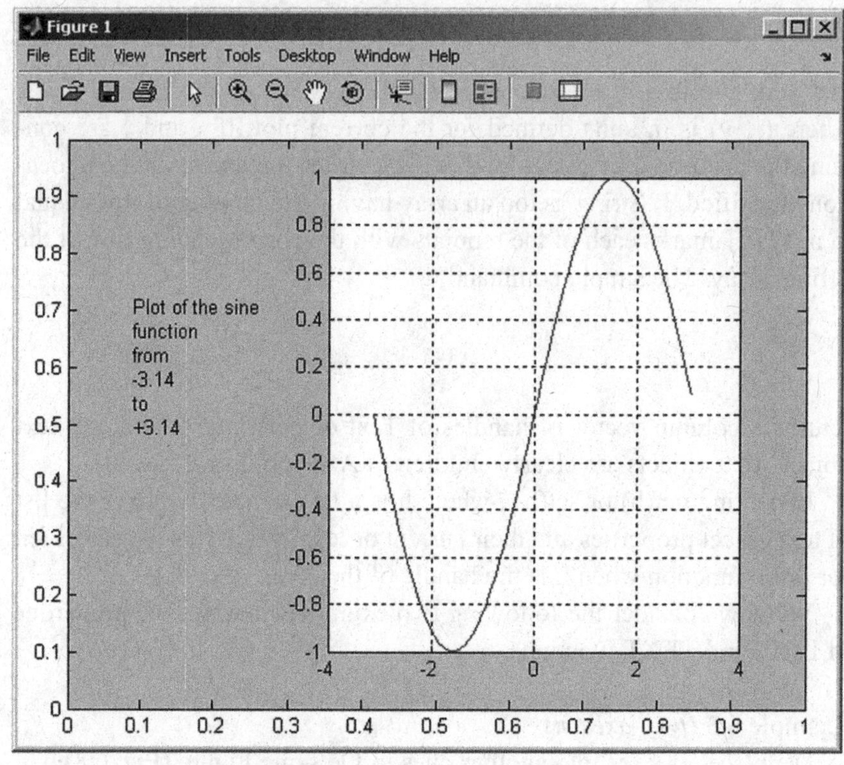

Fig. 6.8 A comment is inserted into the Axes.

```
str(6) = {'+3.14'};
set (gcf, 'CurrentAxes',h2)
h4=text (.09, .6, str, 'FontSize', 10)
h_cur_Axis=get (gcf, 'CurrentAxes')
get (h4)
```

The Command window returns

```
h1 =
    1
h2 =
  158.0111
h3 =
  159.0111
```

```
h4 =
  161.0111
h_cur_Axis =
  158.0111
```

After these results, as we explained before, the command of the last line (*get(h4)*) returns a long list of 41 properties and corresponding values of the *external* Axes . From the list of properties we find

```
Parent = [ 158.0111 ]
Children = [ ]
```

The *internal* Axes (h3 = 159.0111) have the external Axes as parent (h2 = 158.0032) and they haven't children (the list of properties returns for the property ' *Children* ' an empty array). The handle h4 refers to the object graphics 'Text'.

Example 6.4 (*gca_get_set.m*)

The features, or properties, of the lines in a plot are added using the functions GCA,GET and SET

```
Seven_col=get(gca,'ColorOrder')

x=0:0.1:pi/2;y = sin(x);
h1=plot (x, y, x , y+0.2, x, y+0.4, x, y+0.60, x, y+0.8,...
   x, y+1.0, x,y+1.2)

set (gca,'Title',...
   text ('String', 'GCA GET AND SET COMMANDS FOR PLOT',...
   'Color', 'b'))

set (gca, 'XGrid', 'on')

set (gca, 'yTickLabel', {'blue';'green';'red';...
   'cyan'; 'magenta'; 'yellow'})
```

```
h2=gca
h22=get (h1, 'Parent')
ax_children=get (gca, 'children')

c_names={'LineStyle','LineWidth','Marker'}
c_values={'-', 1, '+'; '-.', 1.5, 'o'; '—', 2, 's'; '-', 1.5, 'd';...
   'none', 1, 'p'; '—', 3, 'none'; ':', 2, 'none';}
set (h1, c_names, c_values)

whos
```

Command window returns the following results and the Figure window displays the plot (Fig. 6.9)

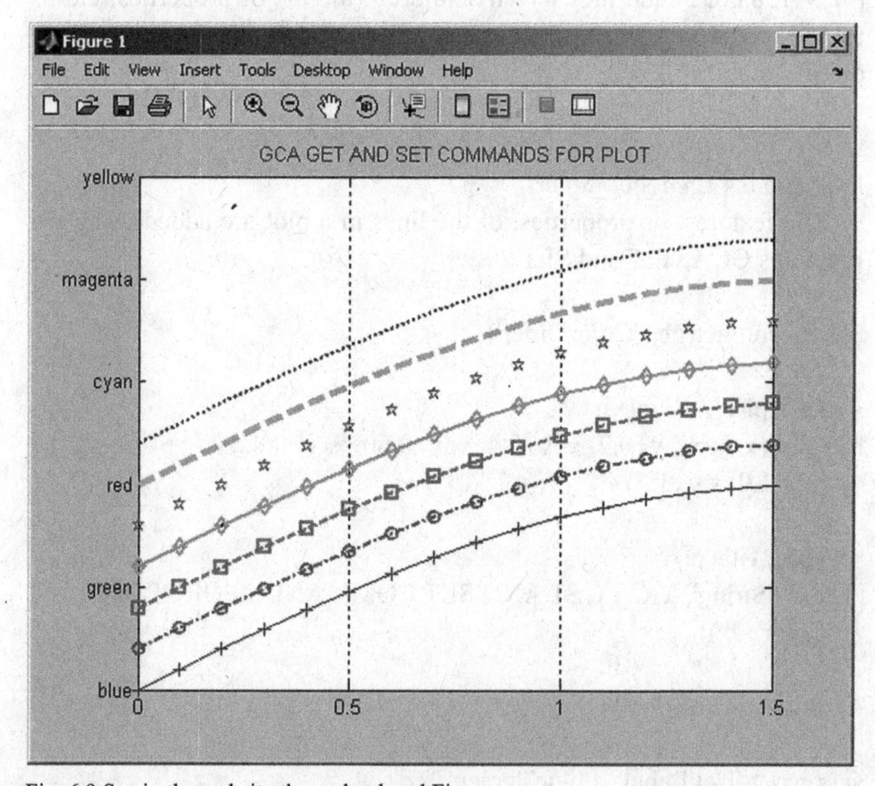

Fig. 6.9 See in the website the real colored Figure.

```
Seven_col =
```

(*The results are reported in the second column of Table 6.4 (See Sec. 6.6). The next array h1 contains th handles of the seven lines*)

```
h1 =
  159.0117
  160.0112
  161.0112
  162.0112
  163.0112
  164.0112
  165.0112
h2 =
  158.0112
h22 =
```

(*The result is an array 1-by-7 with all values equal to 158.0112*)

```
ax_children =
```

(*The result is an array 1-by-7 with all values equal to that of h1 but in reversed order, first 165.0112, then 164.0112, and so on*)

```
c_names =
   'LineStyle'   'LineWidth'   'Marker'
c_values =
```

(*The values of the cell array c_values of size 7-by-3 are reported in Table 6.1*)

Table 6.1 The c_values cell array of size 7-by-3.

LineStyle	**LineWidth**	**Marker**
'-'	[1]	'+'
'-.'	[1.5]	'o'
'—'	[2]	's'
'-'	[1.5]	'd'
'none'	[1]	'p'
'—'	[3]	'none'
':'	[2]	'none'

Name	Size	Bytes	Class
Seven_col	7x3	168	double
ax_children	7x1	56	double
c_names	1x3	228	cell
c_values	7x3	1368	cell
h1	7x1	56	double
h2	1x1	8	double
h22	7x1	476	cell
x	1x16	128	double
y	1x16	128	double

6.6 The Objects Properties

Each graphics object has a number (usually greater than 30) of properties. The names of properties are always *quoted strings* but are *not case sensitive*. Every property defines one or more values (usually numerical or literal) of the object. Some are equal for all objects; others are equal for a group of objects. The remaining properties are unique for each object. For example are common to all objects:

Children – one or more handles of all child objects of an object

HandleVisibility – control of the availability of the object's handle

Parent - the parent of an object

Type - the class of an object (Figure, Axes, Line, Text, *etc.*)

Visible - determines whether or not an object is visible

As examples of properties common to a group of objects we can mention:

color – is a property of Figure, Axes and Text objects, *etc.*

units – is a property of Root, Figure, and Line, *etc.*

In the following Tables we report a partial list of properties of the most significant objects that are of immediate meaning and usefulness. There is a very large number of graphics objects and, correspondingly, of list of properties as we can verify looking through the Appendix 3. As stated in Introduction we have made the choice to highlight only preliminary but fundamental graphics objects: the reader on the basis of his interests and with the aid of the MATLAB Help tools can extend the knowledge of this subject when, if and how he wants.

Table 6.2 Root Properties (6 of 39). Curly braces { } enclose default values.

Property name	Property value	Description
CommandWindowSize	*[columns rows]*	The first element is the number of columns wide and the second element is the number of rows tall.
CurrentFigure	*figure handle*	Handle of the current Figure window, which is the one most recently created, clicked in, or made current with the FIGURE command
ScreenDepth	*bits per pixel*	The maximum number of simultaneously displayed colors on the current graphics device is 2 raised to this power.
ScreenPixelsPerInch	*Display resolution*	DPI setting for our screen
ScreenSize	*four-element rectangle array(read only)*	[left,bottom,width,height] that defines the display size. left and bottom are 0 for all Units except pixels, in which case left and bottom are 1
Type	*string (read only)*	Class of graphics object. For the root object, Type is always 'root'
Units	*{pixels} | normalized | inches | centimeters | points | characters*	Unit of measurement to define size and location
Visible	*{on} | off*	Object visibility. This property has no effect on the root object

Table 6.3 Figure properties (14 of 70). Curly braces { } enclose default values.

Property name	Property value	Description
Children	*Array of handles*	Children of the Figure
Color	*ColorSpec*	Figure background color (See Table 6.4)
CurrentAxes	*handle of current Axes*	Point Axes in the Figure
DockControls	*{on} | off*	Displays controls used to dock Figure
IntegerHandle	*{on} | off*	Figure handle mode. Figure object handles are integers by default
MenuBar	*none | {figure}*	Enable-disable Figure menu bar
Name	*String*	Figure window title. By default, the Figure title is displayed as Figure 1, Figure 2, and so on
NextPlot	*new | {add} | replace | replacechildren*	How to add next plot.
NumberTitle	*{on} | off*	Figure window title number
PaperOrientation	*{portrait} | landscape*	Horizontal or vertical paper orientation
PaperPosition	*four-element rect array*	Location on printed page. rect = [left, bottom, width, height]
PaperUnits	*normalized | {inches} | centimeters | points*	Hardcopy measurement units.
Position	*four-element pos array*	Figure position. pos = [left, bottom, width, height]; left and bottom define the distance from the lower left corner of the screen to the lower left corner of the Figure
Units	*{pixels} | normalized | inches | centimeters | points | characters*	Normalized units map the lower left corner of the Figure window to (0,0) and the upper right corner to (1.0,1.0)
Type	*string (read only)*	For figures, Type is always the string 'figure'.
Visible	*{on} | off*	If the Visible property of a figure is off, the entire figure window is invisible

Table 6.4 ColorSpec.

RGB Value	RGB values from command get(gca,'ColorOrder')	Short Name	Long Name
[1 1 0]	[0, 0, 1]	y	yellow
[1 0 1]	[0, 0.5, 1]	m	magenta
[0 1 1]	[1, 0, 0]	c	cyan
[1 0 0]	[0, 0.75, 0.75]	r	red
[0 1 0]	[0.75, 0, 0.75]	g	green
[0 0 1]	[0.75, 0.75, 0]	b	blue
[1 1 1]		w	white
[0 0 0]	[0.25, 0.25, 0.25]	k	black

Table 6.5a Axes properties (11 of 74) Curly braces { } enclose default values.

Property name	Property value	Description
ActivePositionProperty	*{outerposition} | position*	Use OuterPosition or Position property for resize.
Box	*on | {off}*	The default is to not display the box for 2-D views or a cube for 3-D views
Children	*Array of graphics object handles*	An array of size 1-by-n containing the handles of all graphics objects rendered within the Axes (whether visible or not).
Color For	*{none} | ColorSpec*	Color of the Axes back planes ColorSpec see Table 6.4
ColorOrder	*By default is a 7-by-3 array of RGB values*	Colors to use for multiline plots. The PLOT command, if no color is specified, makes automatic use of seven default colors
FontAngle	*{normal} | italic | oblique*	Select italic or normal font
FontName	*A name such as Courier or the string FixedWidth*	The font family name specifying the font to use for Axes labels. FontName must be a font that our system supports
FontSize	*Font size specified in FontUnitsFont size*	The default point size is 12
FontUnits	*{points} | normalized | inches | centimeters | pixels*	The default units (points), are equal to 1/72 of an inch
FontWeight	*{normal} | bold | light | demi*	Select bold or normal font
GridLineStyle	- | - -| *{:}* | -. | *none*	Line style used to draw grid lines. The default grid line style is dotted
HitTest can	*{on} | off*	HitTest determines if the Axes become the current object

Table 6.5b Axes properties (8 of 74) Curly braces { } enclose default values.

Layer	*{bottom}* | *top*	Draw axis lines below or above graphics objects. This is useful for placing grid lines and tick marks on top of images.
LineStyleOrder	*LineSpec (default: a solid line '-')*	Order of line styles and markers used when creating multiple-line plots (See Table 6.1)
LineWidth	*line width in points*	The width of lines. The default value is 0.5 points (1 point = 1/72 inch).
MinorGridLineStyle	- | - -| {:} | -. | *none*	Line style used to draw minor grid lines. The default minor grid line style is dotted
NextPlot	*add* | *{replace}* | *replacechildren*	Where to draw the next plot
OuterPosition	*1-by-4 array [left bottom width height] where left and bottom define the distance from the lower-left corner of the figure window to the lower-left corner of the Figure*	Position of Axes including labels, title, and a margin. The default value of [0 0 1 1] (normalized units) includes the interior of the Figure
Parent	*Figure or uipanel handle*	Axes parent
Position	*1-by-4 array [left bottom width height] specifying a rectangle that locates the Axes*	Position of Axes within its parent container (figure or uipanel). Where left and bottom define the distance from the lower-left corner of the container to the lower-left cornerof the rectangle
TightInset	*[left bottom right top]*	Read only. Margins added to Position to include text labels
Title	*handle of text object*	Axes title. The handle of the text object that is used for the Axes title.

Table 6.5c Axes properties (14 of 74) Curly braces { } enclose default values.

Type	*string (read only)*	A property that identifies the class of graphics object. For Axes objects, Type is always set to 'Axes'.
Units	*inches | centimeters | {normalized} | points | pixels | characters*	The units used to interpret the Position property. All units are measured from the lower left corner of the figure window
Visible	*{on} | off*	By default, Axes are visible
XAxisLocation	*top | {bottom}*	Location of x-axis tick marks and labels
YAxisLocation	*right | {left}*	Location of y-axis tick marks and labels
XColor, YColor, ZColor	*ColorSpec*	Color of axis lines. A three-element vector specifying an RGB triple, or a predefined MATLAB color string
XDir, YDir, ZDir	*{normal} | reverse*	Direction of increasing values
XLabel, YLabel, ZLabel	*handle of text object*	The handle of the text object used to label the x-, y-, or z-axis, respectively
XMinorGrid, YMinorGrid, ZMinorGrid	*on | {off}*	Enable or disable minor gridlines
XMinorTick, YMinorTick, ZMinorTick	*on | {off}*	Enable or disable minor tick marks
XScale, YScale, ZScale	*{linear} | log*	Axis scaling
XTick, YTick, ZTick	*Array 1-by-m locating tick marks*	Tick spacing
XTickLabel, YTickLabel, ZTickLabel	*String*	Tick labels. An array of strings to use as labels for tick marks along the respective axis
XTickMode, YTickMode, ZTickMode	*{auto} | manual*	MATLAB or user-controlled tick spacing
XTickLabelMode, YTickLabelMode, ZTickLabelMode	*{auto} | manual*	Tick labels by default or user determined

Table 6.6 List of graphics objects.

Reference group	**List**
Core Object	*Image*
Core Object	*Line*
Core Object	*Rectangle*
Core Object	*Text*
Core Object	*Light*
Core Object	*Patch*
Core Object	*Surface*
Plot Objects	Lineseries
Plot Objects	Areaseries
Plot Objects	Barseries
Plot Objects	Contourgroup
Plot Objects	Errorbarseries
Plot Objects	Quivergroup
Plot Objects	Scattergroup
Plot Objects	Starseries
Plot Objects	Stemseries
Plot Objects	Surfaceplot
Group Object	*Hggroup*
Group Object	*Hgtransform*
Annotation Object	Arrow
Annotation Object	Doublearrow
Annotation Object	Textarrow
Annotation Object	Textbox
Annotation Object	Line (annotation)
Annotation Object	Rectangle (annotation)
Annotation Object	Ellipse

Table 6.7 Line properties (14 of 31). Curly braces { } enclose default values.

Property name	Property value	Description
Children	*Empty array*	Line objects have no children
Color	*A three-element RGB Array or a name*	See Table 6.4
HandleVisibility	*{on} | off*	Control access to object's handle by command-line users and GUIs.
LineStyle	*{-} | — | : | -. | none*	The available line styles are always used as quoted strings
LineWidth	*A single value in points*	The default LineWidth is 0.5 points.
Marker	*character*	Property specifies marks that display at data points. See Table 6.8
MarkerEdgeColor	*ColorSpec | none | {auto}*	For ColorSpec see Table 6.4. The color of the marker or the edge color for filled markers
MarkerFaceColor	*ColorSpec | none | {auto}*	The fill color for markers that are closed shapes. For ColorSpec see Table 6.4.
MarkerSize	*A single value in points*	The default value for MarkerSize is six points
Parent	*Handle of Axes*	This property contains the handle of the line object's parent
Type	*string (read only)*	Class of graphics object. For line objects, Type is always the string 'line'.
Visible	*{on} | off*	Line visibility. By default, all lines are visible.
XData	*An array of x-coordinates defining the line*	YData and ZData must be the same length and have the same number of rows
YData	*An array of y-coordinates defining the line*	XData and ZData must be the same length and have the same number of rows
ZData	*An array of z-coordinates defining the line*	XData and YData must have the same number of rows

Table 6.8 Marker.

Marker	Name
'+'	*Plus sign*
'o'	*Circle*
'*'	*Asterisk*
'.'	*Point*
'x'	*Cross*
's'	*Square*
'd'	*Diamond*
'^'	*Upward-point*
'v'	*Downward-point*
'>'	*Right-pointing*
'<'	*Left-pointing*
'p'	*Five-pointed star*
'h'	*Six-pointed star*
'none'	*No marker*

Table 6.9 Text Properties (20 of 39). Curly braces { } enclose default values.

<table>
<tr><th>Property name</th><th>Property value</th><th>Description</th></tr>
<tr><td>BackgroundColor</td><td>ColorSpec | {none}</td><td>define a color for the rectangle that encloses the text</td></tr>
<tr><td>Children</td><td>An empty array (read only)</td><td>Text objects have no children.</td></tr>
<tr><td>Color</td><td>ColorSpec</td><td>Text color. See Table 6.4 for ColorSpec</td></tr>
<tr><td>EdgeColor</td><td>ColorSpec | {none}</td><td>Color of edge drawn around text extent rectangle plus margin.</td></tr>
<tr><td>Editing</td><td>on | {off}</td><td>Enable or disable editing mode</td></tr>
<tr><td>FontAngle</td><td>{normal} | italic | oblique</td><td>A a font is selected from those available on PC system.</td></tr>
<tr><td>FontName</td><td>A font name</td><td>This must be one that PC system supports. The default font is Helvetica</td></tr>
<tr><td>FontSize</td><td>Font size in points</td><td>The default is 10 points</td></tr>
<tr><td>FontWeight</td><td>light | {normal} | demi | bold</td><td>Weight of text characters.</td></tr>
<tr><td>FontUnits</td><td>{points} | normalized | inches | centimeters |</td><td>Font size units</td></tr>
<tr><td>HorizontalAlignment</td><td>{left} | center | right</td><td>Horizontal alignment of text.</td></tr>
<tr><td>LineStyle</td><td>{-} | — | : | -. | none</td><td>Edge line type</td></tr>
<tr><td>LineWidth</td><td>A single value in points</td><td>Width of line used to draw text extent rectangle</td></tr>
<tr><td>Margin</td><td>A single value in pixels</td><td>Distance between the text extent and the rectangle edge</td></tr>
<tr><td>Position</td><td>[x, y]</td><td>Location specifies the location of the text in the plot</td></tr>
<tr><td>Rotation</td><td>A single value in degree</td><td>Text orientation. The default is 0</td></tr>
<tr><td>String</td><td>string</td><td>A quoted string for single-line strings or a cell array of strings</td></tr>
<tr><td>Type</td><td>string (read only)</td><td>Class of graphics object</td></tr>
<tr><td>Units</td><td>pixels | normalized | inches | centimeters | points | {data}</td><td>Units of measurement</td></tr>
<tr><td>VerticalAlignment</td><td>top | cap | {middle} | baseline | bottom</td><td>Vertical alignment specifies the vertical justification of the text</td></tr>
<tr><td>Visible</td><td>{on} | off</td><td>Text visibility. By default, all text is visible.</td></tr>
</table>

About Chapter 7

Graphics objects are used to display ten types of 2-D and 3-D plot subdivided in more than sixty graphs. Among these we will examine only the "*graph*" usually called 2-D plot. This is only one of the nine *Line 2-D graphs* belonging to the *lineseries* type. Most of the features and properties of the graphics objects, that we consider, are however common to all graphs.

A 2-D plot and its associate commands (*subplot, grid, box, label, title, hold, legend*, *etc*.) are formally defined. Examples clarify how the properties *Position*, *OuterPosition* and *TightInset* affect the resize, the print and the export of a 2-D plot.

We can also control interactively the properties of graphics objects and the print and the export of a 2-D plot.

An image is a graphic *core* object represented by an array whose numeric elements contain color or gray data.

We explain the types of images (*indexed, truecolor and gray*) and introduce in a very simplified form some commands (*image, imagesc, imread, imwrite, imfinfo and map*) necessary to execute the examples.

Chapter 7

Plot 2-D and Image

7.1 Plot 2-D

7.1.1 *The objects hierarchy*

We have a great number of graphics objects and among these MATLAB considers ten types of 2-D and 3-D plot objects (Table 7.1) subdivided in more than sixty graphs (Table 7.2).

Table 7.1 Types of plot objects.

Plot Objects	**Used to create**
areaseries	area graphs
barseries	bar graphs
contourgroup	contour graphs
errorbarseries	errorbar graphs
lineseries	***line plotting functions (plot,* plot3, *etc.)***
quivergroup	quiver and quiver3 graphs
scattergroup	scatter and scatter3 graphs
stairseries	stairstep graphs (stairs)
stemseries	stem and stem3 graphs
surfaceplot	the surf and mesh group of functions

Table 7.2 - 2-D and 3-D graphs.

2-D types and their numbers	***3-D types and their numbers***
Line (9)	*Line* (5)
Bar (8)	*Mesh&Bar* (7)
Area (7)	*Area* (6)
Direction (3)	*Surface* (5)
Radial (4)	*Direction* (3)
Scatter (3)	*Volumetric* (5)

As stated in the Introduction we will examine only the "*graph*" usually called *2-D plot*. This is one of the nine *Line* 2-D graphs present in the first column of Table 7.2 belonging to the *lineseries* of Plot Objects present in the fifth row of Table 7.1. Most of the features and properties of the graphics objects, that we are considering, are however common to all *Plot objects* (Table 7.1) and some are common to all graphics objects.

The hierarchy of the main objects implied in a 2-D plot is given in Fig. 7.1. Clearly *objects*, *properties* and *commands* are different things: the name *plot* doesn't refer to an object but it is a *command* by which we can create objects (See next Example 7.1). Then Root, Figure, Axes, Line and Text are objects while color, ticks, width, and position are properties. The list of graphics objects (Table 6.5) and some Tables of properties are located in Sec. 6.6.

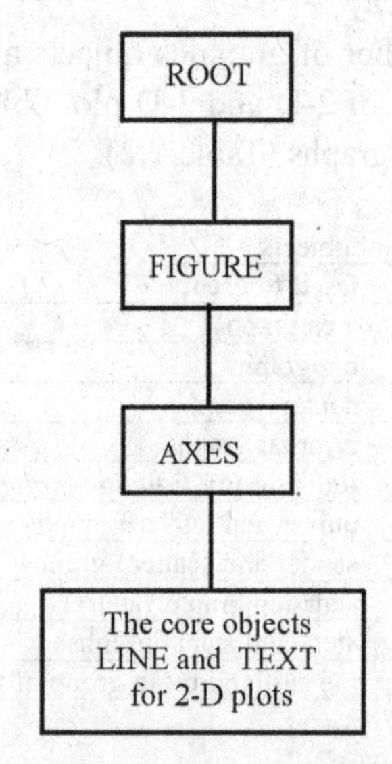

Fig. 7.1 Hierarchy of graphics objects.

Example 7.1 (*hierarchy.m*)

```
%Part a
x = 0:0.1:2*pi; y = sin(x); h4 = figure(4);
h_pl = plot(x, y)
```

```
hs = text('string', 'TITLE OF THE PLOT')
set(gca, 'Title', hs)
class_h_pl = get(h_pl, 'type')
class_hs = get(hs, 'type')
h_title = get(gca ,'Title')
class_h_title = get(h_title, 'type')

%Part b
h_pl_par = get(h_pl, 'parent')
h_pl_chil = get(h_pl,  'children')

hs_par = get(hs,'parent')
hs_chil = get(hs, 'children')

h_ax = gca
h_ax_par = get(h_ax, 'parent')
h_ax_chil = get(h_ax, 'children')
class_ax = get(h_ax, 'type')

h_fig = get(gca, 'parent')
class_pa  r= get(h_fig, 'type')

h_root = get(h_fig, 'parent')
class_root = get(h_root, 'type')
```

The results of the Part a are

```
h_pl =
159.0328
hs =
160.0323
class_h_pl =
line
class_hs =
text
h_title =
```

```
160.0323
class_h_title =
text
```

All results (*Part a* and *Part b*) are visually reported in Fig. 7.2. We observe from the previous Example and the corresponding Fig. 7.2 that

a. the handle (h_pl) created by the command PLOT is the *handle of a line*: if we had ordered the plot of n lines with a command like h_pl = plot(x1, y1, x2, y2, ..., xn, yn) h_pl would have returned an array of n handles,

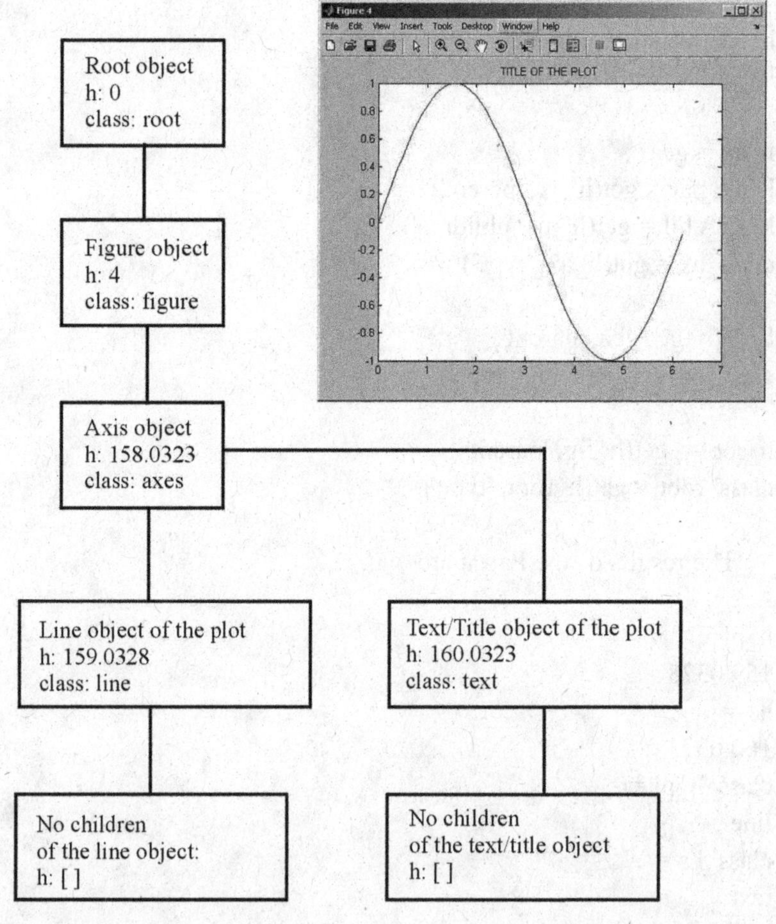

Fig. 7.2 Results of the Example 7.1.

b. the names *text* and *Title* correspond to the same object with the same handle,

c. all other results of the Part b are displayed in Fig. 7.2.

7.1.2 *The PLOT and SUBPLOT commands*

The command PLOT plots the array y versus the array x. Syntax:

```
h = plot (x1, y1, str1, x2, y2, str2, ...)
```

Each pair of x and y arrays must have the same size. The string *str* can have the form '*csm*' where *c* is a color, *s* is a style and *m* a marker of the line. The string *str* can be absent, can contain only one or two properties, and the properties can be in any possible order. For the line object we have defined properties linestyle, color and marker in Table 6.7.

If no color is specified, colors specified by the Axes *ColorOrder* property are used. If a marker type isn't specified, PLOT uses no marker. If a linestyle isn't specified, PLOT uses a solid line.

The handle h is optional. If present the handles of the lines are returned. The (x,y,str) triples, can be followed by parameter/value pairs to specify additional Line properties (Table 6.7). Syntax:

```
plot (x1, y1, str1, prop1, val1, x2, y2, str2, prop2, val2...)
```

For example, plot(x,y, '—rs', 'LineWidth', 2, 'Color',[0.6 0 0]).

The command SUBPLOT breaks the Figure window creating many Axes in tiled positions. Syntax:

h = subplot(m, n, p)

The Figure content is divided into an m-by-n array of small Axes. The command selects the p-th Axes for the current plot. If h is present, it returns the axis handle. Clearly after the SUBPLOT command a PLOT command must follow to create the p-th Axes.

7.1.3 *Commands complementary to PLOT*

The AXIS command controls Axes scaling and appearance. If executed without arguments the command creates a default Figure and Axes without a line. Syntax:

```
axis ([xmin xmax ymin ymax])
```

sets scaling for the x- and y-axis on the current plot.

```
axis off
```

turns off *labeling*, *tick marks* and *background* of the Axes.

```
axis on
```

turns for the Axes *labeling, tick marks* and *background* back on.

```
axis tight
```

sets the limits of the Axes to the range of the data.

With the TITLE command a string is centered at the top of the box containing the plot. Syntax:

```
h = title (string)
```

For example writing title ({'This title', 'has 2 lines' }) the title is displayed in two rows.

```
h = title (string, prop1, val1,.prop2, val2,...)
```

specifies property name and property value pairs for the text graphics object that the TITLE command creates.

If h is present, the handle to the text object used as the title is returned.

The "*major/minor*" grid lines can be added to or removed from a plot, setting (without using the SET command) at a high-level the Axes properties Xgrid, Ygrid. Syntax of some main commands:

```
grid on
```

adds major grid lines to the current Axes.

```
grid off
```

removes major and minor grid lines from the current Axes.

```
grid minor
```

adds the minor grid lines of the current Axes.

The BOX command, without using the SET command for the Box property of Axes, adds a box or takes it off from the current Axes. Syntax:

```
box on
box off
```

The c-LABEL commands add text beside the current c-axis. Syntax:

```
c-label('text')
```

or

```
c-label('text', prop1, val1, prop2, val2,...)
```

where c- stands for x or y. The second form sets the values of the specified properties of the c-label.

The HOLD command refers to the *NextPlot* property of the current Figure (Table 6.2). Syntax:

```
hold on
```

holds the current plot and all Axes properties so that subsequent commands operate on the existing graph. It sets the *NextPlot* property of the current Figure to "add".

hold off

returns to the default mode whereby PLOT commands erase the previous plots and reset all Axes properties before drawing. It sets the *NextPlot* property to "replace".

hold all

holds the plot, the current color and linestyle so that subsequent plotting commands will not reset the color and linestyle.

The comand LEGEND puts a legend on the current plot. Syntax:

legend(string)

puts a *legend* on the current plot using the specified string as label. The *fontsize* and *fontname* for the legend string matches the corresponding Axes properties (Table 6.4a).

legend off

removes the legend from the current Axes and deletes the legend handle.

legend boxoff
legend boxon

make legend background box invisible/visible when legend is visible/invisible.

legend (string, 'location', loc)

adds a legend in the specified location, *loc*, with respect to the Axes. The location *loc* may be either a 1x4 position vector or a defined string. Some of about 20 defined *loc* strings are in Table 7.3.

Table 7.3 Some *loc* strings.

The loc string	Its meaning
'NorthEast'	inside top right (default)
'Best'	least conflict with data in plot
'BestOutside'	least unused space outside plot
'North'	inside plot box near top
'South'	inside bottom
'East'	inside right
'West'	inside left

7.1.4 *Resize, print and export of a plot*

The Axes properties (Table. 6.4b) contain, in three arrays 1-by-4, values that define the locations and sizes of

a. the Axes (*Position*),

b. the rectangle equal to the Figure space (*OuterPosition*)

c. the margin around the Axes including xlabel at the bottom, ylabels on the left, the title at the top and a blank space at the right of the Axes (*TightInset*).

The space between the TightInset box and the OuterPosition box remain blank.

Calling p and t respectively the arrays containing the properties of Position and TightInset, Fig. 7.3 gives a visual meaning of all the values. Fig. 7.4 shows how the margin defined by the t array of the TightInset property changes if xlabel, ylabels and title are either absent or not. In Fig. 7.4 when these texts are not present the values of t in centimeters, rounded to two decimal digits, are

t = [0.66, 0.45, 0.21, 0.21]

But if the texts are added in the plot the array t becomes

t = [1.35, 1.00, 0.21, 0.61]

We see that has not changed only the third element of t, corresponding to the right margin of the TightInset where hasn't been added any text.

The array defining the values of OuterPosition properties are those of the Figure. If normalized units are used the array is [0 0 1 1]. But, if other units are used, the first two elements are measured from the lower left corner of the screen.

The next example shows how we can change the position and the size of a Figure content.

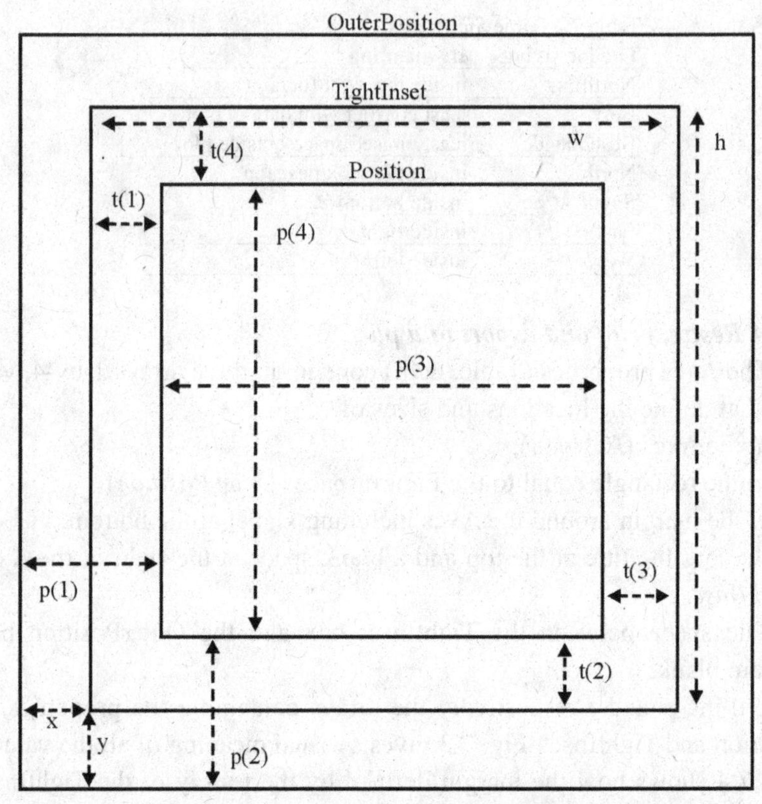

Fig. 7.3 The array p contains the left (p(1)), the bottom (p(2)), the width (p(3)) and the height (p(4)) values of the rectangle Position; the TightInset array t contains the left (t(1)), bottom (t(2)), right (t(3)) and top (t(4)) distances from the Position rectangle. If normalized units are used [0, 0, 1, 1] are the values defining the OuterPosition and Figure box. The array [x, y, w, h] contains the values of the rectangle TightInset + Position.

Example 7.2 (*plot_pos_size.m*)

```
set(gca,'units','normalized')
p = get(gca, 'Position')
t = get(gca, 'TightInset')
outp = get(gca, 'outerposition')

x = -pi:.1:pi; y = sin(x); plot(x,y); axis tight;
title('The sine function'); legend('sine','location','best');
```

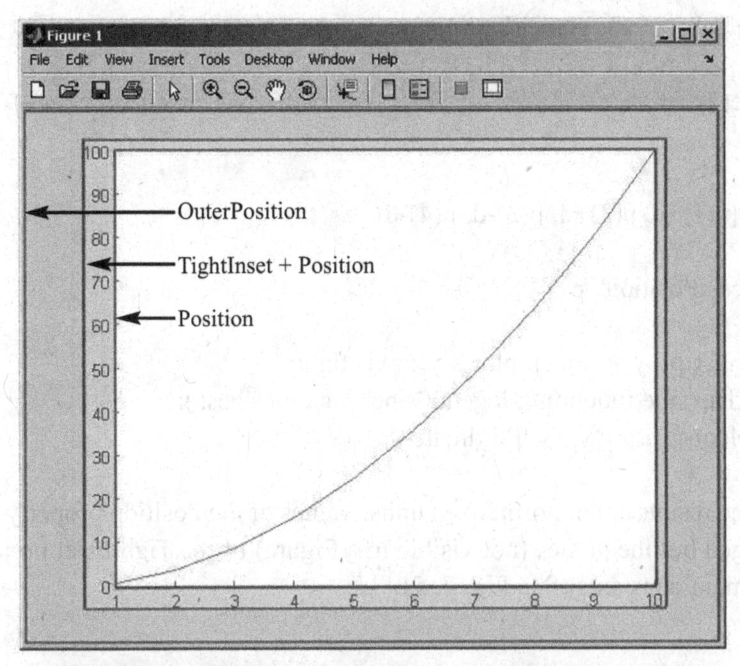

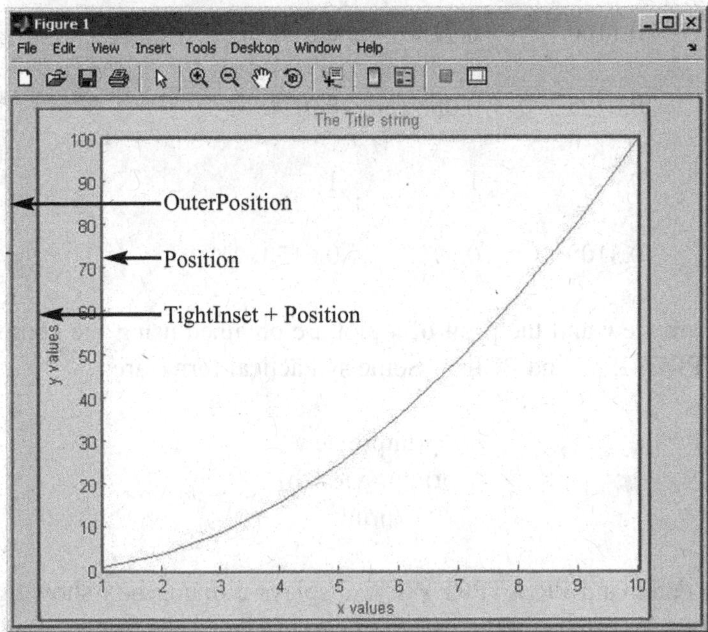

Fig. 7.4 In the second Figure labels and title are added.

```
xlabel('abscissa'); ylabel('ordinate')

figure(2)

d = 0.2;
p1 = [p(1)+d, p(2)+d, p(3)-d, p(4)-d]
t1 = t;
set(gca, 'Position', p1)

x = -pi:.1:pi; y = sin(x); plot(x,y); axis tight;
title('The sine function'); legend('sine','location','best');
xlabel('abscissa'); ylabel('ordinate')
```

The results are in normalized units. Values of the Position property are changed but the values (not visible in a Figure) of the TightInset property remain constants (See Fig. 7. 5)

```
p =
0.1300    0.1100    0.7750    0.8150
t =
0.0393    0.0405    0.0089    0.0190
outp =
0         0         1         1
p1 =
0.3300    0.3100    0.5750    0.6150
```

The preview and the print of a plot are obtained using the command PRINTPREVIEW and PRINT. Some syntactical forms are:

```
printpreview
printpreview(h)
print
```

The command PRINTPREVIEW displays a dialog box showing the *content of the Figure* in the currently active Figure window as it will be printed (Fig. 7.6). A scaled version of the Figure is displayed in the right-

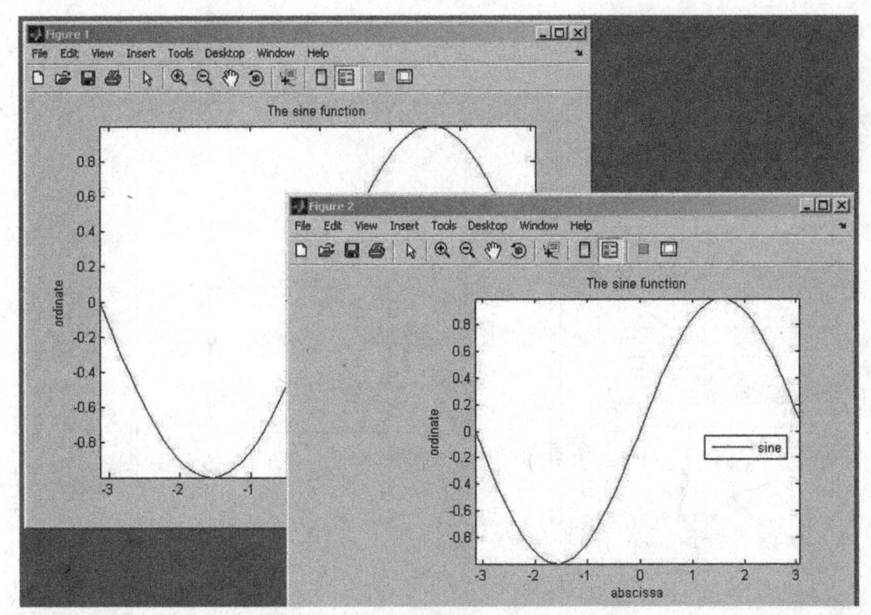

Fig. 7.5 The position and dimensions of the Axes in the overlapped Figure are defined in Example 7.2.

hand pane of the dialog box (this is an example of GUI). If h is present the command displays the dialog box showing the Figure with handle h.

We are showing only the simplest form of the command PRINT, usually sufficient if we have to really print a graph on paper. The PRINTPREVIEW command can be used to inspect the plot to be printed, modify it if necessary and, then, print it using the Print button on the top of the right panel (Fig. 7.6). The print Preview box is treated too in Sec. 7.1.5.

We have to point out attention to *what is printed*. This is not the *content of the Axes* (or of the plot) but the *content of the Figure* that contains the Axes but also the content of the TightInset area and the blank space between the OuterPosition and the TightInset. Besides the Figure properties must be used to specify the position and the size of what we want to print in a page. These considerations will make easy the meaning of the next exercises.

Example 7.3 (*plot_print1.m*)

The default size and position (in centimeters) of the plot in an A4 paper sheet are examined.

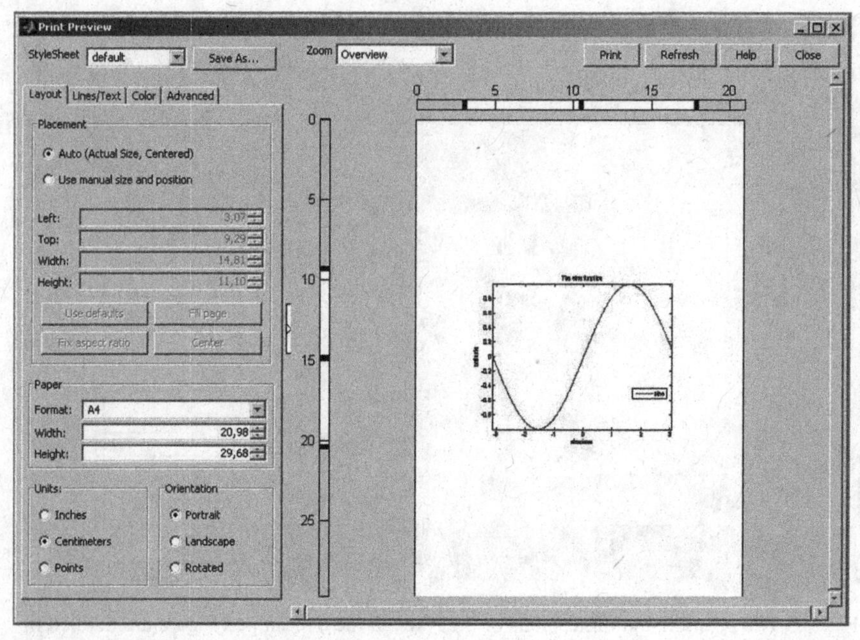

Fig. 7.6 The Print Preview box.

```
x=-pi:.1: pi; y=sin (x); plot (x, y); axis tight;
title ('The sine function'); legend ('sine', 'location', 'best');
xlabel ('abscissa'); ylabel('ordinate')

set (gca, 'units', 'centimeters')
p = get (gca, 'Position')
t= get (gca, 'tightinset')
outp = get (gca, 'OuterPosition')

set (gcf, 'PaperUnits', 'centimeters')
% set (gcf, 'PaperPositionMode', 'manual')
set(gcf, 'PaperPositionMode', 'auto')

paper=get (gcf, 'PaperPosition')
val=[p(1)+paper(1), p(2)+paper(2), p(3), p(4)]

printpreview(gcf)
```

The preview is given in Fig. 7.6. The following results return in Command window

```
p =
1.9247      1.2214      11.47429.0498
t =
1.3748      1.0047      0.0529          0.6081
outp =
0           0           14.8054         11.1041
paper =
3.0668      9.2798      14.805411.1041
val =
4.9915      10.5013     11.4742         9.0498
```

We observe that the distance paper (1) of the printed plot from the left side of the paper referes to left side of Figure (or OuterPosition) but not to the left side of the Axes (Fig. 7.7 and Fig. 7.8).

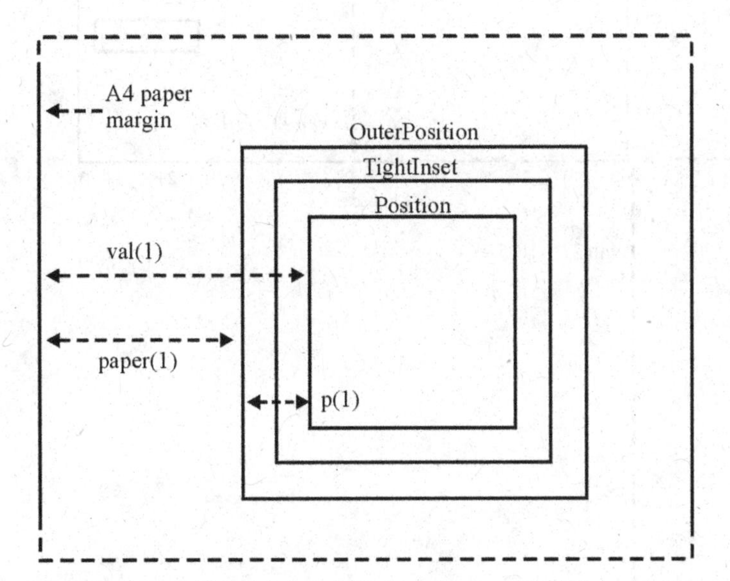

Fig.7.7 The positions and the sizes of the OuterPositions and TightInset, given by the arrays *t* and *outp*, are not visible on the screen and on the paper.

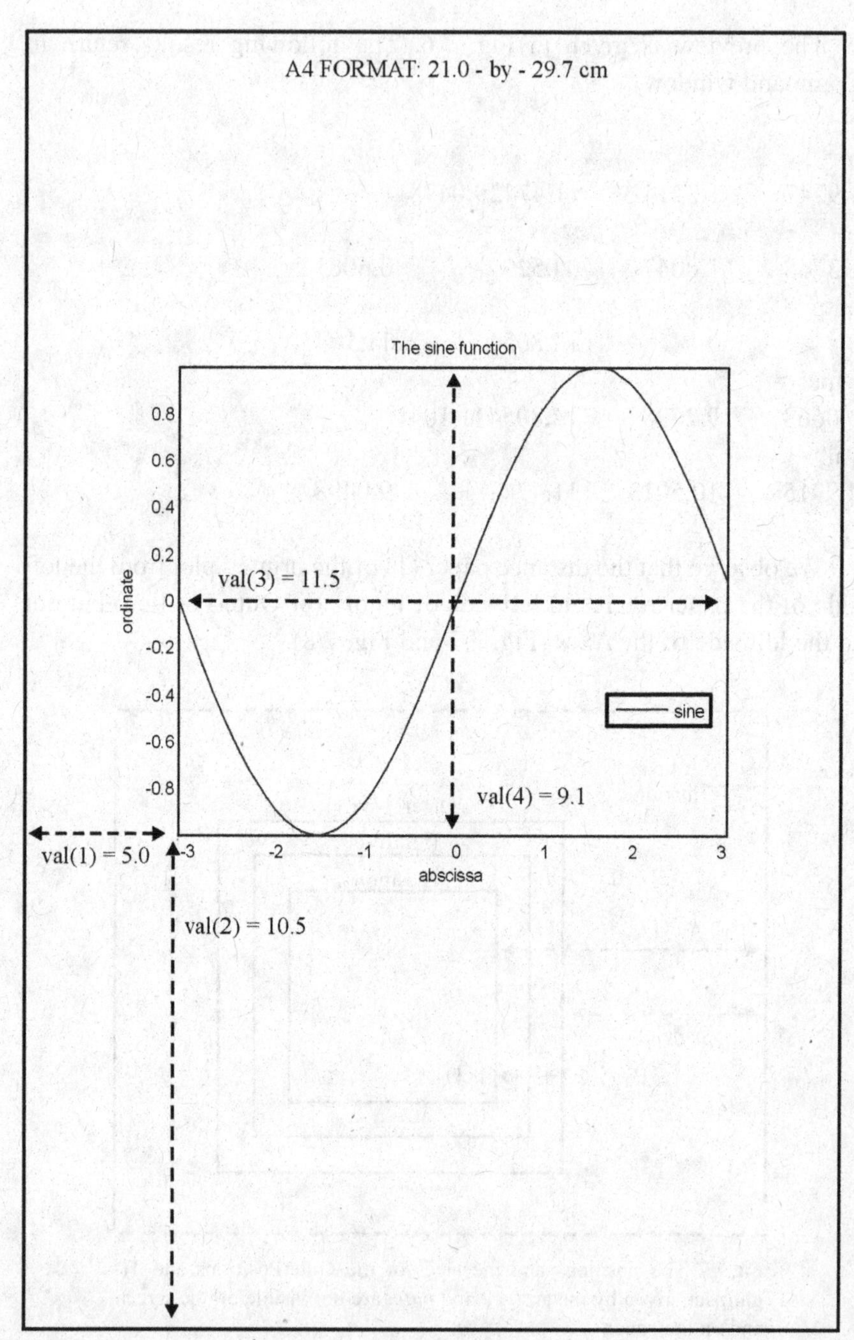

Fig. 7.8 Values are in centimeters.

Example 7.4 (*plot_print2.m*)

The user-defined size and position (in centimeters) of the plot in an A4 paper sheet are examined.

```
set(gcf, 'units', 'centimeters')
set(gca, 'units' ,'centimeters')

set(gca, 'position', [0 0 1 1])
p=get(gca, 'position');
t=get(gca, 'tightInset');
w=[p(1)+4.5, p(2)+4, p(3)+4, p(4)+4]
set(gca, 'position', w)
x=-pi:.1:pi; y=sin(x); plot(x,y); axis tight;

set(gcf, 'PaperUnits', 'centimeters')
set(gcf, 'PaperPositionMode', 'manual')
paper=get(gcf, 'PaperPosition')

a=[paper(1)+6,paper(2)+12,paper(3)-4,paper(4)]
set(gcf,'PaperPosition',a)

printpreview(gcf)
```

The results of the three arrays return in Command window:

```
w =
4.5000    4.0000        5.0000        5.0000
paper =
0.6345    6.3452        20.3046       15.2284
a =
6.6345    18.3452       16.3046       15.2284
```

The meaning of the array *w* and *a* are explained in Fig. 7.9. The plot, as appears in the Figure is reported in Fig. 7.10. We highlight in Fig. 7.9 the shift to the right and toward the top of the dashed sides of OuterPosition rectangle. The left pane (Fig. 7.11) of the PrintPreview gives a par-

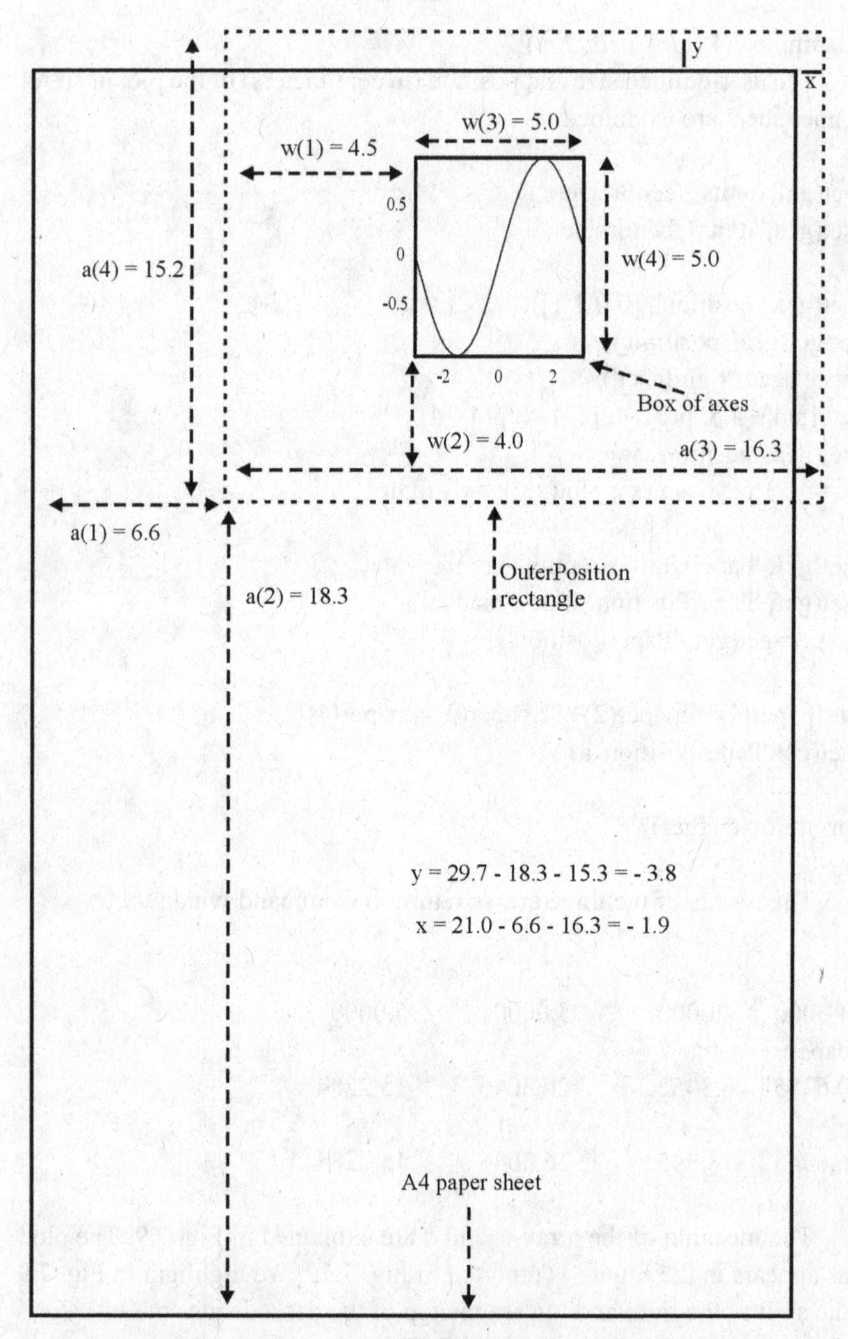

Fig. 7.9 Position and dimensions of the plot in A4 paper sheet. Values are in centimeters.

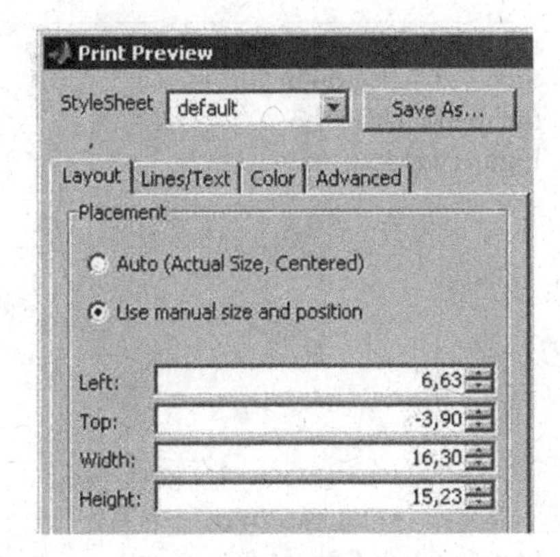

Fig. 7.10 Print Preview (left).

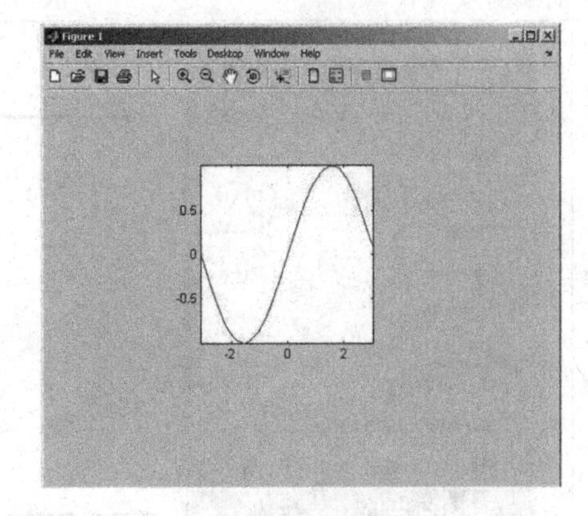

Fig. 7.11 Print Preview (right).

tial account of the shift displaying the value -3.90 in the field Top.

We can export the content of a Figure in a graphics format (tif, jpg, bmp, png, *etc.*; See next Table 7.4) storing it in a disk if we are interested to import it later into another application. The export to a file can be made either from the *Export Setup* dialog box or from a command line. Using the first choice we can perform the operation immediately, as shown in Fig. 7.12. More details about this choice are given in the next Sec. 7.1.5.

7.1.5 *Interactive control over graphics objects*

We have found in the previous Section two dialog boxes: PrintPreview and Export Setup. The Figure window, we have considered until now merely as a black box used as a container of Axes is too a basic interactive tool. Before the standard *editing mode*, the first and simple use of a Figure interactive mode is obtained clicking the various options present in its Menu and Tools bars. We can try especially the options *Edit*, *View*, *Insert* and *Tools* in the menu bar and the *Edit Plot* and *Show Plot Tools and Dock Figure* in the Tools bar.

An exposition of these three interactive doesn't best fit the stiff potentialities of a paper book. However we will examine briefly these tools that serve both the plot objects we have before considered (but also all other graphics objects) and the images, the subject of the next Section.

a. We have seen how to format a plot (setting Figure, Axes, Line and

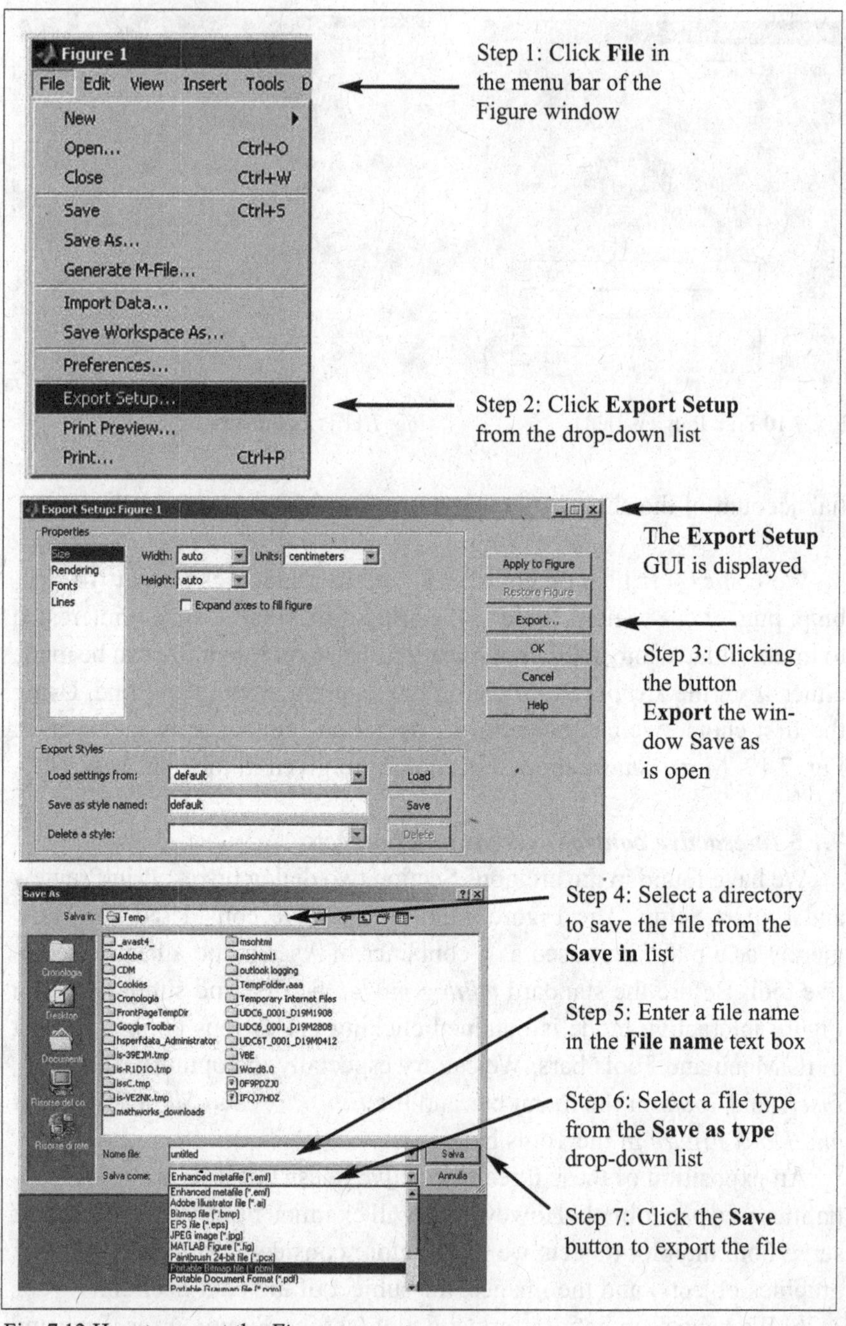

Fig. 7.12 How to export the *Figure content*.

Text properties) writing lines in Command window or in an M-file by the use of functions, like SET, GET, PLOT, *etc*. However, we can change this format, add or modify the properties (labels, titles, legends, *etc*.) enabling the *editing mode* in the Figure window (Fig. 7.13). In this mode we can also select, cut, copy, past, move, resize objects or multiple objects and modify other plot features.

However, we can only access a subset of object properties through the editing mode and sometimes the best solution is the use both of functions and of the interactive mode.

We can activate the edit mode clicking in the Tools bar the icons *Edit Plot* or *Show Plot Tools* (See arrows *a* and *b* in Fig. 7.13).

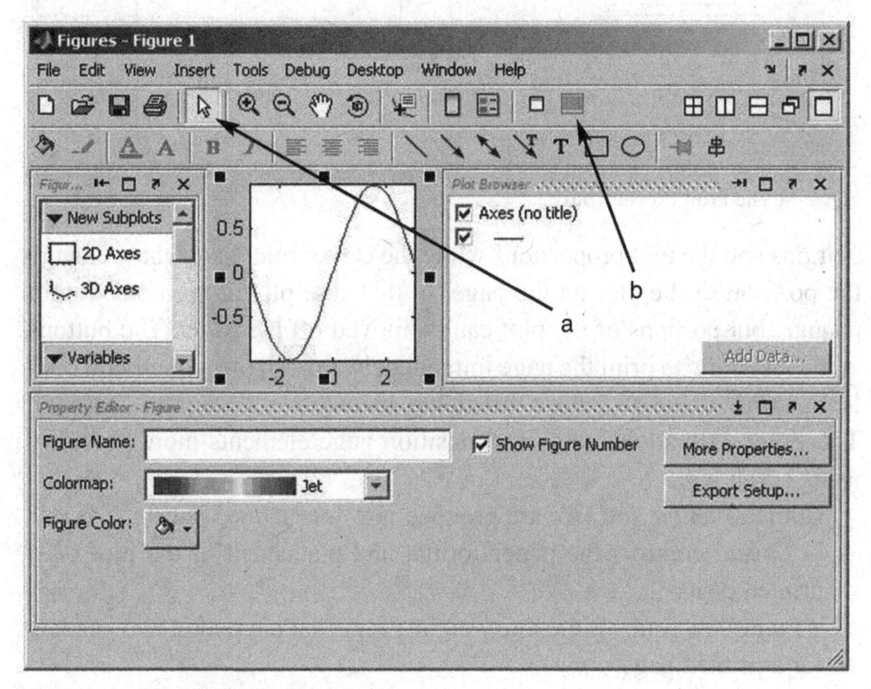

Fig. 7.13 a) Edit Plot, b) Show Plot Tools.

b. The *Print Preview* dialog box (Fig. 7.14) controls the layout and appearance of the content of a Figure before sending it to a printer. Operating on *Right Pane Controls* we can change position and scale of a plot on the printed page using rulers: the outer ruler handlebars change

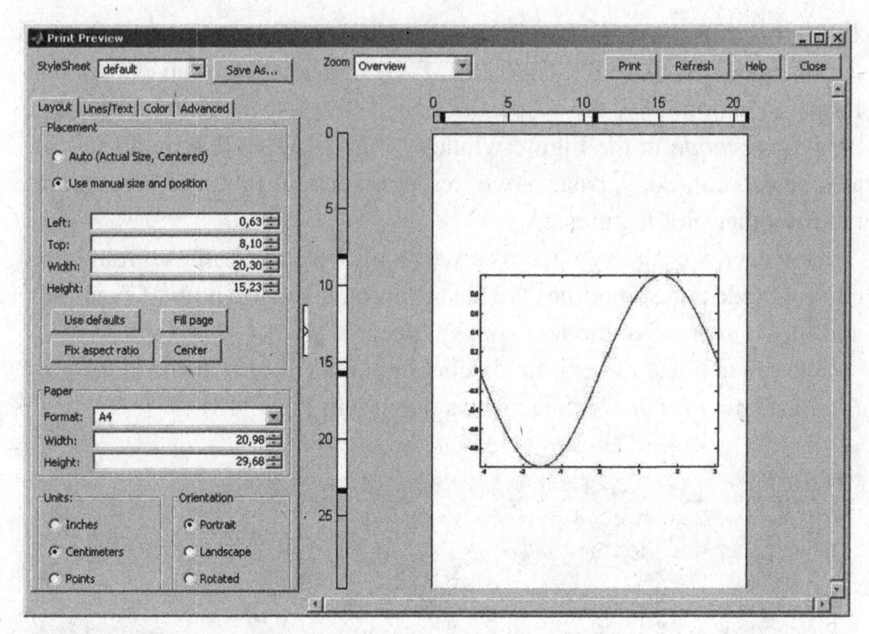

Fig. 7.14 The Print Preview box.

margins and the plot proportions while the center ruler handlebars change the position of the plot on the page. In this case plot proportions do not change, but portions of the plot can be moved off the paper. The buttons at the top allow to print the page immediately, refresh the plot, obtain context-sensitive help and close the dialog (preserving all current settings). The Zoom box allows view and position page elements more precisely using scroll bars.

Controls on the left side are grouped into four tabbed panes:

- *Layout* controls the paper format and placement of the plot on a printed page;

- *Lines/Text* controls the line weights, font characteristics, and headers for a printed page

- *Color* controls how colors are printed for lines and backgrounds

- *Advanced* controls finer details of printing, such as limits, ticks, renderer, resolution, *etc*.

c. The content of a Figure can be exported to a file using a command (the PRINT function) or the Export Setup GUI (Fig. 7.15) that has four

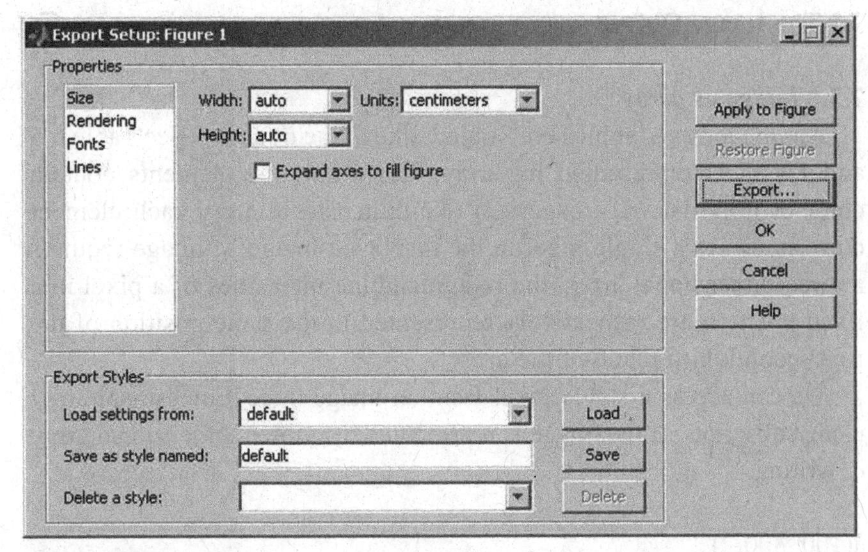

Fig. 7.15 Export Setup.

dialog boxes in the pane labeled *Properties* that enable to adjust properties prior to exporting Figure:

- *Adjusting the Figure Size*: This dialog box modifies the size of the Figure content as it will appear when imported from the export file into another application;
- *Changing the Rendering*: we can change "Colorspace" using a drop-down list, click the check boxex "Custom Color" or "Custom Renderer", select resolution from the drop-down list and click the check boxes "keep axis limits" and "show uicontrols";
- *Changing Font Characteristics*: click the check boxes, the radio buttons and the drop-down lists to define the properties of the text objects in the Figure
- *Changing Line Characteristics*: click the check boxes and the radio buttons to define the properties of the line objects in the Figure.

Below the pane labeled *Properties* appears the pane *Export Styles* where load, save and delete operation about a style can be made.

When we finish the settings in the two panes, the Figure content can be exported to a file by clicking the *Export* button on the right side of the panes.

7.2 The Image Object

7.2.1 *Image as array*

An image is a graphics *core* object like a line or a text (See Table 6.5 and Fig. 7.1) represented by array whose numeric elements contain color or gray data. If image is a two-dimensional array each element corresponds to a single pixel in the displayed image. If image requires a three-dimensional array, the red/green/blue intensities of a pixel in a fixed position are respectively represented in the same position of the first/second/third plane of the array.

We can access a single pixel from an image three-dimensional array using subscripts. If the image is represented by a three-dimensional array *a*, writing

```
a(100, 300, :)
```

the three values of the red/green/blue intensities of the pixel located at row 100, column 300 are returned.

The elements of the image array can be numbers of class double (double-precision floating-point), uint16 (16-bit unsigned integer), and uint8 (8-bit unsigned integer). Because the number of pixels in an image are often very large to reduce memory requirements the elements of the image array in some cases are defined as 8-/16-bit unsigned integers.

The main graphics file formats are given in Table 7.4.

Table 7.4 Formats and file extensions for some graphics files.

Graphics file formats	**file extensions**
Windows Bitmap (BMP)	'bmp'
Graphics Interchange Format (GIF)	'gif'
Joint Photographic Experts Group (JPEG)	'jpg' or 'jpeg'
Portable Network Graphics (PNG)	'png'
Tagged Image File Format (TIFF)	'tif' or 'tiff'

7.2.2 *The image functions*

The IMAGE function displays image object. The main syntactical form of the function is

```
h = image (a)
```

displays the array *a* as an image and returns, if *h* is present, the handle of the image object it creates. *The handle can be obtained too with all the following functions, if requested.*

The function IMAGESC displays image object and can scale data. The main syntactical form of the function is

```
imagesc(I)
```

that displays *I* as an image. Each element of *I* corresponds to a pixel position in the image. The values of the elements of *I* are indices into the current colormap that determine the color of image pixels (See indexed images in the next Sec.7.2.3).

```
imagesc(I, lim)
```

normalizes the values in *I* to the range specified by *lim* and displays *I* as an image; *lim* is a two-element array that limits the range of data values in *I*. These values map to the full range of values in the current colormap.

The IMREAD function reads image from a graphics file. The main syntactical form of the function can be used in the following two ways

```
a = imread ('filename', 'fmt')
a = imread ('filename.fmt')
```

Both read a gray or color image from the file specified by the string filename. The full pathname must be specified if the file is not in the current directory, or in a directory on the MATLAB path. The string *fmt* specifies the format of the file by its standard file extension (Table 7.4). The value *a* is an array containing the image data. If the file contains a grayscale image, *a* is an m-by-n array. If the file contains a truecolor image, *a* is an m-by-n-by-3 array. For TIFF files containing color images that use the CMYK (cyan, magenta, yellow, black) color space, *a* is an m-by-n-by-4 array.

```
[x, map] = imread ('filename', 'fmt')
[x, map] = imread ('filename. fmt')
```

Both read an indexed image into *x* and its associated colormap into *map*.

The function IMWRITE writes image to a graphics file. The main syntactical form of the function can be used in the following two ways

```
imwrite(a, 'filename', 'fmt')
imwrite(a, 'filename.fmt')
```

Both write the image *a* to the file specified by the string filename with the format specified by the string fmt.

```
imwrite(x, map, 'filename', 'fmt')
imwrite(x, map, 'filename.fmt)
```

Both write the indexed image in *x* and its associated colormap *map* to filename in the format specified by fmt.

The function IMFINFO returns information about a graphics file. The main syntactical forms of the function can be used in the following two ways:

```
info = imfinfo('filename','fmt')
info = imfinfo('filename.fmt')
```

This returns a structure, info, whose fields contain information about a graphics file. The string filename specifies the name of the graphics file and fmt the extension format of the file. The file must be in the current directory or in a directory on the MATLAB path. If the extension is not present the function attempts to infer the file format from its contents.

The function IND2RGB converts indexed image to truecolor (RGB) image. Syntax:

```
a = ind2rgb(x, map)
```

converts the array *x* and corresponding colormap *map* to the RGB (truecolor) format. The class of *x* can be uint8, uint16, or double. The array *a* has size m-by-n-by-3 and class double.

7.2.3 *Image types*

An *indexed image* is stored using an array *x* of size m-by-n and a colormap array *map* of size p-by-3. The number *tot* (the product of m by n) of elements of the array *x* is equal to the number of pixels into the image. All the *tot* pixels of an image don't have *tot* different colors: usually the number of colors present in an image is $p < tot$. Each row of the array *map* contains a triple of floating-point RGB values in the range [0, 1]. Then the color of each pixel is defined using the integer values of *x* as an *index* into map: the integer elements of the array *x,* 1 or $k < p$ or *p*, point ("are *indexed*") to the rows 1 or *k* or *p* of the array *map*. An indexed image is displayed with the statements

```
image(x); colormap(map)
```

A *truecolor* (RGB) image is stored as an m-by-n-by-3 array that defines red, green, and blue intensities for each pixel. For a pixel located in fixed location (in a fixed row and column of the plane of the image) the corresponding same positions of the three pages gives the color intensities of the pixel. Graphics file formats can store RGB images as 24-bit images, where the red, green, and blue components are 8 bits each with a potential of about 16 million colors. To display the truecolor image *a* the following command can be used

```
image(a)
```

An *intensity* (or gray) image is a data array, *I*, whose values represent intensities within some range. MATLAB stores an intensity image as a single array, with each element of the matrix corresponding to one image pixel. The array can be of class double, uint8, or uint16. Even if intensity images are rarely saved with a colormap, MATLAB uses a colormap to display intensity images and handles intensity images as indexed images.

Colormap is a three-column array, with each row defining a particular color by the three RGB values in the range [0, 1]. A colormap enables to control how data values can be mapped to colors in images and in many other graphics objects: MATLAB supports a number of about twenty built-in colormaps. The gray colormap, for example, is used to display intensity images. Some colormaps are listed in Table 8.3.

The function COLORMAP has the following syntactical forms

```
colormap(map)
map = colormap
```

in the first form the function sets the colormap of the *current Figure* to map. In the second form the *current colormap* is retrieved.

7.2.4 *Examples*[1]

Example 7.5 (*four_images.m*)

Four images of different types are read and displayed.

```
[x1,map1]=imread('Pesaro.gif');
info1=imfinfo('Pesaro','gif')
whos
image(x1);
colormap(map1);

figure
[x2 map2]=imread('clown','bmp');
imagesc(x2)
info2=imfinfo('clown','bmp')
whos
colormap(gray);
```

[1] *In the web site are stored the image files, the M-files and the resulting colored Figures; when we use M-files that have to read image files stored in a disk, the current directory containing these files must be specified in the Command window (See Fig. 1.2d) if the full pathname is not specified*

Fig. 7.16a A gif image.

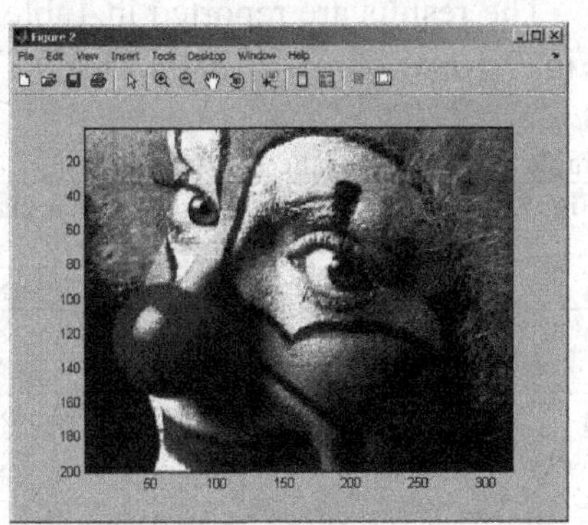

Fig. 7.16b A bmp image.

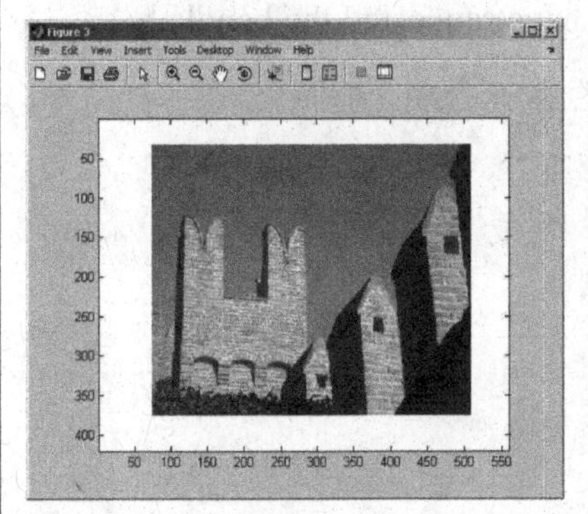

Fig. 7.16c A jpg image.

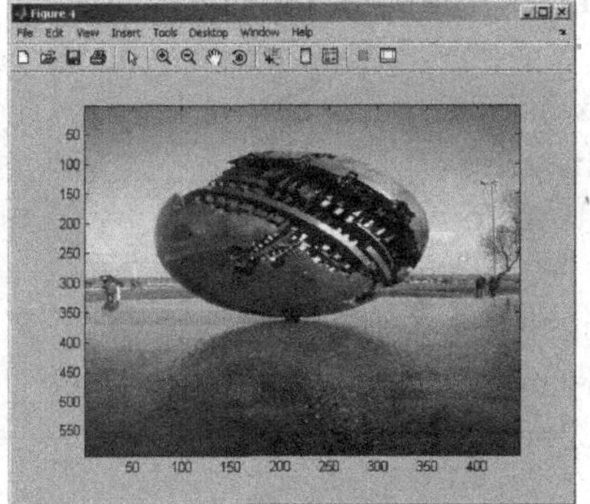

Fig. 7.16d A tif image.

```
figure
x3=imread('Gradaragray','jpg');
info3=imfinfo('Gradaragray','jpg')
whos
image(x3)

figure
x4=imread('Pomodoro.tif');
info4=imfinfo('Pomodoro','tif')
whos
image(x4);
```

The results are reported in Table 7.5 and the displayed Figures are in Fig. 7.16

Table 7.5 Results of the Example 7.5.

Fig. 7.16x	x array	x size	x class	map size	map class	format	colortype
a	Pesaro	443x591	uint8	256x3	double	gif	indexed
b	Clown	200x320	uint8	256x3	double	bmp	indexed
c	Gradara	420x561x3	uint8	0x0	double	jpg	truecolor
d	Pomodoro	591x443x3	uint8	0x0	double	tif	truecolor

Example 7.6 (*color_to_gray.m*)

The first colored image, that is not displayed, is converted to gray (Fig. 7.16b). For the gray image we have requested the handle h.

```
[x map]=imread('clown','bmp');
image(x)
C1=colormap(map);

figure(2)
h=imagesc(x)
C2=colormap(gray).
```

Example 7.7 (*Image_size.m*)

An image is displayed on the screen with different sizes and on different positions (Fig. 7.17).

```
%unit of measurement
unitScreen=get(0,'units')
%the size of the screen array is read
screen=get(0,'ScreenSize')
% the width of the screen is assigned to Sx
Sx=screen(3)
% the height of the screen is assigned to Sy
Sy=screen(4)
%%
%==================================================
```

Fig. 7.17 Three images of different size are displayed on the screen in different positions.

```
%A PLOT IS DEFINED WITH POSITION AND SIZE FIXED BY MATLAB
%============================================================

x=imread('owl.png');

image(x); axis off;
set(gcf,'Menubar','none','Toolbar','none')
set(gca,'position',[0,0,1,1])

unitFP=get(gcf,'units')

pos=get(gcf,'position')
% unitFI=get(gcf,'units')
%the width of the Figure is assigned to Pc
%(the number of pixels columns)
Pc=pos(3)
%the height of the Figure is assigned to Pr
%(the number of pixels rows)
Pr=pos(4)
%the ratio between Pc and Pr
```

```
R=Pc/Pr
%%
%==================================================================
%A NEW POSITION WITH A SMALLER SIZE OF THE FIGURE AND IMAGE
%==================================================================
%
%the distance of the left side of the figure
%from the left side of the screen
dx1=670;
%the distance of the bottom side of the figure
%from the bottom side of the screen
dy1=100;
%
%the desired height of the Figure is assigned
H1=250;
%
%the width consistent with Pr and Pc is calculated
W1=R*H1;
%the new position and size are assigned
%with the figure command
figure('Position',[dx1 dy1 W1 H1])

image(x);
axis off;
set(gcf,'Menubar','none','Toolbar','none')
% set(gca,'position',[0.25,0.25,0.5,0.5])
set(gca,'position',[0,0,1,1])

% set(gcf,'Menubar','none','Toolbar','none')
%new position and size are given in the Command Window
get(gcf,'position')
%
%%
%==================================================================
%A NEW POSITION WITH A GREATER SIZE OF THE FIGURE AND IMAGE
%==================================================================
```

```
%
%%the distance of the left side of the figure
%from the left side of the screen
% dx2=30;
dx2=1;

%the distance of the bottom side of the figure
%from the bottom side of the screen
% dy2=30;
dy2=1;

%
%the desired height of the Figure is assigned
H2=490;
%
%the width consistent with Pr and Pc is calculated
W2=R*H2;
%the new position and size are assigned
%with the figure command
figure('Position',[dx2 dy2 W2 H2])
%the greater figure of the plot is read

% x=imread('owl.png');
image(x); axis off;
set(gcf,'Menubar','none','Toolbar','none')
% set(gca,'position',[0.25,0.25,0.5,0.5])
set(gca,'position',[0,0,1,1])

set(gcf,'Menubar','none','Toolbar','none')
%new position and size are given in the Command Window
get(gcf,'position')
```

Example 7.8 (*print1_image.m*)

We can define different positions and sizes of the image in Figure and print it in A4 paper sheet with default size and position (Fig. 7.18 and Fig. 7.19)

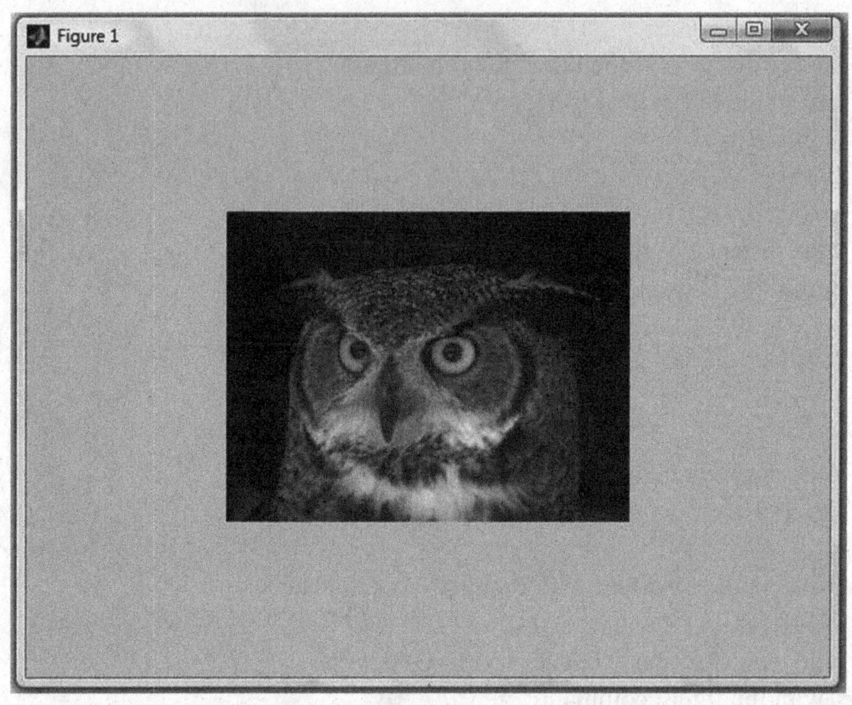

Fig. 7.18 Size and position of the image in Figure window changed using set command.

```
%DIFFERENT SIZES AND POSITIONS OF THE IMAGE IN FIGURE
x=imread('owl.png');
image(x)
axis off
set(gcf,'Menubar','none','Toolbar','none')

%image fills all Figure space
% set(gca,'position',[0,0,1,1])

%image position is resized and centered
set(gca,'position',[0.25,0.25,0.5,0.5])

%image resized and placed at the bottom left corner
% set(gca,'position',[0,0,0.4,0.4])

%image is resized and shifted to the top right corner
```

Fig. 7.19 Default position and size of the image in A4 paper sheet.

```
% set(gca,'position',[0.75,0.75,0.25,0.25])

%PRINT IMAGE WITH DEFAULT POSITION AND SIZE
set(gcf,'PaperPositionMode','auto')
set(gcf,'PaperUnits','centimeters')
paper=get(gcf,'PaperPosition')

printpreview(gcf)
```

Example 7.9 (*print2_image.m*)

The image in Figure can be printed in A4 paper sheet in a user-defined position (Fig. 7.20). The same rules applied to change the size of a printed plot (Sec. 7.1.4) can be used with an image.

```
x=imread('Owl.png');
image(x)
```

Fig. 7.20 The position of the image in A4 paper sheet defined by the user.

```
axis off
set(gcf,'Menubar','none','Toolbar','none')
set(gca,'position',[0,0,1,1])

set(gcf,'PaperUnits','centimeters')
set(gcf,'PaperPositionMode','manual')
paper=get(gcf,'PaperPosition')
ratio=paper(3)/paper(4)

left=3.0
bottom=9.0
h=8
w=ratio*h
set(gcf,'PaperPosition',[left, bottom, w, h])

printpreview(gcf)
```

About Chapter 8

Computers and programming languages are both born at the same time since they are each other indispensable. Exploiting the standard features of a computer soon appeared necessary in a programming language to create some basic tools. An example is the loop: running a block of code either a specified number of times or until a particular condition prevails. Some names for the constructs of the flow control continues to remain the same in all languages, others have changed. In this Chapter we treat the MATLAB versions of these.

With the *if* (and its additional options *else* or *elseif*) the selection is based on whether a condition is true or false.

With the *switch* and *case* statements (which may include the *otherwise* line) the selection is made from a number of possible options.

The *for* statement allows to move in a loop a predetermined number of times.

The *while* loop executes one or more statements repeatedly as long as the controlling expression gives the logical true as result.

Chapter 8
Flow Control

8.1 The Programming Constructs

The flow control statements allow to select a block of code, among many, which has to be executed at run-time if a condition is verified or to run it either a specified number of times or until a particular condition prevails.

Together with the M-file functions (Chapter 3), the flow control constructs we are considering in this chapter exponentially decrease the number of code lines of a real program and allow exerting an easy control over all its parts. In a real program some blocks of code have to be executed many times either with different initial values (in M-file functions) or when some conditions are verified (flow control constructs).

As an M-file function can be nested and one function may have within it functions of other kind (Sec. 3.7) so a flow control construct can be nested with others of the same or different type.

Besides both the flow control constructs and the M-file functions are present, as necessary building blocks of programming, within almost all earlier programming languages.

The last chapter seems the right place where to treat the flow control constructs because these have data as regular inner components and, as optional, also graphics objects. Both seem apparently ready to understand, but nevertheless their applications are not always quite simple.

8.2 The Conditional Control *if*

With the *if* (and its additional options *else* or *elseif*) the selection is based on whether a *condition is true or false*. The *if* construct evaluates a logical expression and executes a group of statements based on the value of the expression. In its simplest form, the syntax is

```
if logical_expression
    statements
end
```

If the logical_expression returns the *true* value (that is the logical 1), all the statements between the *if* and *end* lines are executed and then the execution continues at the line following the *end* statement. If the condition is false (evaluating the logical 0), all the statements between the *if* and *end* lines are skipped and the execution resumes at the line following the *end* statement.

When *elseif* and *else* are present the syntax is

```
if logical_expression1
statements1
elseif logical_expression2
statements2
            elseif logical_expression2
            statements2
                 .........
                 elseif logical_expression_n
                 statements_n
            else
            statements3
end
```

The *elseif* statements have logical conditions that are evaluated if the preceding *if* or *elseif* conditions return the *false* value. The statements1 or the statements2, . . ., or the statements_n associated with the corresponding *elseif* are executed if one of the associated logical_expression1 or logical_expression2, . . . , or logical_expression_n evaluates the *true* value (logical 1). We can have also only one *elseif* statement within the construct.

The *else* line doesn't contain any logical condition and the statements associated with it are executed if the preceding *if* and *elseif* conditions give as results the false value (logical 0).

If the *if* construct is nested, with any number of other *if*, the syntax is

```
if logical_expression1
statements1
        if logical_expression2
        statements2
            ...........  ......
            if logical_expression_n
            statements_n
        end
            ...........  ......
end

end
```

Example 8.1 (*serial_if.m*)

```
a = 6; b = 1:5;

if a = = b(1)
  display ('a is equal to b(1)')
end
  if a = = b(2)
    display ('a is equal to b(2)')
  end
    if a = = b(3)
      display ('a is equal to b(3')
    end
      if a = = b(4)
```

```
        display ('a is equal to b(4')
    end
        if a = = b(5)
          display ('a is equal to b(5)')
        end
```

display ('no element of b is equal to a').

In this example none of the *if* constructs return a logical 1 in their logical_expressions. So the result appearing in Command window is only the content of the last display command (*no element of b is equal to a*)

Example 8.2 (*nested_if*)

```
a = 5; b = 1:5;

j = 1;
if a = = b(end)
  c(1,j) = 1;
  j = j+1;

  if a = = b(end)
     c(1,j) = 2;
     j = j+1;

     if a = = b(end)
     c(1,j) = 3;
     j = j+1;

        if a = = b(end)
        c(1,j) = 4;
        j = j+1;
        end
     end
  end
end
c
```

The intent of this example is not, obviously, the creation of the simple array *c* (= [1 2 3 4]) but to demonstrate how the *if* constructs can be nested.

8.3 The Conditional Control *switch*

With the *switch* and *case* statements (which may include the *otherwise* line) the selection is made from *a number of possible options* depending on the value of a variable or an expression. The basic form of the *switch* statement is

```
switch expression
  case value1
    statements1
  case value2
    statements2
.................
  otherwise
    statements_n
end
```

Where the expression must be a numeric or literal constant. The *statements i* following the *case valuei* (i = 1, 2, …, n) are executed when the implicit (in the MATLAB code) command

```
if (valuei = = expression)
```

returns the logical 1 when the *expression* is numeric. If the *expression* is literal the implicit command

```
strcmp(valuei,expression)
```

would return the logical 1.

The statements1 are executed if value1 = expression, statements2 are executed if value2 = expression and statements_n if the expression does not match any valuei (i = 1, 2, …,n). The word *case* is followed by a value that can or cannot match expression. The statements1, statemets2, . . ., statements_n can consist of any valid MATLAB statement *including* other switch blocks. Execution of a *case* group ends when the next *case* or *otherwise* lines are encountered. Only the statements following the first matching *case* or the optional *otherwise* line are executed. For example, if the first *case* statement is true, the other *case* statements do not execute. There must always be an *end* line to match the *switch* line.

Example 8.3 (*switch_and_cell.m*)

```
values={10,3,'<word>'};
for i=1:3

switch values{i}
   case 1
      disp('the value is 1')
   case {2,3,4}
      switch values{i}
         case 3
         disp('the value 3 was found')
         case 2
         disp('the value 2 was found')
         case 4
         disp('the value 4 was found')
      end
   case '<word>'
      disp('the string <word> was found')
   otherwise
      disp('any values was found in the block')
end
end
```

In this example the nested *switch* construct is executed three times because it is placed within a simple *for* construct (Sec. 8.4). The results are strings we report in the Table 8.1.

Table 8.1 Results for Example 8.3.

Steps of the *for* construct	**The string**	**is displayed by**
First (i = 1)	*any values was found in the block*	the *otherwise* line
Second (i = 2)	*the value 3 was found*	the nested *switch*
Third (i = 3)	*the string <word> was found*	the external *switch*

8.4 The Loop Control *for*

We use the *for* statement to move in a loop a predetermined number of times. With loop control constructs we can repeatedly execute a block of code, looping back through it while keeping track of each iteration with an incrementing index variable.

The syntax of *for* loop is

```
for index = start: increment: end
statements
end
```

If increment is omitted, the default value 1 is assumed. The increment can be either positive or negative. For positive indices, execution terminates when the value of the index exceeds the end value; for negative increments, it terminates when the index is less than the end value. Nesting multiple loops with the *for* statement is an usual occurrence:

```
for index1 = start1: increment1: end1
statements1
        for index2 = start2: increment2: end2
        statements2
        ................
                for index_n = start_n: increment_n1: end_n
                statements_n
                end
        end
end
```

Example 8.4 (*sequence_for_if.m*)

```
b=[-5 3 6;3 6 -5;6 -5 3];
for k=1:3
a=b(k,:)

 for i=1:3

   if a(i) < 0;
   disp('a is negative');
   step1 = 1;
   check=[step1 a(i)]

   elseif rem(a(i),2) = = 0;
   disp('a is positive and even');
   A1 = a(i)/2;
   step2 = 2;
   check = [step2 a(i)]

   else
   A2 = (a(i)+1)/2;
   disp('a is positive and odd')
   step3 = 3;
   check = [step3 a(i)]

   end

 end

end
```

The sequence of the blocks executed is shown in Table 8.2 and the content of the corresponding *disp* command returns in the Command window.

Table 8.2 Sequence in the nested *if* loop.

for i =	the array used is	It is executed the code within the block	It is executed the code within the block	It is executed the code within the block
1	[-5 3 6]	*if*	*else*	*elseif*
2	[3 6 -5]	*else*	*elseif*	*if*
3	[6 -5 3]	*elseif*	*if*	*else*

Example 8.5 (*cell_and_num*)

```
a{1,1} = [1 2; 3 4];
a{1,2} = [-1 0; 0 1];
a{2,1} = [7 8; 4 1];
a{2,2} = [4i 3+2i; 1-8i 5];
a;
for k = 1:4
  for m = 1:2
    for n = 1:2
      a3d(m,n,k) = a{k}(m,n);
    end
  end
end
a3d;

b = cell(1,16);
for m = 1:16
  b{m} = a3d(m);
end
b;
whos
```

Information returned in Command window by the execution of the final *whos* command explains the operations made by the script: the numeric elements of the cell array *a* (size 2-by-2 and class cell) are disposed first in the numeric array *a3d* (size 2-by-2-by-4 and class double) and then in a new cell array *b* (size 1-by-16 and class cell). We remember (Sec 5.5) that the command *cell(1,16)* creates a 1-by-16 cell array of empty arrays.

Example 8.6 (*struct_and_for*)

```
for k = 1:2
  s12(k) = struct('a', 10*k, 'b', 10*k+1);
end
s12(1)
s12(2)

s21 = reshape(s12, 2, 1);
s21(1,1)
s21(2,1)

val12=s12
val21=s21
whos
```

With the *for* construct the structure array *s12* (size 1-by-2) is created that the command *reshape* arrange as a new structure array *s21* (size 2-by-1). In both cases each of the four elements contain the fields *a* and *b*. For example the first element of the row-wise *s12* and of column-wise *s21* contains the field $a = 10$ and $b = 11$.

Example 8.7 (*for_with_images*)

```
colorlabels = {'summer','autumn', 'winter','copper',...
            'hot','pink','bone','gray'};
load('durer','X','map');
for j=1:8
figure
image(X);
colormap(map);
colormap(colorlabels{j});
map_info=[j size(colormap)];
axis off;
pause(3)
end
```

The Dürer engraving Melencolia I (Fig. 8.1) is displayed in eight Figures with different fine gradations of some RGB colors. The images are obtained using, from the MATLAB built-in colormaps, those that best fit the Dürer image (Table 8.3).

Table 8.3 Some of the MATLAB colormaps.

Colormap	**RGB colors used**	**Fig.**
summer	shades of green and yellow	8.1A
autumn	varying smoothly from red, through orange, to yellow.	8.1B
winter	shades of blue and green	8.1C
copper	varying smoothly from black to bright copper.	8.1D
hot	varies smoothly from black through shades of red, orange, and yellow, to white.	8.1E
pink	pastel shades of pink providing sepia tone colorization of grayscale photographs.	8.1F
bone	grayscale colormap with a higher value for the blue component, useful for adding an "electronic" look to grayscale images.	8.1G
gray	returns a linear grayscale colormap.	8.1H

8.5 The Loop Control *while*

The *while* loop executes one or more statements repeatedly as long as the controlling expression gives as result the logical 1 (true). Syntax:

```
while expression
statements
end
```

We can exit a *while* loop at any time using the *break* statement (Sec. 8.6).

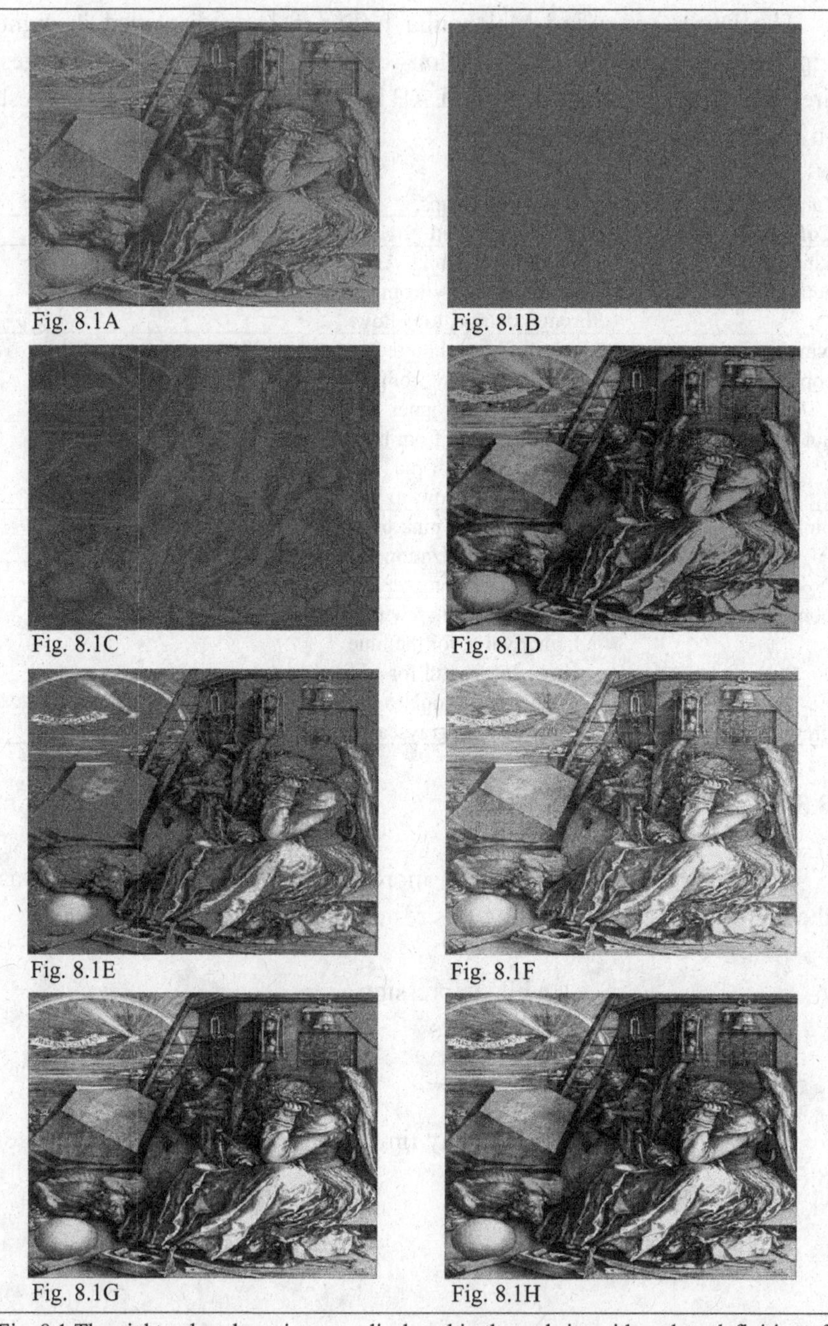

Fig. 8.1 The eight colored versions are displayed in the website with a clear definition of the details.

Example 8.8 (*zero_with_while*)

```
%Part a
t = 1:0.1:3;
f = t.^3-2.*t-5;
plot(t,f),grid on,title('f ( x ) = x^3  -  2 x  -  5');
xlabel('x'); ylabel ('f ( x )')

%Part b
check = [10^-4 10^-6 10^-8 10^-10];
for k = 1:4

x1 = 1.8;
x2 = 2.4;
j = 0;

  while (x2-x1) > check(k)
   j = j+1;
   x = (x1+x2)/2;
   fx = x^3-2*x-5;
     if sign(fx) < 0
        x1 = x;
     else
        x2 = x;
     end

  end
   n_loops(1,k) = j;
   solution(1,k) = x;

end
n_loops
solution
```

From the plot (*Part a*) we see that the mathematical function f=t.^3-2.*t-5 (Fig. 8.2) will assume a value x0 nearer to zero for a value of x contained in the interval (x1 = 2, x2 = 2.2). In the *Part b* we assume x0 equal to the middle point of this interval and we tend to approach a better x0 value making the interval smaller than a fixed check value. In the example we consider four check values placing the *while* block in a *for* construct. The results in the Command window are

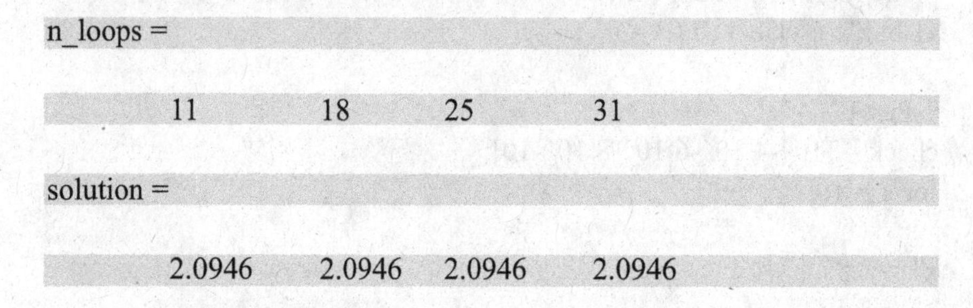

```
n_loops =

    11        18        25        31

solution =

    2.0946    2.0946    2.0946    2.0946
```

A solution with four decimal digits is simply obtained with the smallest check value (0.0001) when the *while* block is repeated only 11 times.

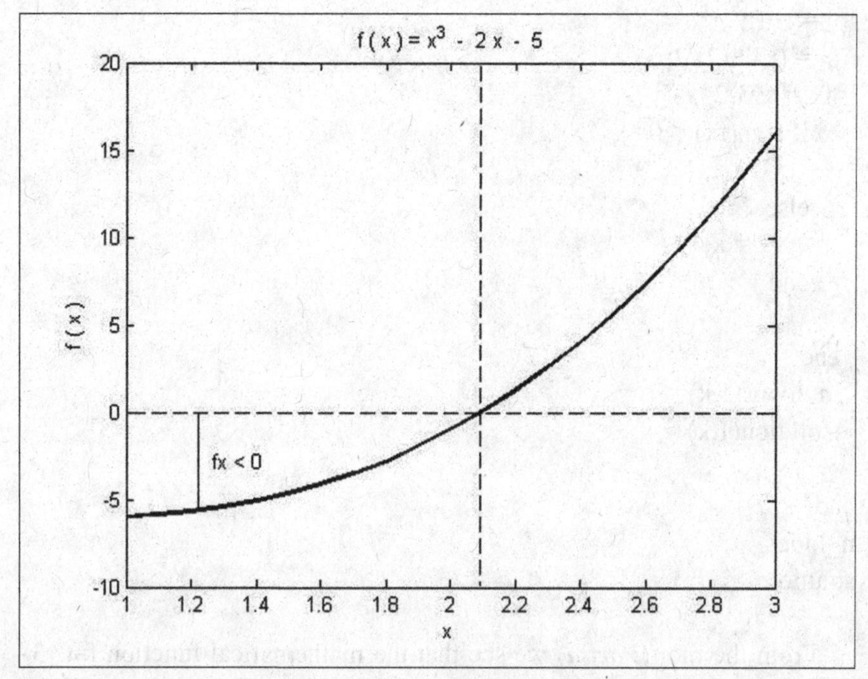

Fig. 8.2 The abscissa value corresponding to a zero value of the function.

8.6 The Loop Control *continue* and *break*

The *continue* and *break* statements give control on exiting a loop. The *continue* statement passes control to the next iteration of the *for* or *while* loop in which it appears, skipping any remaining statements in the body of the loop. In nested loops, *continue* passes control to the next iteration of the *for* or *while* loop enclosing it.

The *break* statement lets an early exit from a *for* or *while* loop, terminating their execution. When a *break* statement is encountered, execution continues with the next statement outside of the loop. In nested loops, *break* exits from the innermost loop only.

About Appendixes

The following three Appendixes are the necessary complement of the book giving the reader a complete view of all MATLAB parts and the chance to choose which part, we do not treat, could be next investigated.

Although their source is the Help Browser, these Appendixes are a fully edited version of the lists reported by MATLAB as "*By Category*" and "*Alphabetical*".

The Appendix 1 details the primary nine categories into which functions and objects properties are grouped. Looking at them the reader can become aware of the topics we haven't considered: parts of the categories 2 (*Mathematics*) and 3 (*Data Analysis*) that require knowledge of advanced calculus, and the full categories 5 (*File I/O*), 7 (*3-D Visualization*), 8 (*Creating Graphical User Interfaces*) and 9 (*External Interfaces*).

The Appendix 2 reports the whole list of 1300 MATLAB functions and properties. In the previous Chapters we have treated only about 200 of them (See their list in Index).

The Appendix 3 contains all the 40 MATLAB operators of which we haven't used only the five ones concerning matrix operations.

Appendix 1

MATLAB Functions Categories

1. DESKTOP TOOLS AND DEVELOPMENT ENVIRONMENT

- 1.1 Startup and Shutdown
- 1.2 Command Window and History
- 1.3 Help for Using MATLAB
- 1.4 Workspace, Search Path, File Operations:
  - 1.4.1 *Workspace*
  - 1.4.2 *Search Path*
  - 1.4.3 *File Operations*
- 1.5 Programming Tools:
  - 1.5.1 *Edit and Debug M-Files*
  - 1.5.2 *Improve Performance and Tune M-Files*
  - 1.5.3 *Source Control*
  - 1.5.4 *Publishing*
- 1.6 System:
  - 1.6.1 *Operating System Interface*
  - 1.6.2 *MATLAB Version and License*

2. MATHEMATICS

- 2.1 Arrays and matrices:
  - 2.1.1 *Basic Information*
  - 2.1.2 *Operators*
  - 2.1.3 *Elementary Matrices and Arrays*
  - 2.1.4 *Array Operations*
  - 2.1.5 *Array manipulation*
  - 2.1.6 *Specialized Matrices*
- 2.2 Linear algebra:
  - 2.2.1 *Matrix Analysis*
  - 2.2.2 *Linear Equations*
  - 2.2.3 *Eigenvalues and Singular Values*
  - 2.2.4 *Matrix Logarithms and Exponential*
  - 2.2.5 *Factorization*
- 2.3 Elementary Math:
  - 2.3.1 *Trigonometric*
  - 2.3.1 *Exponential*
  - 2.3.1 *Complex*
  - 2.3.1 *Rounding and Remainder*
  - 2.3.1 *Discrete Math (e.g. Prime Factors)*
- 2.4 Polynomials
- 2.5 Interpolation and Computational Geometry:
  - 2.5.1 *Interpolation*
  - 2.5.2 *Delaunay Triangulation and Tessellation*
  - 2.5.3 *Convex Hull*
  - 2.5.4 *Voronoi Diagrams*
  - 2.5.5 *Domain Generation*
- 2.6 Cartesian Coordinate System Conversion
- 2.7 Nonlinear Numerical Methods:
  - 2.7.1 *Ordinary Differential Equations*
  - 2.7.2 *Delay Differential Equations*
  - 2.7.3 *Boundary Value Problems*
  - 2.7.4 *Partial Differential Equations*

2.7.5 *Optimization*
2.7.6 *Numerical Integration (Quadrature)*
2.8 Specialized Math
2.9 Sparse Matrices
2.9.1 *Elementary Sparse Matrices*
2.9.2 *Full to Sparse Conversion*
2.9.3 *Working with Sparse Matrices*
2.9.4 *Reordering Algorithms*
2.9.5 *Linear Algebra*
2.9.6 *Linear Equations (Iterative Methods)*
2.9.7 *Tree Operations*
2.10 Math Constants

3. DATA ANALYSIS
3.1 Basic Operations
3.2 Descriptive Statistics
3.3 Filtering and Convolution
3.4 Interpolation and Regression
3.5 Fourier Transforms
3.6 Derivatives and Integrals
3.7 Time Series Objects
3.7.1 *General Purpose*
3.7.2 *Data Manipulation*
3.7.3 *Event Data*
3.7.4 *Descriptive Statistics*
3.8 Time Series Collections
3.8.1 *General Purpose*
3.8.2 *Data Manipulation*

4. PROGRAMMING AND DATA TYPES:
4.1 Numeric Types
4.1.1 *Characters and Strings*
4.1.2 *Structures*
4.1.3 *Cell Arrays*
4.1.4 *Function Handles*
4.1.5 *MATLAB Classes and Objects*
4.1.6 *Java Classes and Objects*
4.1.7 *Data Type Identification*
4.2 Data Type Conversion:
4.2.1 *Numeric*
4.2.2 *String to Numeric*
4.2.3 *Numeric to String*
4.2.4 *Other Conversions*

4.3 Operators and Special Characters:
4.3.1 *Arithmetic Operators*
4.3.2 *Relational Operators*
4.3.3 *Logical Operators*
4.3.4 *Special Characters*
4.4 String Functions:
4.4.1 *Description of Strings in MATLAB*
4.4.1 *String Creation*
4.4.2 *String Identification*
4.4.3 *String Manipulation*
4.4.4 *String Parsing*
4.4.5 *String Evaluation*
4.4.6 *String Comparison*
4.5 Bit-wise Functions
4.6 Logical Functions
4.7 Relational Functions
4.8 Set Functions
4.9 Date and Time Functions
4.10 Programming in MATLAB:
4.10.1 *M-Files Functions and Scripts*
4.10.2 *Evaluation of Expressions and Functions*
4.10.3 *Timer Functions*
4.10.4 *Variables and Functions in Memory*
4.10.5 *Control Flow*
4.10.6 *Error Handling*
4.10.7 *MEX Programming*

5. FILE I/O
5.1 File Name Construction
5.2 Opening, Loading, Saving Files
5.3 Memory Mapping
5.4 Low-Level File I/O
5.5 Text File
5.6 XML Documents
5.7 Spreadsheets:
5.7.1 *Microsoft Excel Functions*

- 5.7.2 *Lotus 1-2-3 Functions*
- 5.8 Scientific Data:
  - 5.8.1 *Common Data Format (CDF)*
  - 5.8.2 *Flexible Image Transport System*
  - 5.8.3 *Hierarchical Data Format (HDF)*
  - 5.8.4 *Band-Interleaved Data*
- 5.9 Audio and Audio/Video:
  - 5.9.1 *General*
  - 5.9.2 *SPARC station-Specific Sound Functions*
  - 5.9.3 *Microsoft WAVE Sound Functions*
  - 5.9.4 *Audio/Video Interleaved (AVI) Functions*
- 5.10 Images
- 5.11 Internet Exchange:
  - 5.11.1 *URL, Zip, Tar, E-Mail*
  - 5.11.2 *FTP Functions*

6. GRAPHICS

- 6.1 Basic Plots and Graphs
- 6.2 Plotting Tools
- 6.3 Annotating Plots
- 6.4 Specialized Plotting:
  - 6.4.1 *Area, Bar, Pie Plots*
  - 6.4.2 *Contour Plots*
  - 6.4.3 *Direction and Velocity Plots*
  - 6.4.4 *Discrete Data Plots*
  - 6.4.5 *Function Plots*
  - 6.4.6 *Histograms*
  - 6.4.7 *Polygons and Surfaces*
  - 6.4.8 *Scatter/Bubble Plots*
  - 6.4.9 *Animation*
- 6.5 Bit-Mapped Images Printing
- 6.6 Handle Graphics:
  - 6.6.1 *Finding and Identifying Graphics Objects*
  - 6.6.2 *Object Creation Functions*
  - 6.6.3 *Plot Objects*
  - 6.6.4 *Figure Windows*
  - 6.6.5 *Axes Operations*
  - 6.6.6 *Operating on Object Properties*

7. 3-D VISUALIZATION

- 7.1 Surface and mesh plots:
  - 7.1.1 *Creating Surfaces and Meshes*
  - 7.1.2 *Domain Generation*
  - 7.1.3 *Color Operations*
  - 7.1.4 *Colormaps*
- 7.2 View control:
  - 7.2.1 *Controlling the Camera Viewpoint*
  - 7.2.2 *Setting the Aspect Ratio and Axis Limits*
  - 7.2.3 *Object Manipulation*
  - 7.2.4 *Selecting Region of Interest*
- 7.3 Lighting
- 7.4 Transparency,
- 7.5 Volume Visualization

8. CREATING GRAPHICAL USER INTERFACES

- 8.1 Predefined Dialog Boxes
- 8.2 Deploying User Interfaces
- 8.3 Developing User Interfaces
- 8.4 User Interfaces Objects
- 8.5 Finding Objects from Callbacks
- 8.6 GUI Utility Functions
- 8.7 Controlling Program Execution

9. EXTERNAL INTERFACES

- 9.1 Dynamic Link Libraries Java
- 9.2 Component Object Model and Activex
- 9.3 Dynamic Data Exchange
- 9.4 Web Services
- 9.5 Serial Port Devices
- 9.6 Interfaces to DLLs, Java

Appendix 2

MATLAB Functions and Objects Properties

List of Functions and Objects Properties (A)

Name	Description	Categories
abs	Absolute value and complex magnitude	Complex-Fourier Transforms
accumarray	Construct array with accumulation	Array Operations
acos	inverse cosine; result in radians	Trigonometric
acosd	Inverse cosine; result in degrees	Trigonometric
acosh	Inverse hyperbolic cosine	Trigonometric
acot	Inverse cotangent; result in radians	Trigonometric
acotd	Inverse cotangent; result in degrees	Trigonometric
acoth	Inverse hyperbolic cosine	Trigonometric
acsc	Inverse cosecant; result in radians	Trigonometric
acscd	Inverse cosecant; result in degrees	Trigonometric
acsch	Inverse hyperbolic cosecant	Trigonometric
actxcontrol	Create ActiveX control in figure window	External Interfaces
actxcontrollist	List all currently installed ActiveX controls	External Interfaces
actxcontrolselect	Open GUI to create ActiveX control	External Interfaces
ActxGetRunning Server	Get handle to running instance of Automation server	External Interfaces

actxserver	Create COM server	External Interfaces
addevent	Add event to timeseries object	Time Series Objects
addframe	Add frame to Audio/Video Interleaved (AVI) file	File I/O
AddOptional (inputParser)	Add optional argument to input Parser schema	M-File Functions and Scripts
AddParamValue (inputParser)	Add parameter-value argument to inputParser schema	M-File Functions and Scripts
addpath	Add directories to MATLAB search path	Search Path
addpref	Add preference (see rmpref)	Creating GUI
addproperty	Add custom property to object	External Interfaces
AddRequired (inputParser)	dd required argument to inputParser schema	M-File Functions and Scripts
addsample	Add data sample to timeseries object	Time Series Objects
Addsampleto· collection	Add sample to tscollection object	Time Series Collections
addtodate	Modify date number by field	Date and Time Functions
addts	Add timeseries object to tscollection object	Time Series Collections
airy	Airy functions	Specialized Math
align	Align user interface controls (uicontrols) and Axes	Creating GUI
alim	Set or query Axes alpha limits	3-D Visualization
all	Determine whether all array elements are nonzero	Logical Functions
allchild	Find all children of specified objects	Handle Graphics
alpha	Set transparency properties for objects in current Axes	3-D Visualization
alphamap	Specify figure alphamap (transparency)	3-D Visualization
amd	Approximate minimum degree permutation	Sparse Matrices
ancestor	Ancestor of graphics object	Handle Graphics
and	Find logical AND of an array	Logical Functions
angle	Phase angle	Complex-Fourier Transforms

annotation	Create annotation objects	Annotating Plots
Annotation Arrow Properties	Define annotation arrow properties	Plot Objects
Annotation Doublearrow Properties	Define annotation doublearrow properties	Plot Objects
Annotation Ellipse Properties	Define annotation ellipse properties	Plot Objects
Annotation Line Properties	Define annotation line properties	Plot Objects
Annotation Rectangle Properties	Define annotation rectangle properties	Plot Objects
Annotation Textarrow Properties	Define annotation textarrow properties	Plot Objects
Annotation Textbox Properties	Define annotation textbox properties	Plot Objects
ans	Most recent answer	Evaluation of Expressions and Functions-Variables and Functions in Memory
any	Determine whether any array elements are nonzero	Logical Functions
area	Filled area 2-D plot	Specialized Plotting
Areaseries Properties	Define areaseries properties	Plot Objects
arrayfun	Apply function to each element of array	Array Operations-Numeric Types-Structures -Evaluation of Expressions and Functions
ascii	Set FTP transfer type to ASCII	File I/O
asec	Inverse secant; result in radians	Trigonometric
asecd	Inverse secant; result in degrees	Trigonometric
asech	Inverse hyperbolic cosecant	Trigonometric
asin	Inverse sine; result in radians	Trigonometric
asind	Inverse sine; result in degrees	Trigonometric
asinh	Inverse hyperbolic sine	Trigonometric
assert	Generate error when condition is violated	Evaluation of Expressions and Functions Error Handling
assignin	Assign value to variable in specified workspace	Workspace -Variables and Functions in Memory
atan	Inverse tangent; result in radians	Trigonometric

atan2	Four-quadrant inverse tangent	Trigonometric
atand	Inverse tangent; result in degrees	Trigonometric
atanh	Inverse hyperbolic tangent	Trigonometric
audioplayer	Create audio player object	File I/O
audiorecorder	Create audio recorder object	File I/O
aufinfo	Information about NeXT/SUN (.au) sound file	File I/O
auread	Read NeXT/SUN (.au) sound file	File I/O
auwrite	Write NeXT/SUN (.au) sound file	File I/O
avifile	Create new Audio/Video Interleaved (AVI) file	File I/O
aviinfo	Information about Audio/Video Interleaved (AVI) file	File I/O
aviread	Read Audio/Video Interleaved (AVI) file	File I/O
Axes	Create Axes graphics object	Handle Graphics
Axes Properties	Define Axes Properties	Plot Objects
axis	Axis scaling and appearance	Handle Graphics

List of Functions and Objects Properties (B - C)

Name	Description	Categories
balance	Diagonal scaling to improve eigenvalue accuracy	Eigenvalues and Singular Values&Factorization
bar, barh	Plot bar graph (vertical and horizontal)	Specialized Plotting
bar3, bar3h	Plot 3-D bar chart	Specialized Plotting
Barseries Properties	Define barseries properties	Plot Objects
base2dec	Convert base N number string to decimal number	Data Type Conversion
beep	Produce beep sound	File I/O
besselh	Bessel function of third kind (Hankel function)	Specialized Math
besseli	Modified Bessel function of first kind	Specialized Math
besselj	Bessel function of first kind	Specialized Math
besselk	Modified Bessel function of second kind	Specialized Math
bessely	Bessel function of second kind	Specialized Math
beta	Beta function	Specialized Math
betainc	Incomplete beta function	Specialized Math
betaln	Logarithm of beta function	Specialized Math
bicg	Biconjugate gradients method	Linear Equations (Iterative Methods)
bicgstab	Biconjugate gradients stabilized method	Linear Equations (Iterative Methods)
bin2dec	Convert binary number string to decimal number	Data Type Conversion
binary	Set FTP transfer type to binary	File I/O
bitand	Bitwise AND	Bit-wise Functions
bitcmp	Bitwise complement	Bit-wise Functions
bitget	Bit at specified position	Bit-wise Functions
bitmax	Maximum double-precision floating-point integer	Bit-wise Functions
bitor	Bitwise OR	Bit-wise Functions
bitset	Set bit at specified position	Bit-wise Functions
bitshift	Shift bits specified number of places	Bit-wise Functions
bitxor	Bitwise XOR	Bit-wise Functions
blanks	Create string of blank characters	String Functions
blkdiag	Construct block diagonal matrix from input arguments	Elementary Matrices and Arrays&Array Manipulation

box	Axes border	Basic Plots and Graphs Handle Graphics
break	Terminate execution of for or while loop	Control Flow
brighten	Brighten or darken colormap	3-D Visualization
builtin	Execute built-in function from overloaded method	Evaluation of Expressions and Functions
bsxfun	Applies element-by-element binary operation to two arrays with singleton expansion enabled	Array Operations
bvp4c	Solve boundary value problems for ordinary differential equations	Boundary Value Problems
bvpget	Extract properties from options structure created with bvpset	Boundary Value Problems
bvpinit	Form initial guess for bvp4c	Boundary Value Problems
bvpset	Create or alter options structure of boundary value problem	Boundary Value Problems
bvpxtend	Form guess structure for extending boundary value solutions	Boundary Value Problems
calendar	Calendar for specified month	Date and Time Functions
calllib	Call function in external library	External Interfaces
callSoapService	Send SOAP message off to endpoint	External Interfaces
camdolly	Move camera position and target	3-D Visualization
cameratoolbar	Control camera toolbar programmatically	3-D Visualization
camlight	Create or move light object in camera coordinates	3-D Visualization
camlookat	Position camera to view object or group of objects	3-D Visualization
camorbit	Rotate camera position around camera target	3-D Visualization
campan	Rotate camera target around camera position	3-D Visualization
campos	Set or query camera position	3-D Visualization
camproj	Set or query projection type	3-D Visualization
camroll	Rotate camera about view axis	3-D Visualization

camtarget	Set or query location of camera target	3-D Visualization
camup	Set or query camera up vector	3-D Visualization
camva	Set or query camera view angle	3-D Visualization
camzoom	Zoom in and out on scene	3-D Visualization
cart2pol	Transform Cartesian coordinates to polar or cylindrical	Cartesian Coordinate
cart2sph	Transform Cartesian coordinates to spherical	Cartesian Coordinate
case	Execute block of code if condition is true	Control Flow
cast	Cast variable to different data type	Array Operations Numeric Types Data Type Conversion
cat	Concatenate arrays along specified dimension	Array Manipulation Numeric Types
catch	Specify how to respond to error in a try statement	Control Flow Error Handling
caxis	Color axis scaling	3-D Visualization
cd	Change working directory	File Operations
cd (ftp)	Change current directory on FTP server	File I/O
cdf2rdf	Convert complex diagonal form to real block diagonal form	Eigenvalues and Singular Values-Factorization
cdfepoch	Construct cdfepoch objec for Common Data Format	File I/O
cdfinfo	Information about Common Data Format (CDF) file	File I/O
cdfread	Read data from Common Data Format (CDF) file	File I/O
cdfwrite	Write data to Common Data Format (CDF) file	File I/O
ceil	Round toward infinity	Rounding and Remainder
cell	Construct cell array	Cell Arrays&Java Classes and Objects
cell2mat	Convert cell array of arrays to single matrix	Cell Arrays &Data Type Conversion
cell2struct	Convert cell array to structure array	Structures-Cell Arrays Data Type Conversion
celldisp	Cell array contents	Cell Arrays

cellfun	Apply function to each cell in cell array	Cell Arrays-Evaluation of Expressions and Functions
cellplot	Graphically display structure of cell array	Cell Arrays
cellstr	Create cell array of strings from character array	Characters and Strings Cell Arrays &String Functions
cgs	Conjugate gradients squared method	Linear Equations (Iterative Methods)
char	Convert to character array (string)	Characters and Strings Data Type Conversion String Functions
checkin	Check files into source control system (UNIX)	Source Control
checkout	Check files out of source control system (UNIX)	Source Control
chol	Cholesky factorization	Linear Equations Factorization
cholinc	Sparse incomplete Cholesky and Cholesky-Infinity factorizations	Linear Equations Factorization
cholupdate	Rank 1 update to Cholesky factorization	Factorization
circshift	Shift array circularly	Array Manipulation
cla	Clear current Axes	Handle Graphics
clabel	Contour plot elevation labels	Annotating Plots
class	Create object or return class of object	Numeric Types Structures-Cell Arrays Function Handles MATLAB Classes and Objects Java Classes and Objects String Functions External Interfaces
clc	Clear Command Window	Command Window and History
clear	Remove items from workspace, freeing up system memory	Workspace Java Classes and Objects
clear (serial)	Remove serial port object from MATLAB workspace	External Interfaces
clf	Clear current figure window	Handle Graphics
clipboard	Copy and paste strings to and from system clipboard	Edit and Debug M-Files Operating System Interface
clock	Current time as date vector	Date and Time Functions
close	Remove specified figure	Handle Graphics
close (avifile)	Close Audio/Video Interleaved (AVI) file	File I/O

close (ftp)	Close connection to FTP server	File I/O
closereq	Default figure close request function	Handle Graphics
cmopts	Name of source control system	Source Control
colamd	Column approximate minimum degree permutation	Sparse Matrices
colmmd	obsolete	Sparse Matrices
colorbar	Colorbar showing color scale	3-D Visualization
colordef	Set default property values to display different color schemes	3-D Visualization
colormap	Set and get current colormap	3-D Visualization
colormapeditor	Start colormap editor	3-D Visualization
ColorSpec	Color specification. ColorSpec is not a function	3-D Visualization
colperm	Sparse column permutation based on nonzero count	Sparse Matrices
comet	2-D comet plot	Specialized Plotting
comet3	3-D comet plot	Specialized Plotting
commandhistory	Open Command History window or select it if already open	Command Window and History
commandwindow	Open Command Window or select it if already open	Command Window and History
compan	Companion matrix	Specialized Matrices
compass	Plot arrows emanating from origin	Specialized Plotting
complex	Construct complex data from real and imaginary components	Complex
computer	Information about computer on which MATLAB is running	Operating System Interface
cond	Condition number with respect to inversion	Matrix Analysis Linear Equations
condeig	Condition number with respect to eigenvalues	Matrix Analysis Eigenvalues and Singular Values
condest	1-norm condition number	
estimate	Linear Equations	
coneplot	Plot velocity vectors as cones in 3-D vector field	3-D Visualization
conj	Complex conjugate	Complex

continue	Pass control to next iteration of for or while loop	Control Flow
contour	Contour plot of matrix	Specialized Plotting
contour3	3-D contour plot	Specialized Plotting
contourc	Low-level contour plot computation	Specialized Plotting
contourf	Filled 2-D contour plot	Specialized Plotting
Contourgroup Properties	Define contourgroup properties	Plot Objects
contourslice	Draw contours in volume slice planes	3-D Visualization
contrast	Grayscale colormap for contrast enhancement	3-D Visualization
conv	Convolution and polynomial multiplication	Polynomials Filtering and Convolution
conv2	2-D convolution	Filtering and Convolution
convhull	Convex hull	Convex Hull Specialized Plotting
convhulln	N-D convex hull	Convex Hull
convn	N-D convolution	Filtering and Convolution
copyfile	Copy file or directory	File Operations
copyobj	Copy graphics objects and their descendants	Handle Graphics
corrcoef	Correlation coefficients	Descriptive Statistics
cos	Cosine of argument in radians	Trigonometric
cosd	Cosine of argument in degrees	Trigonometric
cosh	Hyperbolic cosine	Trigonometric
cot	Cotangent of argument in radians	Trigonometric
cotd	Cotangent of argument in degrees	Trigonometric
coth	Hyperbolic cotangent	Trigonometric
cov	Covariance matrix	Descriptive Statistics
cplxpair	Sort complex number into complex conjugate pairs	Complex Fourier Transforms
cputime	Elapsed CPU time	Date and Time Functions
createClass FromWsdl	Create MATLAB object based on WSDL file	External Interfaces
createCopy (inputParser)	Create copy of inputParser object	M-File Functions and Scripts
createSoap Message	Create SOAP message to send to server	External Interfaces
cross	Vector cross product	Array Operations
csc	Cosecant of argument in radians	Trigonometric

cscd	Cosecant of argument in degrees	Trigonometric
csch	Hyperbolic cosecant	Trigonometric
csvread	Read comma-separated value file	File I/O
csvwrite	Write comma-separated value file	File I/O
Ctranspose (timeseries)	Transpose timeseries object	Time Series Objects
cumprod	Cumulative product	Array Operations
cumsum	Cumulative sum	Array Operations
cumtrapz	Cumulative trapezoidal numerical integration	Derivatives and Integrals
curl	Compute curl and angular velocity of vector field	3-D Visualization
customverctrl	Allow custom source control system (UNIX)	Source Control
cylinder	Generate cylinder	Specialized Plotting

List of Functions and Objects Properties (D - E)

Name	Description	Categories
daqread	Read Data Acquisition Toolbox (.daq) file	File I/O
daspect	Set or query Axes data aspect ratio	3-D Visualization
datacursormode	Enable or disable interactive data cursor mode	Annotating Plots
datatipinfo	Produce short description of input variable	Edit and Debug M-Files &Variables and Functions in Memory
date	Current date string	Date and Time Functions
datenum	Convert date and time to serial date number	Date and Time Functions
datestr	Convert date and time to string format	Data Type Conversion Date and Time Functions
datetick	Date formatted tick labels	Annotating Plots
datevec	Convert date and time to array of components	Date and Time Functions
dbclear	Clear breakpoints	Edit and Debug M-Files
dbcont	Resume execution	Edit and Debug M-Files
dbdown	Change local workspace context when in debug mode	Edit and Debug M-Files
dblquad	Numerically evaluate double integral	Numerical Integration (Quadrature)
dbmex	Enable MEX-file debugging	MEX Programming
dbquit	Quit debug mode	Edit and Debug M-Files
dbstack	Function call stack	Edit and Debug M-Files
dbstatus	List all breakpoints	Edit and Debug M-Files
dbstep	Execute one or more lines from current breakpoint	Edit and Debug M-Files
dbstop	Set breakpoints	Edit and Debug M-Files
dbtype	List M-file with line numbers	Edit and Debug M-Files
dbup	Change local workspace context	Edit and Debug M-Files
dde23	Solve delay differential equations (DDEs) with constant delays	Delay Differential Equations
ddeadv	Set up advisory link	External Interfaces
ddeexec	Send string for execution	External Interfaces
ddeget	Extract properties from delay differential equations options structure	Delay Differential Equations
ddeinit	Initiate Dynamic Data Exchange (DDE) conversation	External Interfaces

ddepoke	Send data to application	External Interfaces
ddereq	Request data from application	External Interfaces
ddesd	Solve delay differential equations (DDEs) with general delays	Delay Differential Equations
ddeset	Create or alter delay differential equations options structure	Delay Differential Equations
ddeterm	Terminate Dynamic Data Exchange (DDE) conversation	External Interfaces
ddeunadv	Release advisory link	External Interfaces
deal	Distribute inputs to outputs	Structures Cell Arrays
deblank	Strip trailing blanks from end of string	String Functions
debug	List M-file debugging functions	Edit and Debug M-Files
dec2base	Convert decimal to base N number in string	Data Type Conversion
dec2bin	Convert decimal to binary number in string	Data Type Conversion
dec2hex	Convert decimal to hexadecimal number in string	Data Type Conversion
decic	Compute consistent initial conditions for ode15i	Ordinary Differential Equations
deconv	Deconvolution and polynomial division	Polynomials-Filtering and Convolution
del2	Discrete Laplacian	Derivatives and Integrals
delaunay	Delaunay triangulation	Delaunay Triang-Tess
delaunay3	3-D Delaunay tessellatio	Delaunay Triang-Tess Specialized Plotting
delaunayn	N-D Delaunay tessellation	Delaunay Triang-Tess Specialized Plotting
delete	Remove files or graphics objects	File Operations Handle Graphics
delete (COM)	Remove COM control or server	External Interfaces
delete (ftp)	Remove file on FTP server	File I/O
delete (serial)	Remove serial port object from memory	External Interfaces
delete (timer)	Remove timer object from memory	Timer Functions
deleteproperty	Remove custom property from object	External Interfaces

delevent	Remove tsdata.event objects from timeseries object	Time Series Objects
delsample	Remove sample from timeseries object	Time Series Objects
delsample fromcollection	Remove sample from tscollection object	Time Series Collections
demo	Reference page in Help browser	Help for Using MATLAB
depdir	List dependent directories of M-file or P-file	M-File Functions and Scripts
depfun	List dependencies of M-file or P-file	M-File Functions and Scripts Java Classes and Objects
det	Matrix determinant	Matrix Analysis
detrend	Remove linear trends	Filtering and Convolution
detrend (timeseries)	Subtract mean or best-fit line and all NaNs from time series	Time Series Objects
deval	Evaluate solution of differenti al equation problem	Ordinary Differential Equations Delay Differential Equations Boundary Value Problems
diag	Diagonal arrays and diagonals of an array	Elementary Matrices and Arrays-Array Manipulation
dialog	Create and display dialog box	Creating GUI
diary	Save session to file	Command Window and History
diff	Differences and approximate derivatives	Derivatives and Integrals
diffuse	Calculate diffuse reflectance	3-D Visualization
dir	Directory listing	File Operations
dir (ftp)	Directory contents on FTP server	File I/O
disp	Display text or array	Array Basic Information
disp (memmapfile)	Information about memmapfile object	File I/O
disp (serial)	Serial port object summary information	External Interfaces
disp (timer)	Information about timer object	Timer Functions
display	Display text or array (overloaded method)	Array Basic Information
divergence	Compute divergence of vector field	3-D Visualization
dlmread	Read ASCII-delimited file of numeric data into matrix	File I/O
dlmwrite	Write matrix to ASCII-delimited file	File I/O

dmperm	Dulmage-Mendelsohn decomposition	Sparse Matrices
doc	doc opens the Help browser	Help for Using MATLAB
docopt	Web browser for UNIX platforms	Help for Using MATLAB
docsearch	Open Help browser Search pane and search for specified term	Help for Using MATLAB
dos	Execute DOS command and return result	Command Window and History-Operating System Interface
dot	Vector dot product	Array Operations
double	Convert to double precision	Data Type Conversion
dragrect	Drag rectangles with mouse	3-D Visualization
drawnow	Complete pending drawing events	Handle Graphics
dsearch	Search Delaunay triangulati on for nearest point	Interpolation&Delaunay Triang-Tess-Voronoi Diagrams Specialized Plotting
dsearchn	N-D nearest point	Interpolation Delaunay Triang-Tess Specialized Plotting
echo	Echo M-files during execution	M-File Functions and Scripts Evaluation of Expressions and Functions
echodemo	Run M-file demo step-by-step in Command Window	Help for Using MATLAB
edit	Edit or create M-file	Edit and Debug M-Files
eig	Find eigenvalues and eigenvectors	Eigenvalues and Singular Values
eigs	Find largest eigenvalues and eigenvectors of sparse matrix	Eigenvalues and Singular Values Linear Algebra
ellipj	Jacobi elliptic functions	Specialized Math
ellipke	Complete elliptic integrals of first and second kind	Specialized Math
ellipsoid	Generate ellipsoid	Specialized Plotting
else	Execute statements if condition is false	Control Flow
elseif	Execute statements if additional condition is true	Control Flow
enableservice	Enable, disable, or report status of Automation server enable DDE server	External Interfaces

end	Terminate block of code or indicate last array index	Array Manipulation M-File Functions and Scripts Control Flow
eomday	Last day of month	Date and Time Functions
eps	Floating-point relative accuracy	Math Constants
eq	Test for equality	Relational Functions
erf, erfc, erfcx erfinv, erfcinv	Error functions	Specialized Math
error	Display message and abort function	Error Handling
errorbar	Plot error bars along curve	Basic Plots and Graphs
Errorbarseries Properties	Define errorbarseries properties	Plot Objects
errordlg	Create and open error dialog box	Creating GUI
etime	Time elapsed between date vectors	Date and Time Functions
etree	Elimination tree	Tree Operations
etreeplot	Plot elimination tree	Tree Operations
eval	Execute string containing MATLAB expression	Characters and Strings String Functions Evaluation of Expressions and Functions
evalc	Evaluate MATLAB expression with capture	String Functions Evaluation of Expressions and Functions
evalin	Execute MATLAB expression in specified workspace	Workspace&String Functions Evaluation of Expressions and Functions
eventlisteners	List of events attached to listeners	External Interfaces
events	List of events control can trigger	External Interfaces
Execute	Execute MATLAB command in server	External Interfaces
exifread	Read EXIF information from JPEG and TIFF image files	File I/O
exist	Check existence of variable, function, directory, or Java class	Workspace&File Operations Java Classes and Objects
exit	Terminate MATLAB (same as quit)	Startup and Shutdown
exp	Exponential	Exponential
expint	Exponential integral	Specialized Math
expm	Matrix exponential	Matrix Log and Exp

expm1	Compute exp(x)-1 accurately for small values of x	Exponential
export2wsdlg	Export variables to workspace	Creating GUI
eye	Identity matrix	Elementary Matrices and Arrays
ezcontour	Filled 2-D contour plot	Specialized Plotting
ezcontourf	Easy-to-use filled contour plotter	Specialized Plotting
ezmesh	Easy-to-use contour plotter	Specialized Plotting
ezmeshc	Easy-to-use filled contour plotter	Specialized Plotting
ezplot	Easy-to-use function plotter	Specialized Plotting
ezplot3	Easy-to-use 3-D parametric curve plotter	Specialized Plotting
ezpolar	Easy-to-use polar coordinate plotter	Specialized Plotting
ezsurf	Easy-to-use 3-D colored surface plotter	Specialized Plotting
ezsurfc	Easy-to-use combination surface/contour plotter	Specialized Plotting

List of Functions and Objects Properties (F - G)

Name	Description	Categories
factor	Prime factors	Discrete Math
factorial	Factorial function	Discrete Math
false	Logical 0 (false)	Logical Functions
fclose	Close one or more open files	File I/O
fclose (serial)	Disconnect serial port object from device	External Interfaces
feather	Plot velocity vectors	Specialized Plotting
feof	Test for end-of-file	File I/O
ferror	Query MATLAB about errors in file input or output	Error Handling File I/O
feval	Evaluate function	Function Handles Evaluation of Expressions and Functions
Feval (COM)	Evaluate MATLAB function in server	External Interfaces
fft	Discrete Fourier transform	Fourier Transforms
fft2	2-D discrete Fourier transform	Fourier Transforms
fftn	N-D discrete Fourier transform	Fourier Transforms
fftshift	Shift zero-frequency component to center of spectrum	Fourier Transforms
fftw	Interface to FFTW library run-time algorithm tuning control	Fourier Transforms
fgetl	Read line from file discarding newline character	File I/O
fgetl (serial)	Read line of text from device and discard terminator	External Interfaces
fgets	Read line from file keeping newline characte	File I/O
fgets (serial)	Read line of text from device and include terminator	External Interfaces
fieldnames	Field names of structure or public fields of object	Structures&MATLAB Classes and Objects Java Classes and Objects External Interfaces
figure	Create figure graphics object	Handle Graphics
Figure Properties	Define Figure Properties	Plot Objects
figurepalette	Show or hide figure palette	Plotting Tools
fileattrib	Set or get attributes of file or directory	File Operations
filebrowser	Current Directory browser	File Operations

File Formats	Readable file formats. It's not a function	Not included in the MATLAB categories
filemarker	Character to separate file name and internal function name	File I/O
fileparts	Returns parts of file name and path	File I/O
filehandle	Construct file handle object	File I/O
filesep	Directory separator for current platform	File I/O
fill	Filled 2-D polygons	Specialized Plotting
fill3	Filled 3-D polygons	Specialized Plotting
filter	1-D digital filter	Filtering and Convolution
filter (timeseries)	Shape frequency content of time series	Time Series Objects
filter2	2-D digital filter	Filtering and Convolution
find	Find indices and values of nonzero elements	Numeric Types Logical Functions Sparse Matrices
findall	Find all graphics objects	Handle Graphics Creating GUI
findfigs	Find visible offscreen figures	Handle Graphics Creating GUI
findobj	Locate graphics objects with specific properties	Handle Graphics Creating GUI
findstr	Find string within another longer string	Characters and Strings String Functions
finish	MATLAB termination M-file	Startup and Shutdown
fitsinfo	Information about FITS file	File I/O
fitsread	Read data from FITS file	File I/O
fix	Round toward zero	Rounding and Remainder
flipdim	Flip array along specified dimension	Array Manipulation
fliplr	Flip array left to right	Array Manipulation
flipud	Flip array up to down	Array Manipulation
floor	Round toward minus infinity	Rounding and Remainder
flow	Simple function of three variables	3-D Visualization
fminbnd	Find minimum of single-variable function on fixed interval	Optimization
fminsearch	Find minimum of unconstrained multivariable function using derivative-free method	Optimization
fopen	Open file, or obtain information about open files	File I/O

fopen (serial)	Connect serial port object to device	External Interfaces
for	Execute block of code specified number of times	Control Flow
format	Set display format for output	Command Window and History
fplot	Plot function between specified limits	Specialized Plotting
fprintf	Write formatted data to file	File I/O
fprintf (serial)	Write text to device	External Interfaces
frame2im	Convert movie frame to indexed image	Specialized Plotting Bit-Mapped Images
frameedit	Edit print frames for Simulink and Stateflow block diagrams	Printing
fread	Read binary data from file	File I/O
fread (serial)	Read binary data from device	External Interfaces
freqspace	Frequency spacing for frequency response	Elementary Matrices and Arrays
frewind	Move file position indicator to beginning of open file	File I/O
fscanf	Read formatted data from file	File I/O
fscanf (serial)	Read data from device and format as text	External Interfaces
fseek	Set file position indicator	File I/O
ftell	File position indicator	File I/O
ftp	Connect to FTP serve creating FTP object	File I/O
full	Convert sparse matrix to full matrix	Sparse Matrices
fullfile	Build full filename from parts	File I/O
func2str	Construct function name string from function handle	Function Handles Data Type Conversion
function	Declare M-file function	M-File Functions and Scripts
function handle (@)	Handle used in calling functions indirectly	Function Handles
functions	Information about function handle	Function Handles
funm	Evaluate general matrix function	Linear Equations
fwrite	Write binary data to file	File I/O
fwrite (serial)	Write binary data to device	External Interfaces
fzero	Find root of continuous function of one variable	Optimization

gallery	Test matrices	Specialized Matrices
gamma, gammainc gammaln	Gamma functions	Specialized Math
gca	Current Axes handle	Handle Graphics
gcbf	Handle of figure containing object whose callback is executing	Handle Graphics Creating GUI
gcbo	Handle of object whose callback is executing	Handle Graphics Creating GUI
gcd	Greatest common divisor	Discrete Math
gcf	Current figure handle	Handle Graphics
gco	Handle of current object	Handle Graphics
ge	Test for greater than or equal to	Relational Functions
genpath	Generate path string	Search Path
genvarname	Construct valid variable name from string	Variables and Functions in Memory
get	Query object properties	Handle Graphics
get (COM)	Get property value from interface or display properties	External Interfaces
get (memmapfile)	Memmapfile object properties	File I/O
get (serial)	Serial port object properties	External Interfaces
get (timer)	Timer object properties	Timer Functions
get (timeseries)	Query timeseries object property values	Time Series Objects
get (tscollection)	Query tscollection object property values	Time Series Collections
getabstime (timeseries)	Extract date-string time vector into cell array	Time Series Objects
getabstime (tscollection)	Extract date-string time vector into cell array	Time Series Collections
getappdata	Value of application-defined data	Time Series Objects
GetCharArray	Get character array from server	External Interfaces
getdata samplesize	Size of data sample in timeseries object	Time Series Objects
getenv	Environment variable	Operating System Interface
getfield	Field of structure array	Structures
getframe	Capture movie frame	Specialized Plotting
GetFull Matrix	Get matrix from server	External Interfaces

getinterpmethod	Interpolation method for timeseries	Time Series Objects
getpixelposition	Get component position in pixels	Creating GUI
getpref	Preference	Creating GUI
getqualitydesc	Data quality descriptions	Time Series Objects
getsampleusingtime (timeseries)	Extract data samples into new timeseries object	Time Series Objects
getsampleusingtime (tscollection)	Extract data samples into new tscollection object	Time Series Collections
gettimeseriesnames	Cell array of names of timeseries objects in tscollection object	Time Series Collections
gettsafteratevent	New timeseries object with samples occurring at or after event	Time Series Objects
gettsafterevent	New timeseries object with samples occurring after event	Time Series Objects
gettsatevent	New timeseries object with samples occurring at event	Time Series Objects
gettsbeforeatevent	New timeseries object with samples occurring before or at event	Time Series Objects
gettsbeforeevent	New timeseries object with samples occurring before event	Time Series Objects
gettsbetweenevents	New timeseries object with samples occurring between events	Time Series Objects
GetVariable	Get data from variable in server workspace	External Interfaces
GetWorkspaceData	Get data from server workspace	External Interfaces
ginput	Graphical input from mouse or cursor	Creating GUI
global	Declare global variables	Variables and Functions in Memory
gmres	Generalized minimum residual method (with restarts)	Linear Equations (Iterative Methods)
gplot	Plot nodes and links representing adjacency matrix	Tree Operations
grabcode	MATLAB code from M-files published to HTML	Publishing
gradient	Numerical gradient	Derivatives and Integrals

graymon	Set default figure properties for grayscale monitors	3-D Visualization
grid	Grid lines for 2-D and 3-D plots	Handle Graphics
griddata	Data gridding	Interpolation 3-D Visualization
griddata3	Data gridding and hypersurface fitting for 3-D data	Interpolation
griddatan	Data gridding and hypersurface fitting (dimension >= 2)	Interpolation
gsvd	Generalized singular value decomposition	Eigenvalues and Singular Values-Factorization
gt	Test for greater than	Relational Functions
gtext	Mouse placement of text in 2-D view	Annotating Plots
guidata	Store or retrieve GUI data	Creating GUI
guide	Open GUI Layout Editor	Creating GUI
guihandles	Create structure of handles	Creating GUI
gunzip	Uncompress GNU zip files	File I/O
gzip	Compress files into GNU zip files	File I/O

List of Functions and Objects Properties (H - I)

Name	Description	Categories
hadamard	Hadamard matrix	Specialized Matrices
hankel	Hankel matrix	Specialized Matrices
hdf	Summary of MATLAB HDF4 capabilities	File I/O
hdf5	Summary of MATLAB HDF5 capabilities	File I/O
hdf5info	Information about HDF5 file	File I/O
hdf5read	Read HDF5 file	File I/O
hdf5write	Write data to file in HDF5 format	File I/O
hdfinfo	Information about HDF4 or HDF-EOS file	File I/O
hdfread	Read data from HDF4 or HDF-EOS file	File I/O
hdftool	Browse and import data from HDF4 or HDF-EOS files	File I/O
help	Help for MATLAB functions in Command Window	Help for Using MATLAB
helpbrowser	Open Help browser for all online documentation and demos	Help for Using MATLAB
helpdesk	Open Help browser	Help for Using MATLAB
helpdlg	Create and open help dialog box	Creating GUI
helpwin	Provide access to M-file help for all functions	Help for Using MATLAB
hess	Hessenberg form of matrix	Eigenvalues and Singular Values
hex2dec	Convert hexadecimal number string to decimal number	Data Type Conversion
hex2num	Convert hexadecimal number string to double-precision number	Data Type Conversion
hgexport	Export figure	Printing
hggroup	Create hggroup object	Handle Graphics
Hggroup Properties	Define Hggroup Properties	Plot Objects
hgload	Load Handle Graphics object hierarchy from file	Handle Graphics
hgsave	Save Handle Graphics object hierarchy to file	Handle Graphics
hgtransform	Create hgtransform graphics object	Handle Graphics

Hgtransform Properties	Define Hgtransform Properties	Plot Objects
hidden	Remove hidden lines from mesh plot	3-D Visualization
hilb	Hilbert matrix	Specialized Matrices
hist	Histogram plot	Specialized Plotting
histc	Histogram count	Specialized Plotting
hold	Retain current graph in figure	Basic Plots and Graphs
home	Move cursor to upper-left corner of Command Window	Command Window and History
horzcat	Concatenate arrays horizontally	Array Manipulation
horzcat (tscollection)	Horizontal concatenation for tscollection objects	Time Series Collections
hostid	MATLAB server host identification number	Operating System Interface
hsv2rgb	Convert HSV colormap to RGB colormap	3-D Visualization
hypot	Square root of sum of squares	Trigonometric
i	Imaginary unit	Complex&Math Constants
idealfilter (timeseries)	Apply ideal (noncausal) filter to timeseries object	Time Series Objects
idivide	Integer division with rounding option	Array Operations Rounding and Remainder
if	Execute statements if condition is true	Control Flow
ifft	Inverse discrete Fourier transform	Fourier Transforms
ifft2	2-D inverse discrete Fourier transform	Fourier Transforms
ifftn	N-D inverse discrete Fourier transform	Fourier Transforms
ifftshift	Inverse FFT shift	Fourier Transforms
ilu	Sparse incomplete LU factorization	Linear Equations Factorization
im2frame	Convert image to movie frame	Specialized Plotting Bit-Mapped Images
im2java	Convert image to Java image	Java Classes and Objects File I/O &Bit-Mapped Images
imag	Imaginary part of complex number	Complex
image	Display image object	Bit-Mapped Images Handle Graphics
Image Properties	Define image properties	Plot Objects
imagesc	Scale data and display image object	Bit-Mapped Images

imfinfo	Information about graphics file	File I/O-Bit-Mapped Images
imformats	Manage image file format registry	Bit-Mapped Images
import	Add package or class to current Java import list	Java Classes and Objects External Interfaces
importdata	Load data from disk file	File I/O
imread	Read image from graphics file	File I/O &Bit-Mapped Images
imwrite	Write image to graphics file	File I/O &Bit-Mapped Images
ind2rgb	Convert indexed image to RGB image	Bit-Mapped Images
ind2sub	Subscripts from linear index	Elementary Matrices and Arrays
Inf	Infinity	Math Constants
inferiorto	Establish inferior class relationship	MATLAB Classes and Objects
info	Information about contacting The MathWorks	Help for Using MATLAB
inline	Construct inline object	Array Manipulation
inmem	Names of M-files, MEX-files, Java classes in memory	Java Classes and Objects Variables and Functions in Memory-MEX Programming
inpolygon	Points inside polygonal region	Specialized Plotting
input	Request user input	M-File Functions and Scripts
inputdlg	Create and open input dialog box	Creating GUI
inputname	Variable name of function input	M-File Functions and Scripts
inputParser	Construct input parser object	M-File Functions and Scripts
inspect	Open Property Inspector	Creating GUI-External Interfaces
instrcallback	Event information when event occurs	External Interfaces
instrfind	Read serial port objects from memory to MATLAB workspace	External Interfaces
instrfindall	Find visible and hidden serial port objects	External Interfaces
int2str	Convert integer to string	Data Type Conversion
int8, int16 int32, int64	Convert to signed integer	Data Type Conversion
interfaces	List custom interfaces to COM server	External Interfaces

interp1	1-D data interpolation (table lookup)	Interpolation and Regression
interp1q	Quick 1-D linear interpolation	Interpolation
interp2	2-D data interpolation (table lookup)	Interpolation and Regression
interp3	3-D data interpolation (table lookup)	Interpolation and Regression
interpft	1-D interpolation using FFT method	Interpolation
interpn	N-D data interpolation (table lookup)	Interpolation and Regression
interpstream speed	Interpolate stream-line vertices from flow speed	3-D Visualization
intersect	Find set intersection of two vectors	Set Functions
intmax	Largest value of specified integer type	Math Constants Numeric Types
intmin	Smallest value of specified integer type	Math Constants Numeric Types
intwarning	Control state of integer warnings	Numeric Types Error Handling
inv	Matrix inverse	Linear Equations
invhilb	inverse of Hilbert matrix	Specialized Matrices
invoke	Invoke method on object or interface, or display methods	External Interfaces
ipermute	Inverse permute dimensions of N-D array	Array Manipulation Numeric Types
iqr (timeseries)	Interquartile range of timeseries data	Time Series Objects
is*	Detect state	Data Type Identification
isa	Determine whether input is object of given class	Data Type Identification String Functions Logical Functions External Interfaces
isappdata	True if application-defined data exists	Creating GUI
iscell	Determine whether input is cell array	Cell Arrays Data Type Identification
iscellstr	Determine whether input is cell array of strings	Cell Arrays Data Type Identification String Functions
ischar	Determine whether item is character array	Data Type Identification String Functions
iscom	Is input COM object	External Interfaces

isdir	Determine whether input is a directory	File Operations
isempty	Determine whether array is empty	Array Basic Information
isempty (timeseries)	Determine whether timeseries object is empty	Time Series Objects
isempty (tscollection)	Determine whether tscollection object is empty	Time Series Collections
isequal	Test arrays for equality	Array Basic Information Numeric Types-Structures Cell Arrays-Function Handles
isequalwith equalnans	Test arrays for equality treating NaNs as equal	Array Basic Information Numeric Types
isevent	Is input event	External Interfaces
isfield	Determine whether input is structure array field	Structures Data Type Identification
isfinite	Array elements that are finite	Array Basic Information Numeric Types
isfloat	Determine whether input is floating-point array	Array Basic Information Data Type Identification
isglobal	Determine whether input is global variable	Variables and Functions in Memory
ishandle	Is object handle valid	Handle Graphics
ishold	Current hold state	Handle Graphics
isinf	Array elements that are infinite	Array Basic Information
isinteger	Determine whether input is integer array	Array Basic Information Data Type Identification
isinterface	Is input COM interface	External Interfaces
isjava	Determine whether input is Java object	Java Classes and Objects Data Type Identification External Interfaces
iskeyword	Determine whether input is MATLAB keyword	Logical Functions Evaluation of Expressions and Functions
isletter	Array elements that are alphabetic letters	String Functions
islogical	Determine whether input is logical array	Array Basic Information Data Type Identification
ismac	Determine whether running Macintosh OS X versions of MATLAB	MATLAB Version and License
ismember	Array elements that are members of set	Set Functions
ismethod	Determine whether input is object method	External Interfaces

isnan	Array elements that are NaN	Array Basic Information Numeric Types
isnumeric	Determine whether input is numeric array	Array Basic Information Numeric Types Data Type Identification
isobject	Determine whether input is MATLAB OOPs object	MATLAB Classes and Objects Data Type Identification
isocaps	Compute isosurface end-cap geometry	3-D Visualization
isocolors	Calculate isosurface and patch colors	3-D Visualization
isonormals	Compute normals of isosurface vertices	3-D Visualization
isosurface	Extract isosurface data from volume data	3-D Visualization
ispc	Determine whether PC (Windows) version of MATLAB	MATLAB Version and License
ispref	Test for existence of preference	Creating GUI
isprime	Array elements that are prime numbers	Discrete Math
isprop	Determine whether input is object property	External Interfaces
isreal	Determine whether input is real array	Complex-Numeric Types-Data Type Identification
isscalar	Determine whether input is scalar	Array Basic Information Numeric Types-Structures Cell Arrays-String Functions
issorted	Determine whether set elements are in sorted order	Set Functions
isspace	Array elements that are space characters	String Functions
issparse	Determine whether input is sparse	Array Basic Information Sparse Matrices
isstr	Determine whether input is character array	Characters and Strings Data Type Identification
isstrprop	Determine whether string is of specified category	String Functions
isstruct	Determine whether input is structure array	Structures Data Type Identification
isstudent	Determine whether Student MATLAB Version	MATLAB Version and License
isunix	Determine whether UNIX MATLAB version	MATLAB Version and License

isvalid (serial)	Determine whether serial port objects are valid	External Interfaces
isvalid (timer)	Determine whether timer object is valid	Timer Functions
isvarname	Determine whether input is valid variable name	Logical Functions Evaluation of Expressions and Functions
isvector	Determine whether input is vector	Array Basic Information Numeric Types-Structures Cell Arrays-String Functions

List of Functions and Objects Properties (J - M)

Name	Description	Categories
j	Imaginary unit	Complex Math Constants
javaaddpath	Add entries to dynamic Java class path	Java Classes and Objects External Interfaces
javaArray	Construct Java array	Java Classes and Objects External Interfaces
javachk	Generate error message based on Java feature support	MATLAB Version and License Java Classes and Objects External Interfaces
javaclasspath	Set and get dynamic Java class path	Java Classes and Objects External Interfaces External Interfaces
javaMethod	Invoke Java method	Java Classes and Objects External Interfaces
javaObject	Construct Java object	Java Classes and Objects External Interfaces
javarmpath	Remove entries from dynamic Java class path	Java Classes and Objects External Interfaces
keyboard	Input from keyboard	Edit and Debug M-Files
kron	Kronecker tensor product	Array Operations
lasterr	Last error message	Error Handling
lasterror	Last error message and related information	Error Handling
lastwarn	Last warning message	Error Handling
lcm	Least common multiple	Discrete Math
ldl	Block ldl' factorization for Hermitian indefinite matrices	Sparse Matrices
ldivide, rdivide	Left or right array division	Array Operations
le	Test for less than or equal to	Relational Functions
legend	Graph legend for lines and patches	Annotating Plots
legendre	Associated Legendre functions	Numerical Integration
length	Length of array	Array Basic Information
length (serial)	Length of serial port object array	External Interfaces
length (timeseries)	Length of time vector	Time Series Objects
length (tscollection)	Length of time vector	Time Series Collections
libfunctions	Information on functions in external library	External Interfaces
libfunctionsview	Create window displaying information on functions in external library	External Interfaces

libisloaded	Determine whether external library is loaded	External Interfaces
libpointer	Create pointer object for use with external libraries	External Interfaces
libstruct	Construct structure as defined in external library	External Interfaces
license	Return license number or perform licensing task	MATLAB Version and License
light	Create light object	Handle Graphics 3-D Visualization
Light Properties	Define Light Properties	Plot Objects
lightangle	Create or position light object in spherical coordinates	3-D Visualization
lighting	Specify lighting algorithm	3-D Visualization
lin2mu	Convert linear audio signal to mu-law	File I/O
line	Create line object Handle Graphics	Annotating Plots
Line Properties	Define Line Properties	Plot Objects
Lineseries Properties	Define lineseries properties	Plot Objects
LineSpec	Line specification string syntax	Basic Plots and Graphs
linkaxes	Synchronize limits of specified 2-D Axes	Handle Graphics
linkprop	Keep same value for corresponding properties	Handle Graphics
linsolve	Solve linear system of equations	Linear Equations
linspace	Generate linearly spaced arays	Elementary Matrices and Arrays
listdlg	Create and open list-selection dialog box	Creating GUI
listfonts	List available system fonts	Creating GUI
load	Load workspace variables from disk	File I/O
load (COM)	Initialize control object from file	External Interfaces
load (serial)	Load serial port objects and variables into MATLAB workspace	External Interfaces
loadlibrary	Load external library into MATLAB	External Interfaces
loadobj	User-defined extension of load function for user objects	MATLAB Classes and Objects
log	Natural logarithm	Exponential
log10	Common (base 10) logarithm	Exponential
log1p	Compute log(1+x) accurately for small values of x	Exponential

log2	Base 2 logarithm and dissect floating-point numbers into exponent and mantissa	Exponential
logical	Convert numeric values to logical	Data Type Conversion Logical Functions
loglog	Log-log scale plot	Basic Plots and Graphs
logm	Matrix logarithm	Matrix Log and Exp
logspace	Generate logarithmically spaced vectors	Elementary Matrices and Arrays
lookfor	Search for keyword in all help entries	Help for Using MATLAB File Operations
lower	Convert string to lowercase	String Functions
ls	Directory contents on UNIX system	File Operations
lscov	Least-squares solution in presence of known covariance	Linear Equations
lsqnonneg	Solve nonnegative least-squares constraints problem	Linear Equations Optimization
lsqr	LSQR method	Linear Equations (Iterative Methods)
lt	Test for less than	Relational Functions
lu	LU matrix factorization	Linear Equations Factorization
luinc	Sparse incomplete LU factorization	Linear Equations Factorization
magic	Magic square	Specialized Matrices
mkdir	Make new directory	File Operations
makehgtform	Create 4-by-4 transform matrix	Handle Graphics 3-D Visualization
mat2cell	Divide array into cell array of matrices	Cell Arrays Data Type Conversion
mat2str	Convert array to string	Data Type Conversion
material	Control reflectance properties of surfaces and patches	3-D Visualization
matlabcolon (matlab:)	Run specified function via hyperlink	Command Window and Historyry
matlabroot	Root directory of MATLAB installation	File Operations
matlab (UNIX)	Start MATLAB (UNIX systems)	Startup and Shutdown
matlab (Windows)	Start MATLAB (Windows systems)	Startup and Shutdown
matlabrc	MATLAB startup M-file for single-user systems or system administrators	Startup and Shutdown

max	Largest elements in array	Array Basic Information Descriptive Statistics
max (timeseries)	Maximum value of timeseries data	Time Series Objects
Maximize CommandWindow	Open server window on Windows desktop	External Interfaces
mean	Average or mean value of array	Descriptive Statistics
mean (timeseries)	Mean value of timeseries data	Time Series Objects
median	Median value of array	Descriptive Statistics
median (timeseries)	Median value of timeseries data	Time Series Objects
memmapfile	Construct memmapfile object	File I/O
memory	Help for memory limitations	Improve Performance M-Files
menu	Generate menu of choices for user input	Creating GUI
mesh, meshc meshz	Mesh plots	3-D Visualization
meshgrid	Generate X and Y arrays for 3-D plots	Elementary Matrices and Arrays Interpolation Domain Generation 3-D Visualization
methods	Information on class methods	MATLAB Classes and Objects Java Classes and Objects External Interfaces
methodsview	Information on class methods in separate window	MATLAB Classes and Objects Java Classes and Objects External Interfaces
mex	Compile MEX-function from C or Fortran source code	MEX Programming
mexext	MEX-filename extension	MEX Programming
mfilename	Name of currently running M-file	M-File Functions and Scripts
mget	Download file from FTP server	File I/O
min	Smallest elements in array	Array Basic Information Descriptive Statistics
min (timeseries)	Minimum value of timeseries data	Time Series Objects
Minimize CommandWindow		External Interfaces
minres	Minimum residual method	Linear Equations (Iterative Methods)
mislocked	Determine whether M-file or MEX-file cannot be cleared from memory	Variables and Functions In Memory

mkdir	Make new directory	File Operations
mkdir (ftp)	Create new directory on FTP server	File I/O
mkpp	Make piecewise polynomial	Interpolation
mldivide \ mrdivide /	Left or right matrix division	Interpolation and Regression
mlint	Check M-files for possible problems	Improve Performance M-Files
mlintrpt	Run mlint for file or directory, reporting results in browser	Improve Performance M-Files
mlock	Prevent clearing M-file or MEX-file from memory	Variables and Functions in Memory
mmfileinfo	Information about multimedia file	File I/O
mod	Modulus after division	Rounding and Remainder
mode	Most frequent values in array	Descriptive Statistics
more	Control paged output for Command Window	Command Window and History
move	Move or resize control in parent window	External Interfaces
movefile	Move file or directory	File Operations
movegui	Move GUI figure to specified location on screen	Creating GUI
movie	Play recorded movie frames	Specialized Plotting
movie2avi	Create Audio/Video Interleaved (AVI) movie from MATLAB movie	File I/O
mput	Upload file or directory to FTP server	File I/O
msgbox	Create and open message box	Creating GUI
mtimes	Matrix multiplication	Matrix analysis
mu2lin	Convert mu-law audio signal to linear	File I/O
multibandread	Read band-interleaved data from binary file	File I/O
multibandwrite	Write band-interleaved data to file add Top Of Section Buttons;	File I/O
munlock	Allow clearing M-file or MEX-file from memory	Variables and Functions in Memory

List of Functions and Objects Properties (N - P)

Name	Description	Categories
namelengthmax	Maximum identifier length	M-File Functions and Scripts Variables and Functions in Memory
NaN	Not-a-Number	Math Constants
nargchk	Validate number of input arguments	M-File Functions and Scripts
nargin, nargout	Number of function arguments	M-File Functions and Scripts
nargoutchk	Validate number of output arguments	M-File Functions and Scripts
native2unicode	Convert numeric bytes to Unicode characters	Data Type Conversion
nchoosek	Binomial coefficient or all combinations	Discrete Math
ndgrid	Generate arrays for N-D functions and interpolation	Elementary Matrices and Arrays–Interpolation Domain Generation
ndims	Number of array dimensions	Array Basic Information
ne	Test for inequality	Relational Functions
newplot	Determine where to draw graphics objects	Handle Graphics
nextpow2	Base 2 logarithm and dissect floating-point numbers into exponent and mantissa	Exponential Fourier Transforms
nnz	Number of nonzero matrix elements	Sparse Matrices
noanimate	Change EraseMode of all objects to normal	Specialized Plotting
nonzeros	Nonzero array elements	Sparse Matrices
norm	Vector and matrix norms	Matrix Analysis
normest	2-norm estimate	Matrix Analysis
not	Find logical NOT of array or scalar input	Logical Functions
notebook	Open M-book in Microsoft Word (Windows)	Publishing
now	Current date and time	Date and Time Functions
nthroot	Real nth root of real numbers	Exponential
null	Null space	Matrix Analysis
num2cell	Convert numeric array to cell array	Cell Arrays Data Type Conversion
num2hex	Convert singles and doubles to IEEE hexadecimal strings	Data Type Conversion

num2str	Convert number to string	Data Type Conversion
numel	Number of elements in array or subscripted array expression	Array Basic Information
nzmax	Amount of storage allocated for nonzero matrix elements	Sparse Matrices
ode15i	Solve fully implicit differential equations, variable order method	Ordinary Differential Equations
ode23, ode45 ode113, ode15s ode23s, ode23t ode23tb	Solve initial value problems for ordinary differential equations	Ordinary Differential Equations
odefile	Define differential equation problem for ordinary differential equation solvers	Ordinary Differential Equations
odeget	Ordinary differential equation options parameters	Ordinary Differential Equations
odeset	Create or alter options structure for ordinary differential equation solvers	Ordinary Differential Equations
odextend	Extend solution of initial value problem for ordinary Differential equation	Ordinary Differential Equations
ones	Create array of all ones	Elementary Matrices and Arrays
open	Open files based on extension	File I/O
openfig	Open new copy or raise existing copy of saved figure	Creating GUI
opengl	Control OpenGL rendering	Handle Graphics
openvar	Open workspace variable in Array Editor or other tool for graphical editing	Workspace
optimget	Optimization options values	Optimization
optimset	Create or edit optimization options structure	Optimization
or	Find logical OR of array	Logical Functions
ordeig	Eigenvalues of quasitriangular matrices	Eigenvalues and Singular Values
orderfields	Order fields of structure array	Structures
ordqz	Reorder eigenvalues in QZ factorization	Eigenvalues and Singular Values
ordschur	Reorder eigenvalues in Schur factorization	Eigenvalues and Singular Values
orient	Hardcopy paper orientation	Printing

orth	Range space of matrix	Matrix Analysis
otherwise	Default part of switch statement	Control Flow
pack	Consolidate workspace memory	Workspace/Improve Performance M-Files Variables and Functions in Memory
pagesetupdlg	Page setup dialog box	Printing – Creating Gui
pan	Pan view of graph interactively	Plotting Tools 3-D Visualization
pareto	Pareto chart	Specialized Plotting
parse (inputParser)	Parse and validate named inputs	M-File Functions and Scripts
parseSoap Response	Convert response string from SOAP server into MATLAB data types	External Interfaces
partialpath	Partial pathname description	Search Path
pascal	Pascal matrix	Specialized Matrices
patch	Create patch graphics object	Convex Hull Voronoi Diagrams Handle Graphics
Patch Properties	Define Patch Properties	Plot Objects
path	View or change MATLAB directory search path	Search Path
path2rc	The "savepath" function is replacing path2rc	Search Path
pathdef	Directories in MATLAB search path	Search Path
pathsep	Path separator for current platform	Search Path
pathtool	Open Set Path dialog box to view and change MATLAB path	Search Path
pause	Halt execution temporarily	Evaluation of Expressions and Functions
pbaspect	Set or query plot box aspect ratio	3-D Visualization
pcg	Preconditioned conjugate gradients method	Linear Equations (Iterative Methods)
pchip	Piecewise Cubic Hermite Interpolating Polynomial (PCHIP)	Interpolation
pcode	Create preparsed pseudocode file (P-file)	M-File Functions and Scripts

pcolor	Pseudocolor (checkerboard) plot	Specialized Plotting
pdepe	Solve initial-boundary value problems for parabolic-elliptic PDEs in 1-D	Partial Differential Equations
pdeval	Evaluate numerical solution of PDE using output of pdepe	Partial Differential Equations
peaks	Example function of two variables	3-D Visualization
perl	Call Perl script using appropriate operating system executable	Command Window and History-Operating System Interface
perms	All possible permutations	Discrete Math
permute	Rearrange dimension of N-D array	Array Manipulation Numeric Types
persistent	Define persistent variable	Variables and Functions in Memory
pi	Ratio of circle's circumference to its diameter,	Math Constants
pie	Pie chart	Specialized Plotting
pie3	3-D pie chart	Specialized Plotting
pinv	Moore-Penrose pseudoinverse of matrix	Linear Equations
planerot	Givens plane rotation	Factorization
playshow	Run M-file demo (use "echodemo" instead)	Help for Using MATLAB
plot	2-D line plot	Basic Plots and Graphs
plot (timeseries)	Plot time series	Time Series Objects Time Series Collections
plot3	3-D line plot	Basic Plots and Graphs
plotbrowser	Show or hide figure plot browser	Plotting Tools
plotedit	Interactively edit and annotate plots	Plotting Tools
plotmatrix	Scatter plot matrix	Specialized Plotting
plottools	Show or hide plot tools	Plotting Tools
plotyy	2-D line plots with y-axis on both left and right side	Basic Plots and Graphs
pol2cart	Transform polar or cylindrical coordinates to Cartesian	Cartesian Coordinate
polar	Polar coordinate plot	Basic Plots and Graphs
poly	Polynomial with specified roots	Eigenvalues and Singular Values-Polynomials
polyarea	Area of polygon	Specialized Plotting
polyder	Polynomial derivative	Polynomials Derivatives and Integrals

polyeig	Polynomial eigenvalue problem	Eigenvalues and Singular Values-Polynomials
polyfit	Polynomial curve fitting	Polynomials Interpolation and Regression
polyint	Integrate polynomial analytically	Polynomials Derivatives and Integrals
polyval	Polynomial evaluation	Polynomials Interpolation and Regression
polyvalm	Matrix polynomial evaluation	Polynomials
pow2	Base 2 power and scale floating-point numbers	Exponential
power	Array power	Exponential
ppval	Evaluate piecewise polynomial	Interpolation
prefdir	Directory containing preferences history, and layout files	Startup and Shutdown MATLAB Version and License
preferences	Open Preferences dialog box for MATLAB and related products	Startup and Shutdown
primes	Generate list of prime numbers	Discrete Math
print, printopt	Print figure or save to file and configure printer defaults	Printing
printdlg	Print dialog box	Printing (graphics) Creating GUI
printpreview	Preview figure to print	Printing-Creating GUI
prod	Product of array elements	Array Operations
profile	Profile execution time for function	Improve Performance M-Files
profsave	Save profile report in HTML format	Improve Performance M-Files
propedit	Open Property Editor	Handle Graphics
propedit (COM)	Open built-in property page for control	External Interfaces
propertyeditor	Show or hide property editor	Plotting Tools
psi	Psi (polygamma) function	Specialized Math
publish	Publish M-file containing cells, saving output to file of specified type	Publishing
PutCharArray	Store character array in server	External Interfaces
PutFullMatrix	Store matrix in server	External Interfaces
PutWorkspace Data	Store data in server workspace	External Interfaces
pwd	Identify current directory	File Operations

List of Functions and Objects Properties (Q - S)

Name	Description	Categories
qmr	Quasi-minimal residual method	Linear Equations (Iterative Methods)
qr	Orthogonal-triangular decomposition	Linear Equations Factorization
qrdelete	Remove column or row from QR factorization	Factorization
qrinsert	Insert column or row into QR factorization	Factorization
qrupdate	Rank 1 update to QR factorization	Factorization
quad	Numerically evaluate integral, adaptive Simpson quadrature	Numerical Integration (Quadrature)
quadl	Numerically evaluate integral, adaptive Lobatto quadrature	Numerical Integration (Quadrature)
quadv	Vectorized quadrature	Numerical Integration (Quadrature)
questdlg	Create and open question dialog box	Creating GUI
quit	Terminate MATLAB	Startup and Shutdown
Quit (COM)	Terminate MATLAB server	External Interfaces
quiver	Quiver or velocity plot	Specialized Plotting
quiver3	3-D quiver or velocity plot	Specialized Plotting
Quivergroup Properties	Define Quivergroup properties	Plot Objects
qz	QZ factorization for generalized eigenvalues	Factorization
rand	Uniformly distributed and Arrays	Elementary Matrices pseudorandom numbers
randn	Normally distributed random numbers	Elementary Matrices and Arrays
randperm	Random permutation	Sparse Matrices
rank	Rank of matrix	Matrix Analysis
rat, rats	Rational fraction approximation	Discrete Math
rbbox	Create rubberband box for area selection	3-D Visualization
rcond	Matrix reciprocal condition number estimate	Matrix Analysis Linear Equations
readasync	Read data asynchronously from device	External Interfaces
real	Real part of complex number	Complex

reallog	Natural logarithm for nonnegative real arrays	Exponential
realmax	Largest positive floating-point numbe	Math Constants Numeric Types
realmin	Smallest positive floating-point number	Math Constants Numeric Types
realpow	Array power for real-only output	Exponential
realsqrt	Square root for nonnegative real arrays	Exponential
record	Record data and event information to file	External Interfaces
rectangle	Create 2-D rectangle object	Annotating Plots Handle Graphics
Rectangle Properties	Define Rectangle Properties	Plot Objects
rectint	Rectangle intersection area	Specialized Plotting
recycle	Set option to movedeleted files to recycle folder	File Operations
reducepatch	Reduce number of patch faces	3-D Visualization
reducevolume	Reduce number of elements in volume data set	3-D Visualization
refresh	Redraw current figure	Handle Graphics
refreshdata	Refresh data in graph when data source is specified	Handle Graphics
regexp, regexpi	Match regular expression	Characters and Strings String Functions
regexprep	Replace string using regular expression	String Functions
regexptranslate	Translate string into regular expression	String Functions
registerevent	Register event handler with control's event	External Interfaces
rehash	Refresh function and file system path caches	File Operations-Improve Performance M-Files Variables and Functions in Memory
release	Release interface	External Interfaces
rem	Remainder after division	Rounding and Remainder
rmdir	Remove directory	File Operations
removets	Remove timeseries objects from tscollection object	Time Series Collections
rename	Rename file on FTP server	File I/O

repmat	Replicate and tile array	Array Manipulation
resample (timeseries)	Select or interpolate timeseries data using new time vector	Time Series Objects
resample (tscollection)	Select or interpolate data in tscollection using new time vector	Time Series Collections
reset	Reset graphics object properties to their defaults	3-D Visualization
reshape	Reshape array	Array Manipulation Numeric Types
residue	Convert between partial fraction expansion and polynomial coefficients	Polynomials
Restore defaultpath	Restore default MATLAB search path	Search Path
rethrow	Reissue error	Error Handling
return	Return to invoking function	Control Flow
rgb2hsv	Convert RGB colormap to HSV colormap	3-D Visualization
rgbplot	Plot colormap	3-D Visualization
ribbon	Ribbon plot	Specialized Plotting
rmappdata	RemoveCreating GUI application-defined data	
rmdir	Remove directory	File I/O
rmdir (ftp)	Remove directory on FTP server	File I/O
rmfield	Remove fields from structure	Structures
rmpath	Remove directories from MATLAB search path	Search Path
rmpref	Remove preference	Creating GUI
root object	Root object properties	Handle Graphics
Root Properties	Define Root Properties	Plot Objects
roots	Polynomial roots	Polynomials
rose	Angle histogram plot	Specialized Plotting
rosser	Classic symmetric eigenvalue test problem	Specialized Matrices
rot90	Rotate array 90 degrees	Array Manipulation
rotate	Rotate object in specified direction	3-D Visualization
rotate3d	Rotate 3-D view using mouse	Plotting Tools 3-D Visualization
round	Round to nearest integer	Rounding and Remainder
rref	Reduced row echelon form	Matrix Analysis

rsf2csf	Convert real Schur form to complex Schur form	Eigenvalues and Singular Values&Factorization
run	Run script that is not on current path	Evaluation of Expressions and Functions
save	Save workspace variables to disk	File I/O
save (COM)	Serialize control object to file	External Interfaces
save (serial)	Save serial port objects and variables to MAT-file	External Interfaces
saveas	Save figure using specified format	Printing Handle Graphics
saveobj	User-defined extension of save functionand Objects for user objects	MATLAB Classes
savepath	Save current MATLAB search path to pathdef.m file	Search Path
scatter	Scatter plot	Specialized Plotting
scatter3	3-D scatter plot	Specialized Plotting
Scattergroup Properties	Define scattergroup properties	Plot Objects
schur	Schur decomposition	Eigenvalues and Singular Values
script	Script M-file description	M-File Functions and Scripts-Evaluation of Expressions and Functions
sec	Secant of argument in radians	Trigonometric
secd	Secant of argument in degrees	Trigonometric
sech	Hyperbolic secant	Trigonometric
selectmove resize	Select, move, resize or copy Axes and uicontrol graphics objects	3-D Visualization Creating GUI
semilogx semilogy	Semilogarithmic plots	Basic Plots and Graphs
send	Return list of events control can trigger	External Interfaces
sendmail	Send e-mail message to address list	File I/O
serial	Create serial port object	External Interfaces
serialbreak	Send break to device connected to serial port	External Interfaces
set	Set object properties	Handle Graphics
set (COM)	Set object or interface property	External Interfaces

set (serial)	Configure or display serial port object properties	External Interfaces
set (timer)	Configure or display timer object properties	Timer Functions
set (timeseries)	Set properties of timeseries object	Time Series Objects
set (tscollection)	Set properties of tscollection object	Time Series Collections
setabstime (timeseries)	Set times of timeseries object as date strings	Time Series Objects
setabstime (tscollection)	Set times of tscollection object as date strings	Time Series Collections
setappdata	Specify application-defined data	Creating GUI
setdiff	Find set difference of two vectors	Set Functions
setenv	Set environment variable	Operating System Interface
setfield	Set value of structure array fields	Structure
setinterp method	Set default interpolation method for timeseries object	Time Series Objects
setpixel position	Set component position in pixels	Creating GUI
setpref	Set preference	Creating GUI
setstr	This function has been renamed now "char"	
settime seriesnames	Change name of timeseries object in tscollection	Time Series Collections
setxor	Find set exclusive OR of two arrays	Set Functions
shading	Set color shading properties	3-D Visualization
shiftdim	Shift dimensions	Array Manipulation
showplottool	Show or hide figure plot tool	Plotting Tools
shrinkfaces	Reduce the size of patch faces	3-D Visualization
sign	Signum function	Complex
sin	Sine of argument in radians	Trigonometric
sind	Sine of argument in degrees	Trigonometric
single	Convert to single precision	Data Type Conversion
sinh	Hyperbolic sine of argument in radians	Trigonometric
size	Array dimensions	Array Basic Information

size (serial)	Size of serial port object array	External Interfaces
size (timeseries)	Size of timeseries object	Time Series Objects
size (tscollection)	Size of tscollection object	Time Series Collections
slice	Volumetric slice plot	Specialized Plotting 3-D Visualization
smooth3	Smooth 3-D data	3-D Visualization
sort	Sort array elements in ascending or descending order	Array Manipulation
sortrows	Sort rows in ascending order	Array Manipulation
sound	Convert vector into sound	File I/O
soundsc	Scale data and play as sound	File I/O
spalloc	Allocate space for sparse matrix	Sparse Matrices
sparse	Create sparse matrix	Improve Performance M-Files-Sparse Matrices
spaugment	Form least squares augmented system	Linear Algebra
spconvert	Import matrix from sparse matrix external format	Sparse Matrices
spdiags	Extract and create sparse band and diagonal matrices	Sparse Matrices
specular	Calculate specular reflectance	3-D Visualization
speye	Sparse identity matrix	Sparse Matrices
spfun	Apply function to nonzero sparse matrix elements	Sparse Matrices
sph2cart	Transform spherical coordinates to Cartesian	Cartesian Coordinate
sphere	Generate sphere	Specialized Plotting
spinmap	Spin colormap	3-D Visualization
spline	Cubic spline data interpolation	Interpolation
spones	Replace nonzero sparse matrix elements with ones	Sparse Matrices
spparms	Set parameters for sparse matrix routines	Sparse Matrices
sprand	Sparse uniformly distributed random matrix	Sparse Matrices
sprandn	Sparse normally distributed random matrix	Sparse Matrices
sprandsym	Sparse symmetric random matrix	Sparse Matrices

sprank	Structural rank	Linear Algebra
sprintf	Write formatted data to string	Characters and Strings String Functions
spy	Visualize sparsity pattern	Sparse Matrices
sqrt	Square root	Exponential
sqrtm	Matrix square root	Eigenvalues and SingularValues Matrix Log and Exp
squeeze	Remove singleton dimensions	Array Manipulation Numeric Types
ss2tf	Convert state-space filter parameters to transfer function form	Eigenvalues and Singular Values
sscanf	Read formatted data from string	Characters and Strings String Functions
stairs	Stairstep graph	Specialized Plotting
Stairseries Properties	Define stairseries properties	Plot Objects
start	Start timer(s) running	Timer Functions
startat	Start timer(s) running at specified time	Timer Functions
startup	MATLAB startup M-file for user-defined options	Startup and Shutdown
std	Standard deviation	Descriptive Statistics
std (timeseries)	Standard deviation of timeseries data	Time Series Objects
stem	Plot discrete sequence data	Specialized Plotting
stem3	Plot 3-D discrete sequence data	Specialized Plotting
Stemseries Properties	Define stemseries properties	Plot Objects
stop	Stop timer(s)	Timer Functions
stopasync	Stop asynchronous read and write operations	External Interfaces
str2double	Convert string to double-precision value	Data Type Conversion
str2func	Construct function handle from function name string	Function Handles Data Type Conversion
str2mat	Obsolete. Use char instead.	Data Type Conversion
str2num	Convert string to number	Data Type Conversion
strcat	Concatenate strings horizontally	Characters and Strings String Functions
strcmp, strcmpi	Compare strings	Characters and Strings String Functions
stream2	Compute 2-D streamline data	3-D Visualization

stream3	Compute 3-D streamline data	3-D Visualization
streamline	Plot streamlines from 2-D or 3-D vector data	3-D Visualization
streamparticles	Plot stream particles	3-D Visualization
streamribbon	3-D stream ribbon plot from vector volume datan	3-D Visualizatio
streamslice	Plot streamlines in slice planes	3-D Visualization
streamtube	Create 3-D stream tube plot	3-D Visualization
strfind	Find one string within another	String Functions
strings	MATLAB string handling	Characters and Strings String Functions
strjust	Justify character array	Characters and Strings String Functions
strmatch	Find possible matches for string	Characters and Strings String Functions
strncmp strncmpi	Compare first n characters of strings	String Functions String Functions
strread	The textscan function is intended as a replacement for both strread and textread.	Characters and Strings String Functions
strrep	Find and replace substring	Characters and Strings String Functions
strtok	Selected parts of string	String Functions
strtrim	Remove leading and trailing white space from string	Characters and Strings String Functions
struct	Create structure array	Structures
struct2cell	Convert structure to cell array	Structures-Cell Arrays Data Type Conversion
structfun	Apply function to each field of scalar structure	Structures-Data Type Conversion-Evaluation of Expressions and Functions
strvcat	Concatenate strings vertically	Characters and Strings String Functions
sub2ind	Single index from subscripts	Elementary Matrices and Arrays
subplot	Create Axes in tiled positions	Basic Plots and Graphs
subsasgn	Subscripted assignment for objects	MATLAB Classes and Objects
subsindex	Subscripted indexing for objects	MATLAB Classes and Objects

subspace	Angle between two subspaces	Matrix Analysis
subsref	Subscripted reference for objects	MATLAB Classes and Objects
substruct	Create structure argument for subsasgn or subsref	MATLAB Classes and Objects
subvolume	Extract subset of volume data set	3-D Visualization
sum	Sum of array elements	Array Operations
sum (timeseries)	Sum of timeseries data	Time Series Objects
superiorto	Establish superior class relationship	MATLAB Classes and Objects
support	Open MathWorks Technical Support Web page	Help for Using MATLAB MATLAB Classes and Objects
surf, surfc	3-D shaded surface plot	3-D Visualization
surf2patch	Convert surface data to patch data	3-D Visualization
surface	Create surface object	Handle Graphics 3-D Visualization
Surface Properties	Define Surface Properties	Plot Objects
Surfaceplot Properties	Define surfaceplot properties	Plot Objects
surfl	Surface plot with colormap-based lighting	3-D Visualization
surfnorm	Compute and display 3-D surface normals	3-D Visualization
svd	Singular value decomposition	Eigenvalues and Singular Values-Factorization
svds	Find singular values and vectors	Eigenvalues and Singular Values
swapbytes	Swap byte ordering	Bit-wise Functions
switch	Switch among several cases based on expression	Control Flow
symamd	Symmetric approximate minimum degree permutation	Sparse Matrices
symbfact	Symbolic factorization analysis	Tree Operations
symmlq	Symmetric LQ method	Linear Equations (Iterative Methods)
symmmd	Sparse symmetric minimum degree ordering	Sparse Matrices
symrcm	Sparse reverse Cuthill McKee ordering	Sparse Matrices

symvar	Determine symbolic variables in expression	Evaluation of Expressions and Functions
synchronize	Synchronize and resample two timeseries objects using common time vector	Time Series Objects
syntax	Two ways to call MATLAB functions	M-File Functions and Scripts
system	Execute operating system command and return result	Command Window and History-Operating System Interface

List of Functions and Objects Properties (T - Z)

Name	Description	Categories
tan	Tangent of argument in radians	Trigonometric
tand	Tangent of argument in degrees	Trigonometric
tanh	Hyperbolic tangent	Trigonometric
tar	Compress files into tar file	File I/O
tempdir	Name of system's temporary directory	File I/O
tempname	Unique name for temporary file	File I/O
tetramesh	Tetrahedron mesh	Delaunay Triang-Tess 3-D Visualization
texlabel	Produce TeX format from character string	Annotating Plots
text	Create text object in current Axes	Handle Graphics
Text Properties	Define Text Properties	Plot Objects
textread	Read data from text file write to multiple outputs	File I/O
textscan	Read formatted data from text file or string	File I/O
textwrap	Wrapped string matrix for given uicontrol	Creating GUI
tic, toc	Measure performance using stopwatch timer	Evaluation of Expressions and Functions
timer	Construct timer object	Timer Functions
timerfind	Find timer objects	Timer Functions
timerfindall	Find timer objects including invisible objects	Timer Functions
timeseries	Create timeseries object	Time Series Objects
title	Add title to current Axes	Annotating Plots
todatenum	Convert CDF epoch object to MATLAB datenum	File I/O
toeplitz	Toeplitz matrix	Specialized Matrices
toolboxdir	Root directory for specified toolbox	File Operations
trace	Sum of diagonal elements	Matrix Analysis
transpose (timeseries)	Transpose timeseries object	Time Series Objects
trapz	Trapezoidal numerical integration	Derivatives and Integrals
treelayout	Lay out tree or forest	Tree Operations
treeplot	Plot picture of tree	Tree Operations

tril	Lower triangular part of an array	Array Operations
trimesh	Triangular mesh plot	Delaunay Triang-Tess 3-D Visualization
triplequad	Numerically evaluate triple integral	Numerical Integration (Quadrature)
triplot	2-D triangular plot	Delaunay Triang-Tess 3-D Visualization
trisurf	Triangular surface plot	Delaunay Triang-Tess Convex Hull 3-D Visualization
triu	Upper triangular part of an array	Array Operations
true	Logical 1 (true)	Logical Functions
try	Attempt to execute block of code, and catch errors	Control Flow Error Handling
tscollection	Create tscollection object	Time Series Collections
tsdata.event	Construct event object for timeseries object	Time Series Objects
tsearch	Search for enclosing Delaunay triangle	Delaunay Triang-Tess Specialized Plotting
tsearchn	N-D closest simplex search	Interpolation Delaunay Triang-Tess Specialized Plotting
tsprops	Help on timeseries object properties	Time Series Objects
tstool	Open Time Series Tools GUI	Time Series Objects Collections
type	Display contents of file	File Operations
typecast	Convert data types without changing underlying data	Data Type Conversion
uibuttongroup	Create container object to exclusively manage radio buttons and toggle buttons	Creating GUI
Uibuttongroup Properties	Define Uibuttongroup Propertiess	Plot Object
uicontextmenu	Create context menuPlot Objects	Handle Graphics Creating GUI
Uicontextmenu Properties	Define Uicontextmenu Properties	Plot Objects
uicontrol	Create user interface control object	Creating GUI
Uicontrol Properties	Define Uicontrol Properties	Plot Objects

uigetdir	Open standard dialog box for selecting a directory	Creating GUI
uigetfile	Open standard dialog box for retrieving files	Creating GUI
uigetpref	Open dialog box for retrieving preferences	Creating GUI
uiimport	Open Import Wizard to import data	Workspace File I/O
uimenu	Create menus on figure windows	Creating GUI
Uimenu Properties	Define Uimenu Properties	Plot Objects
uint8, uint16, uint32, uint64	Convert to unsigned integer	Data Type Conversion
uiopen	Open file selection dialog box with appropriate file filters	Creating GUI
uipanel	Create panel container object	Creating GUI
Uipanel Properties	Define Uipanel Properties	Plot Objects
uipushtool	Create push button on toolbar	Creating GUI
Uipushtool Properties	Define Uipushtool Properties	Plot Objects
uiputfile	Open standard dialog box for saving files	Creating GUI
uiresume, uiwait	Control program execution	Creating GUI
uisave	Open standard dialog box for saving workspace variablesI	Creating GU
uisetcolor	Open standard dialog box for setting object's ColorSpec	Creating GUI
uisetfont	Open standard dialog box for setting object's font characteristics	Creating GUI
uisetpref	Manage preferences used in uigetpref	Creating GUI
uistack	Reorder visual stacking order of objects	Creating GUI
uitoggletool	Create toggle button on toolbar	Creating GUI
Uitoggletool Properties	Define Uitoggletool Properties	Plot Objects
uitoolbar	Create toolbar on figure	Creating GUI
Uitoolbar Properties	Define Uitoolbar Properties	Plot Objects

undocheckout	Undo previous checkout from source control system (UNIX)	Source Control
unicode2native	Convert Unicode characters to numeric bytes	Data Type Conversion
union	Find set union of two vectors	Set Functions
unique	Find unique elements of vector	Set Functions
unix	Execute UNIX command and return result	Command Window and History Operating System Interface
unloadlibrary	Unload external library from memory	External Interfaces
unmkpp	Piecewise polynomial details	Interpolation
unregisterall events	Unregister all events for control	External Interfaces
unregisterevent	Unregister event handler with control's event	External Interfaces
untar	Extract contents of tar file	File I/O
unwrap	Correct phase angles to produce smoother phase plots	Complex Fourier Transforms
unzip	Extract contents of zip file	File I/O
upper	Convert string to uppercase	String Functions
urlread	Read content at URL	File I/O
urlwrite	Save contents of URL to file	File I/O
usejava	Determine whether Java feature is supported in MATLAB	Java Classes and Objects
vander	Vandermonde matrix	Specialized Matrices
var	Variance	Descriptive Statistics
var (timeseries)	Variance of timeseries data	Time Series Objects
varargin	Variable length input argument list	M-File Functions and Scripts
varargout	Variable length output argument list	M-File Functions and Scripts
vectorize	Vectorize expression	Array Manipulation
ver	Version information for MathWorks products	MATLAB Version and License
verctrl	Source control actions (Windows)	Source Control
verLessThan	Compare toolbox version to specified version string	MATLAB Version and License
version	Version number for MATLAB	MATLAB Version and License
vertcat	Concatenate arrays vertically	Array Manipulation

vertcat (timeseries)	Vertical concatenation of timeseries objects	Time Series Objects
vertcat (tscollection)	Vertical concatenation for tscollection objects	Time Series Collections
view	Viewpoint specification	3-D Visualization
viewmtx	View transformation matrices	3-D Visualization
volumebounds	Coordinate and color limits for volume data	3-D Visualization
voronoi	Voronoi diagram	Voronoi Diagrams Specialized Plotting
voronoin	N-D Voronoi diagram	Voronoi Diagrams
wait	Wait until timer stops running	Timer Functions
waitbar	Open waitbar	Creating GUI
waitfor	Wait for condition before resuming execution	Creating GUI
waitforbutton press	Wait for key press or mouse-button click	Creating GUI
warndlg	Open warning dialog box	Creating GUI
warning	Warning message	Error Handling
waterfall	Waterfall plot	Specialized Plotting
wavfinfo	Information about Microsoft WAVE (.wav) sound file	File I/O
wavplay	Play recorded sound on PC-based audio output device	File I/O
wavread	Read Microsoft WAVE (.wav) sound file	File I/O
wavrecord	Record sound using PC-based audio input device	File I/O
wavwrite	Write Microsoft WAVE (.wav) sound file	File I/O
web	Open Web site or file in Web browser or Help browser	Help for Using MATLAB File Operations
weekday	Day of week	Date and Time Functions
what	List MATLAB files in current directory	File Operations
whatsnew	Release Notes for MathWorks products	Help for Using MATLAB
which	Locate functions and files	Workspace File Operations Java Classes and Objects
while	Repeatedly execute statements while condition is true	Control Flow
whitebg	Change Axes background color	3-D Visualization

who, whos	List variables in workspace	Data Type Identification
wilkinson	Wilkinson's eigenvalue test matrix	Specialized Matrices
winopen	Open file in appropriate application (Windows)	File I/O
winqueryreg	Item from Microsoft Windows registry	Operating System Interface
wk1finfo	Determine whether file contains 1-2-3 WK1 worksheet	File I/O
wk1read	Read Lotus 1-2-3 WK1 spreadsheet file into matrix	File I/O
wk1write	Write matrix to Lotus 1-2-3 WK1 spreadsheet file	File I/O
workspace	Open Workspace browser to manage workspace	Workspace
xlabel, ylabel, zlabel	Label x-, y-, and z-axis	Annotating Plots
xlim, ylim, zlim	Set or query axis limits	3-D Visualization
xlsfinfo	Determine whether file contains Microsoft Excel (.xls) spreadsheet	File I/O
xlsread	Read Microsoft Excel spreadsheet file (.xls)	File I/O
xlswrite	Write Microsoft Excel spreadsheet file (.xls)	File I/O
xmlread	Parse XML document and return Document Object Model node	File I/O
xmlwrite	Serialize XML Document Object Model node	File I/O
xor	Logical exclusive-OR	Logical Functions
xslt	Transform XML document using XSLT engineaddTop OfSectionButtons	File I/O
zeros	Create array of all zeros	Improve Performance M-Files Elementary Matrices and Arrays Numeric Types
zip	Compress files into zip file	File I/O
zoom	Turn zooming on or off or magnify by factor	Plotting Tools 3-D Visualization

Appendix 3

Operators List

Symbol	Operation
+	Addition or unary plus
-	Subtraction or unary minus
*	Matrix multiplication
.*	Array multiplication (element-wise)
/	Matrix right division
\	Matrix left division
./	Array right division (element-wise)
.\	Array left division (element-wise)
^	Matrix power
.^	Array power (element-wise)
'	Matrix transpose
.'	Array transpose. If the array is complex this involves too the conjugation of all its elements
<	Less than
>	Greater than
<=	Not greater than
>=	Not less than
==	Equal to
~=	Not equal to
&	Logical AND for arrays
|	Logical OR for arrays
~	Logical NOT
&&	Logical AND
||	Logical OR
[ ]	Brackets. Construct array, concatenate elements, specify multiple outputs from function
{ }	Curly braces. Construct cell array, index into cell array
( )	Parentheses. Pass function arguments, prioritize operators
.( )	Reference dynamic field of structure
=	Assignment
.	Insert decimal point, define structure field, reference methods of object
..	Reference parent directory
...	Continue statement to next line
,	Comma. Separate rows of array, separate function input/output arguments, separate commands
;	Semicolon. Separate columns of array, suppress output from current command
:	Colon. For array subscripting and for loop iterations
%	Insert comment line into code
%{ %}	Percent-brace. The text enclosed within the %{ and %} symbols is a comment block.
%%	Cell mode for rapid code iteration
!	Exclamation point indicates that the rest of the input line is issued as a command to the operating system
@	Construct function handle, reference class directory

Appendix 4

A Table of Special Ascii Codes

Ascii code	128	129	130	131	132	133	134	135	136	137	138	139
character												
Ascii code	140	141	142	143	144	145	146	147	148	149	150	151
character												
Ascii code	152	153	154	155	156	157	158	159	160	161	162	163
character	˜									¡	¢	£
Ascii code	164	165	166	167	168	169	170	171	172	173	174	175
character	€	¥	ı	§	¨	©	ª	«	¬	–	®	¯
Ascii code	176	177	178	179	180	181	182	183	184	185	186	187
character	°	±	?	?	´	µ	¶	·	¸	?	º	»
Ascii code	188	189	190	191	192	193	194	195	196	197	198	199
character	?	?	?	¿	À	Á	Â	Ã	Ä	Å	Æ	Ç
Ascii code	200	201	202	203	204	205	206	207	208	209	210	211
character	È	É		Ë	Ì	Í	Î	Ï	?	Ñ	Ò	Ó
Ascii code	212	213	214	215	216	217	218	219	220	221	222	223
character	Ô	Õ	Ö	?	Ø	Ù	Ú	Û	Ü	?	?	ß
Ascii code	224	225	226	227	228	229	230	231	232	233	234	235
character	à	á	â	ã	ä	å	æ	ç	è	è	ê	ë
Ascii code	236	237	238	239	240	241	242	243	244	245	246	247
character	ì	í	î	ï	∂	ñ	ò	ó	ô	õ	ö	÷
Ascii code	248	249	250	251	252	253	254	255				
character	ø	ù	ú	û	ü	?	?	ÿ				

INDEX

Bold items are the MATLAB tools (or windows)
Italic items are the MATLAB functions